TALCOTT PARSONS:
ECONOMIC SOCIOLOGIST OF THE 20TH CENTURY

Laurence S. Moss
Andrew Savchenko

Blackwell Publishing

TALCOTT PARSONS:
ECONOMIC SOCIOLOGIST OF THE 20TH CENTURY

Edited by
Laurence S. Moss

and
Andrew Savchenko

Blackwell
Publishing

350 Main Street, Malden, MA 02148-5020, USA
9600 Garsington Road, Oxford OX4 2DQ, UK
550 Swanston Street, Carlton, Victoria 3053, Australia

First published 2006 by Blackwell Publishing Ltd.

Library of Congress Cataloging-in-Publication Data

Parsons, Talcott, 1902–1979
    Talcott Parsons : economic sociologist of the 20th century / edited by Laurence S. Moss and Andrew Savchenko.
        p.   cm.
    "This book consists of the first written transcription of a videotaped seminar held at Brown University on March 10, 1973. The focus of the seminar was Talcott Parsons himself who traveled down from Harvard University to answer questions about his own intellectual development and his essential ideas. Parsons responded extemporaneously to questions from a panel of distinguished social scientists, historians and philosophers"—P.
    Includes index.
    ISBN-12: 978-1-4051-5529-8 (casebound)
    ISBN-10: 1-4051-5529-9 (casebound)
    ISBN-13: 978-1-4051-5530-4 (pbk.)
    ISBN-10: 1-4051-5530-2 (pbk.)
    1. Economics—Sociological aspects.   2. Sociology—Economic aspects.   3. Parsons, Talcott, 1902—Criticism and interpretation.   4. Sociology—History—20th century.
I. Moss, Laurence S., 1944–   II. Savchenko, Andrew.
III. Title.
HM548.P37   2005
301.092—dc22
                                                    2005055311

A catalogue record for this title is available from the Library of Congress.

Set in 10 on 13pt Garamond Light
by SNP Best-set Typesetter Ltd., Hong Kong
Printed and bound in Singapore

For further information on
Blackwell Publishing, visit our website:
http://www.blackwellpublishing.com

Talcott Parsons on a break during the March 10 seminar. (Courtesy of Harvard University Archives).

Videotaping of the March 10, 1973 seminar. (Courtesy of Harvard University Archives).

Talcott in discussion with panel during the March 10, 1973 seminar.
(Courtesy of Harvard University Archives).

An artist's sketch of Talcott Parsons in action at the March 10, 1973 seminar. (This sketch appears on the front cover of the transcript of the seminar.)

Professor Martin Martel at his home in Providence, Rhode Island circa 1995. (Family photo supplied by Mr. John Kulig).

Description

This book consists of the first written transcription of a video-taped seminar held at Brown University on March 10, 1973. The focus of the seminar was Talcott Parsons himself, who traveled down from Harvard University to answer questions about his own intellectual development and his essential ideas. Parsons responded extemporaneously to questions from a panel of distinguished social scientists, historians, and philosophers. More specifically, Parsons was asked to recall the major intellectual influences on his life and to define more precisely the character of his basic insights about society and social organization. Since this is a valuable addition to our collection of Parsons's ideas and comments, the editors invited several commentators to respond to this conversation. Also, this book contains original essays by Milan Zafirovski, Paul Dalziel, Jane Higgins, John Holmwood, Alexandra Hessling and Hanno Pahl. The essay by Jens Beckert is a revised version of an article that first appeared in German in the *Beiliner Journal für Soziologie* in 2002.

Contents

Introduction

In 1987, JEFFREY ALEXANDER pointed to an important pedagogic aspect of modern sociology that sets this discipline apart from the other social sciences such as economics. In sociology, the history of sociology matters. It gives shape to the field and drives its discourse. When surveying the field of sociology and trying to map the line of demarcation separating economic sociology and economics proper, Neil Smelser and Richard Swedberg (1994: 7, 8) emphasized that a positive attitude toward prior intellectual tradition was one of the most significant differentiating characteristics of sociology. In economics, theory and the past history of theories are separate matters. The prevailing attitude among economists is that "the classics belong to the past" or to a specialized area in economics called the history of economic thought, but in sociology, and especially among the "new" economic sociologists, the history of sociology lies at the core of many of the ongoing debates. Indeed, "the classics are constantly reinterpreted and taught" (Swedberg and Smelser 1994: 4). Not only theoretical sociology but also the analytical and methodological frameworks of the field continue to evolve in constant interaction with past debates. The classical writers in sociology remain part of the canon taught today.

*The artist's sketch of Talcott Parsons was drawn during the March 10th seminar. Other photographs of the March 10th seminar were taken by Mr. Steven Dunwell of Providence, Rhode Island, and copies are in the Harvard University Archives in Pusey Library (HUGFP 42.65). The picture of Martel is a family picture. Ms. Michelle Gachette, who serves as a research assistant in the Harvard University Archives, deserves a special thanks for helping us secure copies and permissions for a variety of items that we used in this introduction. Finally, we offer a special word of thanks to Mr. John Kulig for supplying us with a variety of information about Professor Martin U. Martel, who died on December 20, 1995. Mr. Kulig is a relative of the Martels and the executor of Mrs. Martel's estate. Mrs. Martel passed away in 2005 but not before corresponding with the editors about this planned project. During his long tenure at Brown University, Martel was active in the civil rights movement and helped generations of students confront, understand, and contribute to the improvement of race relationships in the United States. He was active at the university with other colleagues in setting up the Center for the Study of Race and Ethnicity in America. Martel was the catalyst in the effort to videotape Talcott Parsons and but for his efforts we would not have a record of Parsons in seminar.

Talcott Parsons' writings are indisputably classics of American sociology. Two writings in particular are constantly cited in the literature as among his best works: *The Structure of Social Action* ([1937] 1949) and (with coauthor Neil J. Smelser) *Economics and Society* (1956). These two works alone are enough to quality Parsons as the preeminent American sociologist of the twentieth century, but there are scores of other books and articles as well (see Parsons 1967: 539–52). Today, more than a quarter of a century after Parsons' death and a full thirty years since he dominated sociological discourse, Parsons' theories still serve as flashpoints in many debates.

Many sociologists engage in what Jonathan Turner called "ritual criticism" of Parsons (Turner 1991: 203). Still, despite the criticisms and attacks, very few can challenge the claim that Parsons was the preeminent figure in twentieth century sociology in America (Turner 1991: 51). During the turbulent 1960s, things began to unravel. Parsons' conceptual framework, once adopted by many scholars, became an object of ridicule and disdain. Many sociologists openly stated their objections to Parsons and his scholarly projects. This practice expanded in frequency after George C. Homans delivered his attack on Parsonian "structural-functionalism" in his presidential address before the American Sociological Association in 1964 (Homans 1964). Homans was Parsons' colleague at Harvard University, and the attack was evidence of a widening schism in American sociology. We shall say more about Homans' criticism below.

Parsons worked his entire life to reconcile the insights of modern economics with modern sociology and to explore how an authentic economic sociology could be developed. Today, there is a subfield within sociology named "economic sociology." Members who pay their dues to the American Sociological Association can declare themselves part of this research group. Had Parsons lived another thirty years, he might be pleased that this subfield now exists. He most assuredly would have been saddened by the fact that his contributions to the field are overlooked and sometimes completely ignored (Krippner 2001). The "new" economic sociologists say little about Parsons' work except to criticize it.

Mark Granovetter and several of the major adherers to this subfield of the "new" economic sociology are explicitly opposed to Parsons'

ideas about economy and society and yet there is some family resemblance between their methods and "Parsons's intellectual maneuver-
ings a half-century before" (Krippner 2001, p. 799). This is a bit
unusual, because sociologists are usually generous with past attribu-
tion. That anomaly motivated this special invited issue of the *American Journal of Economics and Sociology*, which has long stated its
support of this effort to help unify the social sciences by exploring
their special competencies and taking stock of their unique insights.
It is time for another Parsons revival or, at the very least, a "second
look."

I

The March 10th Seminar

IN THE EARLY MORNING HOURS of March 10, 1973, the famed Harvard
sociologist Talcott Parsons drove from his home in Massachusetts to
the campus of Brown University to present a rather special seminar.
The March 10th seminar was not his first appearance at Brown and
probably not the first of his seminars. The evidence in the Parsons
Archives at Harvard suggests that there were several past visits, including one as far back as 1970 (Rueschemeyer 1970: 10).

There was great excitement at Brown about the March 10th visit.
Professors Martin U. Martel, Robert M. Marsh, and Dietrich
Rueschemeyer, all members of the sociology department at Brown
University, had invited him to come.[1] They had planned something
truly special, a uniquely different academic event.[2] Martel intended to
make this particular seminar an historic event. He arranged to have
the entire seminar videotaped by expert technicians from Rhode
Island Junior College under the direction of Mr. Alan Sondheim of
the Rhode Island School of Design. The taping went exactly as
planned.

In a follow-up letter to Parsons dated April 27, 1973, Martel
explained that he had prepared a typed transcript of the March 10th
session from the videotape and "the video-project has aroused so
much interest that it has become a half-time job for several of us, and
we only are hoping to obtain as professionally competent and complete a historical record as possible" (Martel 1973: 2). In later corre-

spondence, referring to a subsequent visits by Parsons to Brown to deliver the Culver lectures, Martel jokingly referred to the "second coming" of the great sociologist but credited this hagiographic remark to an "unnamed 'student" (Martel 1974: 1).[3] Such hagiography from the Brown faculty may have come mostly from Martel himself, who remained a close friend and admirer of Parsons.

In his follow-up letter to Parsons dated May 1, 1973, thanking Parsons for the seminar, Marsh confessed:

> Frankly, I still feel quite new to the idea of using videotape as a scholarly source; but having looked over the transcription and seen part of the recording, I do think they both together provide a resource and perspective on your work that was not available in the literature before. Martel and others have put in a good deal of time seeking the technical help and funds to work up these materials properly so [that] you could consider their wider distribution. Some of our faculty have been exploring the possibility of starting an interdisciplinary library series of videotapes and books on the "Masters of Social Science" which would permit distribution to the widest audience of serious scholars and students. (Marsh, May 1, 1973:1)

A follow-up seminar was planned for May of 1973, and that one was also to be videotaped.[4]

The March 10th seminar was held in Maxcy Hall at Brown, home of the sociology department. About a dozen people attended this session, including several graduate students, several professors, and Professor Hunter Dupree, the accomplished historian of science (from Brown's history department). The seminar consisted of Parsons seated around a large table with those in attendance asking questions and Parsons answering (see the photos in the frontispiece of this issue).

We were able to locate the original transcript of the seminar held on March 10th. That transcript was first given to Andrew Savchenko by Professor Marsh. Laurence Moss discovered an identical copy in perfect shape, safely housed and brilliantly catalogued among the Parsons Papers at the Harvard University Archives in box 6 of HUG (FP) 42.62. The transcript of the entire March 10, 1973 seminar is now reproduced in full in this volume.

The version that we publish in this issue has been compared against the archived copy at Harvard University, and what editing we have done is limited to supplying some missing first names, always within brackets. In cases where variation in the spelling of names occurred (such as the name of Raymond L. Goldstein, variously spelled "Goldsteen"), we allowed that variation to remain in the published version below since neither of us saw any point in trying to "improve" on the transcript when our main purpose is to preserve it.

We wish to make clear that some of the information presented in the March 10th seminar and the conversations that ensued is known to the scholarly community outside New England. First, Martel published an article titled "Dialogues with Parsons (1973–74)" in the *Indian Journal of Social Research* that included long passages from the March 10 transcript and apparently from several of the other seminars and lectures that followed in subsequent months at Brown University (Martel 1976). Unfortunately, this article contains a confusing variety of spellings of names and presentation dates, making its use as a reliable device for tracking down manuscripts and videotapes somewhat problematic. The editors also learned from the Brown University records that Martel's professional correspondence was bequeathed to the John Hay Library at Brown University for the benefit of future generations of scholars. Unfortunately, the John Hay library staff sadly reported that the valuable videotapes are not available, and if they were part of the Martel legacy, they were perhaps "misplaced."[5] There is, however, good news.

The editors have found another videotape and a large number of audio recordings of Parsons' voice. These finds are in the Harvard University Archives at Pusey Library and they are catalogued and carefully preserved (although the labeling is cursory and inexact). Could this videotape be the missing videotape from the March 10th seminar? Perhaps it is the one made on May 1973? We hope to view the videotape, but in order to do this we need to exhume an older playback machine.[6]

We mentioned that some of the information presented at the March 10th seminar was communicated to the scholarly community in other ways beside the transcripts and besides the videotape. It turns out that the first half the seminar (that is, the morning part of the seminar) tracks quite closely with what Parsons himself said about his own development as an economist-turned-sociologist in an important article published in *Daedalus* one year later (Parsons [1974] 1977). The *Daedalus* piece is an amazingly comprehensive discussion of how Parsons came to develop his system theory and who were the main influences on his work. Still, this piece lacks the more free-wheeling back-and-forth conversational tone of the afternoon seminar session on March 10. Future researchers are encouraged to compare the transcripts of the seminar that is reproduced below with the more formal autobiographical account in the 1974 *Daedalus* article.

It must be remembered that when Parsons drove to Brown University in 1973, his position as the major American sociologist was coming under increasing criticism by the radical sociologists of the late 1960s and 1970s (Marsh 2005). In their view, Parsons had not appreciated what Marx had to say about "classes" and their interests and about conflict as the dynamic element in social change facilitated by the conditions surrounding "commodity" production.

But the Marxists were the least of Parsons' problems. Parsons' own colleague at Harvard University, George C. Homans, challenged his conceptual distinctions and declared them worthless. While hardly radical in tone or content, Homan's 1964 address to the American Sociological Association dealt Parsons' structural functionalist theory the most devastating blow of all. Homans concluded that "with all its talk about theory, the functionalist school did not take the job of theory seriously enough. It did not ask itself what a theory was, and it never produced a functional theory that was in fact an explanation" (Homans 1964: 818). Homans was complaining about Parsons.

These criticisms of Parsons' theory damaged his reputation. That is why the editors of this issue of the *AJES* concluded that publishing the March 10th transcript in its entirely would be useful. We concluded that it would be a significant contribution in helping scholars understand Parsons in a more balanced way. This conclusion is corroborated by three leading sociologists who offered to read the March 10th transcript and prepare short commentaries on it. Professors Robert Holton, Giuseppe Sciortino, and Richard Swedberg provided their expert reactions to that conversation of more than three decades ago.

Holton points to the "profound interdisciplinary" texture of Parsons' theories and how the simple publication of this transcript might help break down the textbook stereotype of Parsons. He is optimistic that there is still something to be learned from a careful rereading of Parsons' contributions. As for Parsons' future legacy, Holton is quite optimistic that future researchers will find his work important. Holton points to the centrality of money as a medium of exchange and suggests that through the phenomenon of property rights, money has an analytical connection to the medium of influence.

In his comment, Guiseppe Sciortino reminds us that Juergen Habermas once said that Parsons was looking for solutions to the problems other theorists were only starting to realize needed to be addressed. According to Sciortino, while many of the issues Parsons discussed in his seminars have been described as "controversial," they cannot be dismissed as irrelevant for contemporary sociology. For example, Parsons retained a strong respect for economics but strongly opposed extending the insights of economics to areas where they do not truly belong. Classical economics and especially Marxian economic theory does not belong in the subsystems of society because Marxian economics offers a fundamentally flawed understanding of markets. Sciortino also cautions against the overuse of the money metaphor in the discussion of generalized symbolic media of exchange. Three of the media, namely, power, influence, and value commitment, only resemble money and are certainly not money themselves.

Richard Swedberg harks back to some unexplored territory that is worth remapping as we work to improve the subfield of economic sociology: Parsons' relationship with Joseph Schumpeter, especially their participation along with Harvard graduate students in a seminar on the nature of rationality during the early 1940s. This seminar at Harvard spawned some literature that was directed toward a volume that never made it to press. Parsons later confessed, "I remember having reacted rather coolly [to the proposal to publish the papers] and in fact I let it die. I am not wholly clear about my motives, but I think they had to do with the feeling that I needed a relatively complete formal break with economics" (Parsons [1974] 1977: 32–3). Swedberg suggests that we should detail more completely the relationship between Schumpeter and Parsons, especially in light of Parsons' remark that his ideas about pure economics were learned from Schumpeter. Schumpeter heralded the "general equilibrium" approach that was much criticized and attacked from within the economics professions, especially around the time of the March 10th seminar.

Swedberg points to those places in the March 10th seminar in which Parsons stated that an economist must possess some sociological ideas. Schumpeter's strong opposition to the transformation of economics from a theoretical to an empirical discipline—a kind of specialized psychology—is a major point of difference between the two thinkers. Parsons went on to become a student of modern Freudian psychology but, despite this contrasting emphasis, Schumpeter shared with Parsons a concern that sociology might lose its theoretical coherence and fragment into a loosely related series of empirical research projects. Unfortunately, much of contemporary sociology seems sadly fragmented this way. Swedberg is correct that the Schumpeter-Parsons connection deserves a fresh look.

II

New Insights into Parsons's Work

THE EDITORS OF THIS ISSUE would be the last to deny that Talcott Parsons had an impenetrable style of writing. Boy, did he ever! At places and in selected works, it seems almost like a secret code he needed to showcase what many agree is a complex theoretical edifice. This style did not help to make his ideas popular. Almost without exception, followers and critics of Parsons, as well as neutral commentators, reflect on the density of his writing and the obscurity with which he expresses simple ideas. However, those who attended Parsons' lectures, seminars, and presentations recall that he was capable of expressing himself more clearly when he wanted to. These transcripts are evidence that he could speak with forceful lucidity and engaging style, while not losing the theoretical precision that his works are famous for.

Apart from the stylistic and personal attributes of Parsons' intellectual persona, the March 10th transcript illustrates the multidisciplinary appeal of Parsons' theoretical project. Political scientists and philosophers, historians and economists were present at the seminar alongside sociologists, actively participating in the discussion and asking questions relevant to their respective disciplines. This participation of nonsociologists in what was originally conceived as a sociological seminar and their familiarity with Parsons' writings demonstrates that classical functionalism of Parsons could serve as an interface for communication between different disciplines within the broad domain of social sciences. The fact that this has yet to happen would have disappointed Parsons greatly.

The five essays that make up the second half of this special issue of the *AJES* explore Parsons and the precise connection between his work and some of the ideas in the "new" economic sociology. Let us showcase these connections.

Milan Zafirovski insists that Parsons had a version of economic sociology that still has relevance today. The theme of his chapter is best expressed in his subtitle: "Bridges to Contemporary Economics." Parsons came to reject the approach by which aggregate social and economic phenomena are built up and composed out of the separate voluntary acts of individuals. That approach is sometimes termed "methodological individualism" in economics.

Parsons' *systems* approach toward understanding the economy was a "holistic" approach, in which sociological phenomena put limits on and gave shape to economic processes. The economy is *contained* in the broader notion of "society." How that containment is described and maintained over time—the equilibrium notion—was something that Parsons intended to be his major contribution to social science. Zafirovski suggests that the long-standing typography of "market structures" often taught in the university might be reinterpreted by sociologists as "sociological types" of market situations. This would be a bridge connecting Parsonian insights directly to some of the staples of contemporary economics.

The chapter coauthored by Paul Dalziel and Jane Higgins makes a startling point. When in 1937 Parsons offered a précis of Vilfredo Pareto's ideas in his seminal work *The Structure of Social Action*, he may have misinterpreted Pareto's thoughts. This misstatement of Pareto, entirely unintentional, had the unfortunate consequence of misleading generations of sociologists who relied on what Parsons had said about Pareto (Parsons [1937] 1949). A more careful reading of Pareto suggested that he did not separate the rational types of human action from the nonrational types of human action. Nothing was so neatly compartmentalized. Rather, Pareto's considered view was that while human behavior is nearly always rational from the agent's personal, *subjective* point of view, it can appear quite the opposite from the point of view of the sociologist examining and evaluating that same behavior. The sociologist is in a privileged position to pass judgement and somehow stands outside the world of the acting man. This was Pareto's view, as it was Parsons'.

Furthermore, a careful reevaluation of Pareto's ideas about economics and sociology shows that Pareto's ideas probably gave shape to Parsons'. A more sympathetic reading of Pareto in light of Parsons' advanced sociological projects establishes that the Pareto-Parsons line of discussion anticipated some of the major points of contemporary economic sociology. Dalziel and Higgins break new ground when they try to set the historical record straight. Their insights pave the way for a more systematic discussion of to what extent Parsons owed his fundamental reconsideration of the boundary between economics and sociology to Pareto. The modern "economic sociology" school may be unknowingly catching up to Pareto through the work of Parsons.

In the following two chapters, Professors John Holmwood and Jens Beckert each underscore the continuing relevance of Talcott Parsons' work today in light of the rebirth of interest in economic sociology during the last two decades. Holmwood dislikes the attempt in sociology to try to account for sociological phenomena in terms of utility-maximizing agents whose behaviors get aggregated in some simple way to constitute what some refer to as "collective behavior." Parsons realized early in his career that the professions produced a version of "economic man" that was very different from the neoclassical economist's version of economic man. What was so different was the role of "attitudes of social responsibility and professional duty," which intruded, shaped, and influenced selfish economic calculation. A doctor would not prescribe extra tests and treatments (even when it might be personally profitable for him to do so) for the simple reason that this overselling of medical services is "unprofessional." With

Parsons, we have the idea that social interactions give rise to certain features or "emergent properties" that exist to shape human action and that are replicated through existing institutions. These emergent properties are real and measurable but are themselves not reducible to the choices made by separately acting individuals.

Jens Beckert insists that Parsons really came of age in the second part of his massively productive career when he pioneered the idea of symbolic communication and anticipated the ideas of the "embeddedness" school. Beckert credits all of this advanced material to the "systems-functionalist" period around the 1950s, culminating in the master work with Neil Smelser (Smelser and Parsons 1956). The many writers who flock to Mark Granovettor for their economic sociology might consider taking a second look at what Parsons had to offer as well. Parsons, like Granovetter, rejected the reductionist idea that social events can be explained by modeling individuals as pursuing their private goals with little or no consideration of societal institutions. But unlike some extreme sociologists who reject individual choice altogether as real and interesting and advance the strange idea that individuals are like "marionettes being lead by the strings of their functionally integrated culture," Granovetter advocated his concept of "social embeddedness." Social embeddedness was for Granovetter a compromise idea, somewhere in between the two extreme points of rational calculation, individualism and cultural determinism (Granovetter 1985).

However, Beckert is skeptical of this development and especially offended as to the large number of Granovetter-inspired scholars who criticize Parsons unfairly. Parsons has become the undeserved whipping boy for the social embeddedness movement. Beckert argues that the "new" economic sociology is not a successful replacement for the old economic sociology created by Talcott Parsons.

According to Beckert, Parsons got there first, ahead of the Granovetter school, and did a much better job than the Granovetter group. The heart of the Granovetter approach has to do with the importance of "networks of social relations" that economic agents find valuable. But the clear linkages between "networks" and human action is never made quite clear among Granovetter's admirers. Beckert suspects that this important connection will never be made clear at all. Parsons' vision about economics and sociology being complements and not substitutes is the superior idea for the development of the fledgling field of economic sociology. According to Beckert, all the clues and cues for a better approach are already there in Parsons' seminal work with Smelser (Parsons and Smelser 1956). According to Beckert, while Parsons' economic sociology was largely ignored at the time of its emergence, latter-day economic sociologists chose to confine their discussion of Parsons' theory to strong criticism, when praise is what should be given.

The last paper in our issue is by Alexandra Hessling and Hanno Pahl, who demonstrate the continuing importance of Parsons' economic sociology. Parsons provided analytical tools that are useful toward helping us understand the modern economic system, draped as it is in the new global financial order. The authors look for theoretical foundations for their study of the global system of finance and find them in Parsonian theory, as suggested in the writings of Niklas Luhmann. Hessing and Pahl try to explain the uncoupling of financial markets from the real economy by using Parsons' ideas. They consider Parsons' ideas alive and well in the 21st century.

III

Conclusion

WE HAVE SAID MUCH about Talcott Parsons' theories and methods but not as much about his demeanor and sense of humor. According to veteran participant Marsh, during the March 10th seminar,

> Parsons had the annoying practice of giving *extremely* long answers to each question we asked him. Indeed, a pause he might take after a lengthy disquisition might be interpreted by the audience as an indication that had (finally) concluded his response to the question, and someone would venture to direct a new question to the master. But no, Parsons had only paused perhaps to light a new cigarette, and had yet more to say on the previous question, so the next question had to bide his or her time (Marsh 2005).

Dietrich Rueschemeyer, another Brown University professor present at the March 10th seminar and also at many other Parsons events held at Brown during the 1970s, recalled a precious moment from one of

Parsons' many encounters with the Brown faculty. (Rueschemeyer does not remember which particular visit, but the group was at lunch with Parsons in Cambridge, Massachusetts, and having a relaxed conversation.) As Rueschemeyer explained it, Martin Martel surprised everyone by suddenly "remembering an argument that had erupted the day before in [the sociology] department about a Ph.D. student taking unreasonable risks with his dissertation [research]." Martel put the question to Parsons himself and asked Parsons over lunch, somewhat "out of the blue: 'Are you a gambler?'"

Rueschemeyer recalls Parsons pounding on the table and exclaiming, "A gambler? No. I should say not that at all." Perhaps feeling that Parsons did not understand the question, Martel replied "But you took intellectual risks" over the years. Parsons' reply was "Oh, yes. That's true. But those are different [risks], not at all like poker, [because in the academic world] you never know whether you won" (Rueschemeyer 2005). Indeed, how true.

Laurence S. Moss
and
Andrew Savchenko

Notes

1. Robert M. Marsh was influenced by Robert Merton while studying at Columbia University. Merton had studied with Talcott Parsons. Martin U. Martel, like Marsh was a "second generation" Parsonian. Martel was influenced by Robin Williams (another Parsonian) when preparing his dissertation at Cornell University. Both Marsh and Martel were active in inviting Parsons and making the many needed arrangements. Of the two Brown sociologists, Martel was intensely interested in Parsons' work over the years and maintained a close intellectual and personal interaction with the great professor. The editors are grateful to Professor Robert M. Marsh for his personal recollection of that Parsons seminar sent to the editors by private correspondence (Marsh 2005). Professor Martel remained a close family friend of Talcott Parsons and his family and distinguished himself over the years as a staunch advocate of racial tolerance and understanding. After Parsons' death in 1979, Martel continued as an expert on race and ethnicity, heading up Brown's Center for Race and Ethnicity until his death on December 20, 1995. The close personal and intellectual relationship between the "conservative" Parsons and the "radical" Martel gives lie to the claim that Parsons' approach

toward analyzing society rules out or privileges one political position over another. It is "as advertised" just social *science*.

2. During the winter months of 1970, Dietrich Rueschemeyer invited Talcott Parsons to come and give a lecture and a talk. On March 25, 1970, Rueschemeyer thanked Parsons for visiting the university and expressed his appreciation, regretting that "there wasn't more time to talk" (see Rueschemeyer March 25, 1970:1). The historical evidence suggests that Parsons was a welcomed and frequent visitor to Brown University, which has an enclave of Parsons admirers including Ruechemeyer, Robert M. Marsh, and Martin U. Martel, who all directly and indirectly contributed to this issue and the preservation of the March 10th transcript.

3. In October 1973, Martel wrote to Parsons about the lecture series at Brown University entitled "The Evolution of Societies." This series would consist of three presentations on Feburary 27, March 27, and May 1, 1974. Again the expectation was that these lectures would be videotaped and result in a major publication. These lectures were financed as part of the Brown University Culver Lectures. It was historic for two reasons. First, the lecturer was the famous Talcott Parsons. Second, Brown University had never before invited a sociologist to be the Culver lecturer (see Martel October 1973). The story of the Culver Lecture series and the follow-up publications is most properly a topic for a future issue of this journal.

4. This videotape and the transcript of that videotape have not been found, but the search is continuing. Our search for these transcripts is underway and ongoing and the proper subject for a future issue of this journal.

5. Thankfully, the Harvard University Archives have two full boxes of audio and video recordings, the "tapes of Talcott Parsons." We suspect that the videotape in one of these boxes is the one in question, but playing it back on modern equipment is virtually impossible and solutions are underway. The transmission of information from one historical media to another more accessible media is a vibrant field of commerce in New England and should not be a problem. Harvard University archivist Ms. Michelle Gachette is in correspondence with one of the editors, and we shall announce our findings in a subsequent issue of this journal. Hopefully, we can provide a CD version for all scholars through the auspices of Harvard University Archives in conjunction with the *AJES*. The tapes and audio recordings of Parsons are loosely described on the Parsons shelf list with the remark "many of these are unidentified at the time of processing since no equipment is easily available to the Archives" (see Parsons Papers at Harvard University Archives, in boxes 1 and 2 of HUG (FP) 15.80). As this issue of the journal was on its way to press, I connected to Mr. Alan Sondheim who remembers the March 10 seminar taping and the technical problems they tried to overcome. Sondheim explained that "the tapes were black-and-white EIAJ format, which is a very old standard. It is very difficult to find machines to play back

these tapes—but worse . . . these tapes tend to deteriorate—they literally stick to themselves and to the machines and won't run. There is a way to restore them for literally just one run" (Sondheim, 2006). The editors will try their best in the months ahead to find and subsequently restore the video of the March 10 seminar.

6. Efforts are now being considered to move the tapes to professionals who have the proper equipment to view it and perhaps transfer the information to the modern DVD format. See note 5, above.

REFERENCES

Granovetter, Mark. (1985). "Economic Action and Social Structure: The Problem of Embeddedness." *American Journal of Sociology* 91: 481–510.

Homans, George C. (1964). "Bringing Men Back In." *American Sociological Review* 29 (December): 809–18.

Krippner, Greta R. (2001). "The Elusive Market: Embeddedness and the Paradigm of Economic Sociology." *Theory and Society* 30 (December): 775–810.

Marsh, Robert M. (1 May, 1973). Letter to Talcott Parsons. 1 page. HUGFP 42.88. Lectures and Addresses, Box 9. Talcott Parsons papers. Harvard University Archives.

———. (2005). "Personal Recollections on the Parsons Seminars at Brown University." Private MS sent to Professor Savchenko, 3 pages.

Martel, Martin U. (April 27, 1973). Letter to Talcott Parsons. 2 pages. HUGFP 42.88. Lectures and Addresses, Box 9. Talcott Parsons papers. Harvard University Archives.

———. (October 29, 1973). Letter to Talcott Parsons. 2 pages. HUGFP 42.88. Lectures and Addresses, Box 9. Talcott Parsons papers. Harvard University Archives.

———. (March 21, 1974). Letter to Talcott Parsons. 2 pages. HUGFP 42.88. Lectures and Addresses, Box 9. Talcott Parsons papers. Harvard University Archives.

———. (1976). "Dialogues with Parsons (1973–4)." *Indian Journal of Social Research* 17 (April): 1–33.

Parsons, Talcott. (1949 [1937]). *The Structure of Social Action; A Study in Social Theory with Special Reference to a Group of Recent European Writers.* 2 vols. New York: The Free Press.

———. (1967). *Sociological Theory and Modern Society.* New York: The Free Press.

———. (January 5, 1970). Letter to Dietrich Rueschemeyer. 1 page. HUGFP 15.60. Lectures and Addresses, Box 1. Talcott Parsons papers. Harvard University Archives.

———. 1974. "On Building Social System Theory." *Daedalus* (Winter). Rpt in Parsons (1977). *Social Systems and the Evolution of Action Theory*. New York: The Free Press.

Parsons, Talcott, and Neil J. Smelser. (1956). *Economy and Society: A Study in the Integration of Economic and Social Theory*. New York: The Free Press.

Rueschemeyer, Dietrich. (March 25, 1970). Letter to Talcott Parsons. 1 page. HUGFP 42.62. Lectures and Addresses, Box 7. Talcott Parsons papers. Harvard University Archives.

Rueschemeyer, Dietrich. (December 28, 2005). E-mail to Laurence S. Moss.

Sondheim, Alan. (January 28, 2006). E-mail to Laurence S. Moss.

Smelser, Neil, and Richard Swedberg. (1994). *The Handbook of Economic Sociology*. Princeton, NJ: Princeton University Press.

Turner, Jonathan H. (1991). *The Structure of Sociological Theory*. Belmont, CA: Wadsworth.

The March 10, 1973 Seminar

A Seminar with Talcott Parsons at Brown University

"My Life and Work" (in two parts) Saturday, March 10, 1973

Seminar Faculty: Robert M. Marsh, Martin U. Martel, Dietrich Rueschemeyer, Albert F. Wessen, and C. Parker Wolf in sociology; and A. Hunter Dupree in the history of science. **Faculty Visitors**: George H. Borts and Mark B. Schupack (economics), Erwin C. Hargrove (political science), and Philip L. Quinn (philosophy of science). **Seminar Students**: Robert J. Cormack, Inge Corless, Robert B. Corno, Jeffrey J. Cymrot, Robert D. Conway, John Fulton, Raymond L. Goldstein, Adrian Hayes, Gary Kulik (history), Jennie J. Kronenfeld, Jolyon Miller (political science), Brian Nilson (philosophy), Ibitola P. Onoge, James Rafferty, Mark A. Shields, Stanley Tureski (political science), Peter H. Ulbrich, Harry E. Warner II, and Keith Williamson.

Videotaping was directed by Mr. Alan Sondheim (Rhode Island School of Design), with the consulting aid of Frank L. Ryan (Director of our Language Laboratory) and Gerald P. Sadlier (Audiovideo Director at Rhode Island Junior College, formerly with Brown). The camera work and setting up was carried out by Steve McGinnis and other student volunteers with equipment generously provided by the Chemistry Department and the two cooperating institutions mentioned.

SEMINAR PART I

Morning Session

Welcoming Remarks

Professor Martin U. Martel, Sociology: I'd like to welcome you to our seminar, and thank you for driving down from Boston this

American Journal of Economics and Sociology, Vol. 65, No. 1 (January 2006).
© 2006 AJES, Inc.

morning to join us for our final session. This really is the first time that we in sociology at Brown have had a seminar devoted entirely to a single person's work. It may be worth noting that in addition to those of us in sociology, we also had the help of A. Hunter Dupree in the history department. The seminar students also included several from history, political science, and philosophy, which speaks well for the interdisciplinary interest in your work.

I might note that the session today also is a new experience for us in that it is the first time that any of us have tried to "film" (video-tape) a seminar. And some of us still are a little new to the idea.

I wanted to mention that, in preparation for this morning, the seminar members met the other night. We tried to make a list of some of the kinds of topics we were hoping you might discuss. To begin with, we spent about half an hour listing some of our main questions on a blackboard. When we finished we were struck that we had quickly filled up the board, and that our list ranged from questions about basic philosophical issues, to some about contemporary political and economic affairs, extending over into areas of psychology, psychiatry and even as relevant to so wide a range of problem areas.

We also were left wondering how we could ever ask you to discuss a work of such enormous complexity in a four-hour Saturday session. It was for this reason that—when several of us saw you last Tuesday— we asked if you could review for us how your work developed, in something of its chronological order. We are hoping that you might do that in two parts: first (in the morning session) tracing the main developments from your undergraduate days to perhaps the time of World War II; and then, after lunch, discussing the more recent developments since the war. We also thought that perhaps we could bring in at least some of our many questions in relation to your works, at the time they first come up.

Recalling that you started your academic career first as an economist (before venturing into sociology), we partly have the question of: "How is it that a young, respectable economist ever went so wrong?" To help us begin, we are calling on Hunter Dupree, our historian of science, to lead off.

Leibnitz's Challenge

Question (Professor A. Hunter Dupree, History): I'd like to phrase this in the form of a statement and then a question. I may be the only one in the room (since I was not trained as a sociologist) who came to your written work—and it is stacked all around us on the tables—only after I had the good fortune to meet you personally. Therefore, I found that I had many guides, which clarified what your many works had to say, through the benefit of having had conversations with you beforehand.

Actually, this is a very old tradition. Leibnitz, writing to a friend in Venice in 1714, once made this statement: "It is good to study the discoveries of others in a way that discloses to us the source of their inventions, and partly renders them (in a sort) as our own. And I wish that authors would give us a history of their discoveries, and the steps by which they arrived at them." Now, Leibnitz's suggestion bore fruit, even in the early 18th century, in the autobiography of Giovanni Battista Vico. (Chuckling.) I hope some day to convince you to take a look at Vico.

In the meantime, we could all benefit very much if you would, in a sense, take up Leibnitz's challenge, and give us a review of how you came to some of the important discoveries which many now find in your books. It would be of great value if we could have the kind of explication from which I so benefitted, in hearing you discuss your work personally.

TALCOTT PARSONS: Well, I'm not sure exactly how to begin. You may notice that I don't have any notes. (Please feel free to interrupt with your questions at any point along the way.)

It was suggested that I start at the undergraduate phase. I went to Amherst, which has a special relationship to Brown because the first three years I was there the president was Alexander Meiklejohn, who has been a dean here. Now, this was so long ago that many of you will not even have heard that there was a big ruckus over Meiklejohn. And at commencement time of my junior year Meiklejohn was dismissed from the presidency of Amherst. This somewhat disorganized the rest of my program because, of the courses I had signed up for my senior year, not a single one was given.

All the faculty, including Meiklejohn himself (I was supposed to have a seminar with him) were elsewhere by the next September. Now, there are just one or two other points about the Amherst of that day besides the trauma of the Meiklejohn dismissal. Of course, there wasn't any sociology. As a matter of fact, Amherst was one of the very last institutions to accept sociology. (They do have a department there now, but I think it's only about four years old.) I believe Williams College is the last holdout. At any rate, there wasn't any sociology at Amherst.

I had originally been intending to go either into biology or medicine, and I had pretty much taken the whole gamut of the premedical program. I started biology in my freshman year, and had some biology every single year. In fact, I assisted in the main introductory course—going out and catching worms on the fall evenings in the gardens and dissecting the dogfish. I had the Amherst scholarship to Woods Hole during the summer between my junior and senior years, and also two years of chemistry. But in my junior year I was "converted" to social science by a decidedly maverick economist named Walton Hamilton. He was an "institutionalist" and a very satirical man who never tired of making fun of the neo-classical economists. The institutionalist movement, in its form of that period, has not really survived but, among others, the hero of those people was Veblen.

In my senior year, my main influences were a biologist named Otto Glazer and a German professor named Otto Manthey-Zorn, who gave a seminar on German philosophy. My connection with Manthey-Zorn was very important to me for without his assistance I would not have gone to Germany as a student. I didn't really have a major at Amherst at that time because the rules were virtually suspended as a result of the Meiklejohn affair.[1] So the question of what to do next arose—a question that faces every college senior. I decided to do graduate work. At the time, I had one foot in sociology and one foot in economics. I was not very attracted to a regular graduate school program in sociology. At that time, had I chosen sociology, I believe I would have gone to either Columbia [University] or the University of Chicago. But instead, I chose to attend the London School of Economics. I wasn't a degree candidate there—I was completely "free-lance." I was only there for one academic year and had a very mixed bag of exposure. [L.T.] Hobhouse was still teaching then, and Ginsberg was Hobhouse's understudy. Of course, there were a number of famous economists; the main economic theorist was [Edwin] Cannan, and [R.H.] Tawney and [Harold] Laski were there. A particularly important influence on me, however, was [Bronislaw] Malinowski. I'd never heard of Malinowski when I went there and it was Ginsberg who guided me to him, saying he thought I would be interested in Malinowski's lectures.

His lecturing method was a little unusual. He read from a manu-script of his own and then would stop after two or three paragraphs and comment on what he had just been over. The manuscript was *Magic, Science, and Religion,* and I became very much interested right away. And I had the temerity to enroll in Malinowski's seminar the next term. I was an extremely callow young man and the people in that seminar—there were about a dozen—were a very mixed bag of people. But there were two people in that seminar who really seemed to know something about anthropology. Their names were Firth and Evans-Pritchard. I got acquainted with them on that occasion and I kept up with them after that, especially Firth, ever since.

It was a very fruitful year. I'll just remark by the side, I also met a young lady in the student commons room at L.S.E.—an American fellow student whom I married after a couple of years. Well, I cer-tainly got a lot out of that year. I never heard the name of Max Weber mentioned during the whole year I was in London. That was the year 1924–25: Weber had died in 1920. To be sure, nothing Weber wrote had at that time been translated into English, but I suppose there were a few British scholars who read German. Tawney, I know, was acquainted with Weber. He was in fact working on his book, which was published two or three years later, *Religion and the Rise of Cap-italism.* I went to a number of Tawney's lectures and in the lectures I happened to attend he didn't mention Weber. I doubt if Ginsberg had ever heard of Weber.

Well, I did hear about [Emile] Durkheim but what I heard from both Ginsberg and Malinowski was mostly wrong. For example, in his introduction to a volume of essays by Hobhouse, which was published after his death, Ginsberg says that Durkheim was the proponent of "a mystical view of society as a new entity qualitatively distinct from the members composing it, which was always operating in a powerful and distinctive manner, but whose mode of operation remains wrapped in total obscurity." That was Ginsberg's view of Durkheim. I had to un-learn that.

I didn't have any very well crystalized interests during that year in London. But my Amherst teacher, Manthey-Zorn, was on a committee that was working on the establishment of a German-American exchange fellowship program; while I was in London the committee succeeded in setting up a plan. Manthey-Zorn wrote me in London and told me about this and asked whether I'd be interested in applying for one of those fellowships. I didn't have any very special plans and I thought it would be very interesting to see Germany after the First World War and so I accepted his suggestion and applied and was awarded a fellowship. And then by a curious set of serendipity, without having any personal say in it at all, I was assigned to Heidelberg.

Well, I wasn't in Heidelberg very many hours before I began hearing about Max Weber. Though he was no longer alive, in anything having to do with social science, including the historical disciplines, he was still clearly the dominant figure. I stopped in Heidelberg after the end of the London term but I spent most of that summer in Vienna, largely to improve my command of the German language. And when I came back in the fall I set right to work reading Weber and got extraordinarily interested in Weber very fast.

The German Doctorate

When I went to Heidelberg I had no idea of being a degree candidate. But I discovered that I could do so very easily. I still have to go out of my way to explain to people that I don't have a Ph.D. I've given up fighting about it, because I'm listed as Ph.D. again and again and again. Harvard gets it right: it's Doctor Phil., not Ph.D. And the standards are not nearly as high as a good American Ph.D. However that may be, I decided I might just as well become a candidate and a very important early decision was to write a dissertation on the concept of capitalism, linking it to German literature. This was one focal interest in the interpretation of the modern socioeconomic order that began then and has stuck with me ever since. But I gradually developed another interest, namely, in the relation between economic theory and sociological theory.

My supervisor was an economist, Edgar Salin. It was his advice that limited it to German literature, and there were three major figures dealt with, namely, [Karl] Marx—you couldn't very well omit Marx— Werner Sombart who was a contemporary still living at that time, and Weber. Quite obviously, Weber was the centerpiece, from my point of view.

It soon became evident to me that, though he was called an economist, Sombart didn't know the first thing about economic theory. He was a historical economist in the German tradition—he wrote an enormous six-volume thing entitled *Der moderne Kapitalismus*—but his historical economics wasn't what the English-speaking world meant by economics at all. It was essentially economic history. Weber, quite clearly, knew what economic theory was all about; he was professor of economics for a time. It ceased to be his primary interest but he knew what it was about, all right.

I went back to Amherst for a year as an instructor in economics. There was a new chairman of the economics department, Richard Meriam, whom I had never before met. He had come from Harvard and I got to be quite close to him and confided to him my plan of making a real study of the relations between economic theory and sociological theory. Well, he said, very correctly indeed: "If you're going to do that you've got to learn more economic theory than you know now." He was quite right. So the question was what steps to take to do this. He advised going to Harvard and he was instrumental in arranging an appointment for me by virtue of which I could keep body and soul together. I taught introductory economics there and was also a tutor. I didn't know there were even any plans to do anything about sociology at Harvard at the time, when I went there, and I hadn't the slightest idea of making a career of it. That developed step by step, but as it happened I went there in the fall of 1927 and I've been there ever since.

Well, it was a very complicated situation for a person like myself in the Harvard of that period. I was rather largely unaware of certain kinds of things that were happening. In a book edited by Gerald Holton on the 20th-century sciences there's an article by Paul Samuelson which has a certain amount of his autobiographical story in it. Samuelson came to Harvard as a graduate student in economics from the University of Chicago, where he'd been an undergraduate, just about that time. And if you read Samuelson's paper you'll see the direction that economics was beginning to take, which wasn't my direction. It was the highly technical, mathematical type of theory.

I was very fortunate in being exposed to the kind of economic theory that I needed, particularly through F. W. Taussig, who was still active at that time. And I was fortunate that [Joseph] Schumpeter was there on a visiting basis that year. (He later came back on a permanent basis, but it was a very fortunate moment for him to make his acquaintance, from my point of view.) Another very important figure, for me, was the economic historian Edwin F. Gay. Gay had been trained in Germany. He got his doctorate with [Gustav] Schmoller in Berlin and he knew the background that I had been exposed to in Germany, whereas most of the Harvard economists hadn't the slightest idea of what that stuff was all about. And most of them, not knowing anything about it, knew it was bad! I won't go into that, but I was befriended by people like Taussig and Gay and Schumpeter. I was looked upon very skeptically, however, by most of the other senior economists—and rightly, from their point of view. Now it turned out that there was a plan for developing sociology at Harvard and by 1931, four years after I got there, a formal department of sociology was opened with [Pitirim] Sorokin as chairman and I transferred to it.

At that time I was working on not only Weber but also [Vilfredo] Pareto and Durkheim. I had to work on Weber for my dissertation—which I didn't finish until after coming to Harvard—I had to work on Weber or abandon the dissertation project. I got interested in Pareto and had started working on him independently when I encountered L. J. Henderson. That was a very important relationship to me in those early days. I had also started to work on Durkheim entirely on my own. There were two people around Harvard who really knew and, substantially better than Ginsberg or Malinowski, appreciated Durkheim. One was the Australian psychologist Elton Mayo, one of the grandfathers of industrial sociology He got his interest in Durkheim from [Alfred R.] Radcliffe-Brown, whom he knew in Australia. The other was a young anthropologist, Lloyd Warner, later of Yankee City fame. Warner became a very good friend of mine. He was a Berkeley Ph.D. in anthropology but he had gone to Australia for field work and had come to know Radcliffe-Brown there and through Radcliffe-Brown had become interested in Durkheim. He later went to the University of Chicago, where he spent most of his career.

So I had a little better exposure to Durkheim from those two people from what I'd had at L.S.E. And incidentally, it wasn't intensive but one of my very important experiences at Heidelberg was exposure to Karl Jaspers, who later became much more famous as a philosopher. Jaspers in a couple of his lectures talked about Durkheim and Levy-Bruhl. He knew that French literature, which relatively few German scholars did, and his views were—from what came to be my point of view later—essentially correct and understanding.

At any rate, very, very gradually, the idea crystallized of a comparative study of social theorists, which eventually became my *Structure of Social Action*. I was doing this overwhelmingly on my own, with some advice but mostly on particular points. But the crucial breakthrough from my point of view was Taussig's full-year course in economic theory, which was required of all first-year graduate students in economics at Harvard, Economics 11. I audited that quite faithfully (I never took a single course for credit at Harvard) and even went so far as to actually take the mid-year examination, though it was never graded. At least two-thirds of the fall semester Taussig devoted to Alfred Marshall's *Principles of Economics* and I really got to know Marshall. As a matter of fact, before that I'd never even read Marshall at all. It was that that gave me an idea, following up my discussions with Richard Meriam, namely: economists must have some sociological ideas.

I was sensitized to that idea by Schumpeter, to a very considerable degree. Schumpeter was a strict constructionist about economic theory and he wanted to define it technically and relatively narrow. But he knew that there were a lot of other things; he himself wrote a number of essays on sociological topics, for example, a notable one on social stratification.

I decided I would make a study of Marshall to try to tease out his sociological ideas. I wrote what turned out to be two papers, which I submitted to Taussig, who was then editor of the *Quarterly Journal of Economics*, and he kindly accepted them for publication. That was the real starting point of *The Structure of Social Action* because I had a kind of a fulcrum in Marshall for systematizing the comparison between Marshall, English economics, the background in utilitarianism, and so on, with Durkheim, Pareto, and Weber. That was the main jumping-off place of that book and a very decisive one for me. That's something that has stayed with me.

The Structure of Social Action, you may remember, is a rather fat book—over 800 pages. One might say it's an unforgivable sin, especially for a young man, to foist that on his profession. But I did it anyway. And for some reason that I never understood, I got it published without subsidy. And that was in the Depression period, too. Well, naturally, the question arose, what next?

I'd been working on the idea of capitalism. Naturally, I also had to pay some attention to socialist thought. One of my subjects in my dissertation was Marx himself, and both Durkheim and Pareto wrote large books on socialist thought. Pareto's was published in his lifetime and Durkheim's was in the form of a set of lectures, which were published after his death. So all of my authors were mixed up with the problems presented by socialistic ideas. I was suddenly struck by the fact that in all this discussion, which ranged from sheer ideology well into the structure of the social sciences in the late 19th century and the early part of this century, that nothing was said about the profession except casual remarks here and there. Weber made some but he never went seriously into the subject. But the whole theoretical framework in which I approached the relation between economics and sociology had to pay a very strong attention to the famous formula, "the rational pursuit of self-interest."

The Problem of Self-Interest

A lot of economists were bothered about that conception, they were bothered about the problem of rationality, they were bothered about the problem of self-interest. The famous Wesley Mitchell wrote a very interesting article just about that time, in which he went off on what I am sure was a wild goose chase. He said economics ought to absorb the psychology of the nonrational and be a kind of applied psychology which abandoned the postulate of rationality. Schumpeter would have absolutely none of that—I remember talking to him about the problem—he'd have none of it and Schumpeter, I think, was right. If it had gone that way, economics would have had to become primarily empirical, not a theoretical, discipline. That's the way the institutionalists went and, of course, Mitchell was affiliated with that movement. But there was the problem—and the thing that appealed to me about the profession was that in their occupational ideology, whatever the situation might be at other levels, they repudiated the doctrine of self-interest and they self-consciously drew a line between themselves and businessmen.

I decided to look into this and, for a variety of reasons, I decided to do it by way of empirical field work—broadly speaking, interviewing and participant observation. I decided to pick one professional group and I picked medical practice. Now I'm sure there were personal motivations; I myself considered going into medicine, largely because I had a much-admired older brother who had done so. Later on some of my friends said—not unkindly, but a little bit barbed— "Oh, you studied medicine so you could both have your cake and eat it too"—that I studied medical *practice*, not medicine in the usual sense. In other words, you could identify yourself with the medical profession without doing the work of becoming a doctor. At any rate, I did that and one of my most fruitful kinds of experience was hanging around hospitals. Because the practice of medicine in the hospital is quasi-public, I found that the doctors with whom I made contact were quite willing to give me a white coat to wear around the hospital, that being the uniform then as now. Of course, I had the right to be called doctor and nobody needed to point out that it wasn't M.D. So I'd go around with the house staff on ward rounds, and we'd engage in front of patients in learned discussions until they'd say to me, "Doctor, what do you think of that?" and I'd try to look wise. It was a very interesting experience.

This led into an angle of the study of social structure of modern societies which was quite different from the economist's side. Taking that historic formula "The Rational Pursuit of Self-Interest," I started out focusing on the self-interest aspect. I think I got quite sufficient evidence that there was pay-dirt in studying attitudes in this area—that when physicians said their first concern was not their personal monetary gain but the welfare of the patient, they meant that seriously for the most part. Lots of people—the more cynically minded—say: "Oh, there are no greater money-grabbers in the world than doctors. They're just awful; they're much more avaricious than businessmen are." But there is something else there.

The other operative word of that formula is "rational," and the study of medical practice in the medical situation led one directly into a new aspect of the problem of rationality—what Pareto discussed in his "logical"-"non-logical action" and as himself an economist tried to formulate about those things that economics as a science of rational behavior left out. This is a main centerpiece of his sociology. At any rate, I came along on the study of medical practice, both in terms of time and place, at a rather crucial moment—moments that are measured in terms of years. The fact that I was on the Harvard faculty even though, as local phrasing goes, on the other side of the river, meant that I did have rather special access to people involved in the Harvard Medical School—teaching hospitals and so on. For example, I spent a great deal of time at the Massachusetts General Hospital. Now this was a time when intellectually sophisticated medical people were getting very much interested in what they called the "psychic factors" in disease—not only mental illness but what a little later came to be called the "psychosomatic problem." My first contacts there were with physicians, the type called internists for the most part and secondarily the surgeons.

The MGH had a small psychiatric service, of which the chief was Stanley Cobb, whose name is still quite well known. Eric Lindeman, whom I later got to know very well indeed, was Number 2 on that service. Cobb was also the main founder of the Boston Psychoanalytic Institute—he raised the money to get an institute started in Boston—and from the beginning it was all mixed up with psychoanalytic ideas. I couldn't be around the MGH very long without getting pulled into this kind of thinking about certain kinds of health and illness.

About that time came a very interesting specific experience. Henderson was medically trained; he was L. J. Henderson, M.D. You could call him according to emphasis either a physiologist or a biochemist. He never practiced medicine; he was always a medical scientist rather than a practitioner. But he was identified with the medical world, and was for a number of years a member of the faculty at the Harvard Medical School in the "basic science" division. And Mayo was close to medical thinking, though he was not an M.D. I had consulted Henderson and Mayo about my plans for studying medical practice and been substantially helped by them. One day I was talking to Mayo about this psychological interest that I had been encountering among the medical people I'd been observing and talking to, and he suddenly broke in and said: "How much do you know about Freud?" I said: "Frankly, not very much." I'd done a smattering of reading but nothing at all really serious or systematic. "Well," Mayo said, "I strongly advise you to read [Sigmund] Freud thoroughly and carefully. "I was in a position at that time when I had rather few formal obligations. I had a semester off teaching and I took Mayo's advice and really did read Freud. (If I say so now, I was fortunate in one particular respect because after my study in Germany I could read German just about as well as I could English. I wonder how many Americans who talk about Freud have ever read Freud in German. I imagine it's a very small minority. But remember, Freud wrote in German, not in English. To be sure, it was Viennese German, but still German.) Well, that was a major turn for me. The combination of the study of medical practice on one hand and doing the order of careful reading of Freud that I had done in previous years of Durkheim and Weber, led into quite a number of different things.

Interest in the professions had stayed with me ever since, but my empirical focus has moved to the academic world, which I count very much as part of the professional world. I remember talking with a colleague who was a social scientist about my interest in medical practice and he said, somewhat sarcastically: "Why don't you study what's right under your nose, your own profession, the university as a social organization." I lamely tried to explain why I was interested in the medical profession and he burst in and said: "You know you wouldn't dare study the academic profession because you'd stir up too many hornet's nests and you'd probably be thrown out of the profession for it." In recent years I have dared to do so, as a great many other sociologists have, too.

Question (Adrian Hayes): To outline how your interest in questions of rationality developed, could you say what your feelings were with regard to possible styles of analysis at this time? How did you know what type of answer you were looking for these questions? Was it essentially a question extending Kant's analysis on pure and practical reason?

PARSONS: I had become skeptical of utilitarianism, due to some combination of social sciences and philosophical love. A real landmark there was being asked to write the article on [Thomas Robert] Malthus for the old *Encyclopedia of the Social Sciences*. I did quite a lot of reading, not only in Malthus' own publications but also the secondary literature. I found the secondary literature to be deadly dull—just a repetition of arithmetical and geometrical ratios *ad nauseam*. There's a fat book by a man named [James] Bonar which had this formula on every other page. Then I encountered [Elie] Halévy's *The Growth of Philosophical Radicalism*, and that was a revelation. There was a real analytical intellectual history of the utilitarian movement . . . a great classic. Naturally, as immersed in the German tradition as I was, above all via Weber, I couldn't still be a naive utilitarian. I couldn't have understood Weber on that basis.

I had been exposed to Kant in a very good undergraduate seminar on the *Critique of Pure Reason*. Under the guidance of a tiny Scotsman named George Brown, who was a professor of classics, a small group of six of us went right straight through the *Critique of Pure Reason*. Then in Heidelberg two or three years later I had a seminar on the *Critique of Pure Reason*. That time I reread it in German, not in English, and I was examined orally by Jaspers on Kant. So Kant was a very deep-lying influence.

My next encounter was at Harvard with [A.N.] Whitehead. I would call Bertrand Russell a glorified utilitarian, a more sophisticated version of the utilitarian tradition. But Whitehead is not; he was quite different. I can't read their mathematical logic, but I've always regarded Whitehead as the better philosopher. I know this runs grossly contrary to most current belief, but that happens to be my opinion. There are many things that are very impressive about Whitehead, but one very central one was his conception of the "fallacy of misplaced concreteness" and his critique of the people who interpreted scientific theory as essentially empirical generalization. In his *Science and the Modern World*, a very notable book, in my opinion, he discusses classical mechanics as an abstract analytical scheme which simply could not be identified with concrete reality.

Without some such perspective as that I don't think it would have been possible to really get any comparison between the four principal authors whom I used in *The Structure of Social Action*. Look at Pitirim A. Sorokin's *Contemporary Sociological Theories*, which had appeared only a short time before. Of course he doesn't mention Marshall because Marshall was an economist, but the other three he put in totally distinct schools and there's not a word in Sorokin's book that even suggests that they have anything to do with each other. Well, I might be wrong in thinking they had but that's the thesis of my book. I couldn't have written that without the background of Kant and Whitehead's views of the philosophy of science and, I should mention also, Henderson's. Henderson was pretty close to Whitehead in this field; he really was a philosopher of science, I'd say of a very high order. This was very essential background.

Another crucial point concerns the concept of voluntarism. Without Whitehead's exploding of old-fashioned scientific materialistic determinism you couldn't seriously put forward a formula like a voluntaristic theory of action because if it is scientific it has to be deterministic and there's no room for voluntary action. Quite a few years before publication of *The Structure of Social Action*, I became completely convinced that scientific materialism of the old style was untenable. Incidentally, I still marvel at the ideological use of the word "materialism" you hear so frequently.

I think the really decisive turning point for me was going to Germany and falling under the aegis of Weber. If I had gone to either Columbia or Chicago in the late 20s I would not have absorbed Weber. I might have gotten around to it 10 or 15 years later. Among other things I wouldn't have known German well enough to read

Weber in German and the translations wouldn't have begun coming out for quite a while. There was a very brief efflorescence of interest in Pareto for a while. The English translation of Pareto's *Treatise* didn't appear until '35, when I was more than 10 years out of college. I did my work in the French edition of Pareto, but I don't think if I'd gone to Columbia or Chicago I would have read either German or French works on any scale. Now it may be that I missed more than I gained; personally I don't think so.

At that time you had to read French to read Durkheim; the *Elementary Forms* had been translated by 1915, but hardly anything else. And you can't start to understand Durkheim by reading the *Elementary Forms*. This is the end of his development, not a beginning. I remember as an undergraduate I was asked to, as a course assignment, read some selections from the *Elementary Forms*. And I literally shudder now to think what I did not understand of that. Now I didn't have the slightest inkling at what Durkheim was trying to do in that book from reading a few excerpts in isolation from anything else that Durkheim had written. I really got into Durkheim through the *Division of Labor*, and this was logical because that was Durkheim's first major book, but I had to read that in French. The English edition didn't come out until the late '30s. I might just remark parenthetically in the presence of some graduate students: a translation is never a good substitute for the original of things of this sort.

Question (Mr. Wolf): I have two questions, if I could get back to *The Structure of Social Action* for a minute. It was said at the time that that book was intended to end the "war of the schools" and I was wondering what warring the schools were doing at that time and whether the book ended it. And secondly, in your preface to the paperback edition you mention if you were doing it again you'd give more of a role to [Georg] Simmel and Freud. I wonder if you'd care to elaborate on those two points.

PARSONS: I mentioned just a minute ago Sorokin's treatment of Pareto, Durkheim, and Weber as belonging to three quite different schools. Now my thesis of convergence, to my knowledge, has never been seriously challenged. I mean, nobody has sat down, done a careful analysis of my book, and shown that the thesis of convergence is not tenable. If anybody knows such a document I'd very much like to see it. I wouldn't accept it as having proved its point without going over it very carefully. Now did this or didn't this end a "war of schools"? Maybe, maybe not. At the very least it put on record a view that was contrary to the Sorokinian view.

One of the funny things about getting a reputation by way of a book like that is that it has been very widely used as a "trot." There's so little study of foreign languages that many of you don't know what a "trot" is. The people who didn't really read the Latin texts assigned to them in courses in Latin but somehow smuggled in English translations and read those could say something about the content without having mastered the Latin language.

Innumerable students have read what I had to say about Durkheim and never bothered to read Durkheim, Weber, and so on. I suppose that's a price you have to pay. I don't like it; I think it's very low professional and intellectual ethics to pretend that you learn about a major author's work by never reading it. There is the language excuse, but I happen to be one of those old-fashioned people who very much deplores the decline in the knowledge of foreign languages on the part of the scholarly community. The number of my students—and I know because I ask them—who can read Weber in German is minuscule. No, German's a hard language so they don't bother to learn it. We dropped our language requirements for graduate students; you couldn't enforce them, they became a joke. Robert Merton, who was one of my very first graduate students in sociology, went to Germany and spent two summers very largely working on the language. A man of Merton's caliber will do that kind of thing, but you only have to go down a couple of pegs in intellectual caliber and seriousness and they won't do it. They say: "Don't I speak—and read English? Isn't that enough? Translations are just as good as the original." They just aren't.

The Simmel question is interesting. I actually drafted a chapter on Simmel for *The Structure of Social Action*. If you've ever had to deal with publishers you know that they have one argument that they are apt to press rather hard: "Your manuscript's too long. Can't you cut it?" That was one ground on which I left Simmel out, and I reduced what was to be another chapter on [Ferdinand] Tönnies to a long note. Another reason why I was put off Simmel was that there was a certain vogue of so-called formal sociology at just about that time [Howard] Becker's re-working of von Wiese's *Allgemeine Soziologie*, which I suppose can be roughly translated *Theory of Relationships*, was quite popular and was thought to be the thing, much better than Weber. Why? Because it was easier to understand and for no other reason. I really think that's true. Von Wiese was a watered-down version of Simmel, not nearly as good as Simmel himself. In *The Structure of Social Action* I was concerned with conceptual structure in the principal authors whom I presented and analyzed. At that level, Simmel is not in anything like the class of those others. Simmel's strength was as an extremely insightful essayist about quite concrete and very diverse matters—so diverse it's exceedingly difficult to summarize. In contrast with any of these other three (leaving out Marshall, who was also a great theorist) there was relatively little theory in Simmel, and to give it a place comparable to Weber's wouldn't have made sense. This isn't a judgment on its quality in every respect, but it wasn't in the same universe. I was very much concerned with doing a comparative job and to do a comparative job you have to compare comparables. Freud was that kind of a theorist, in a sense in which Simmel was not. To include Freud would have entirely taken you out of sociology in a narrower sense, but in terms of the genre it would have been entirely appropriate to have had a large section on Freud. Just because Simmel is thought to be good wasn't the primary criterion for dealing with his work extensively in that particular book. It was not a history of sociology. It's often been treated as such, but that wasn't what it was meant to be.

Question (Mr. Wessen): This raises a couple of other issues about which you might comment. It seems to me that at least history now would tend to say that Pareto was not either in the same league with Durkheim or Weber, at least in terms of the influence that he's come to have. That leads me to wonder if there might not have been another issue involved here, namely, the fundamental kinds of questions that concerned the theorists we're speaking to.

PARSONS: You're quite right, there was another issue. For my special concern with the problem of the relation of economic and sociological theory, Pareto was a natural. You could formulate certain of the problems with reference to Pareto much more easily than you could with either Durkheim or Weber. Pareto was completely explicit on it: he was an eminent theoretical economist in his own right, which the others were not—except, of course, Marshall. Pareto was uncommonly convenient for my purposes. This is another example, though, of the danger of interpreting that book as essentially a history of sociology or sociological theory.

Martel: Of course, many people think the most conspicuous omission, then, is Karl Marx, particularly since you had treated him in your dissertation. I realize he's a generation earlier than Weber . . .

PARSONS: That's the main point. Again, what would the publisher have said if I had added 200 pages on Marx? I wouldn't have gotten it published without subsidy, I'm sure of that. And where was I going to raise the money for the subsidy? But I would defend something on a slightly different level. All four of my authors (but Marshall somewhat less so in a different context) were very much concerned with the problems of socialism and socialist thought. Pareto wrote a large book on socialist thought. Durkheim gave a voluminous set of lectures, which were posthumously published, called "Les Socialisme." Weber didn't in a comparable sense devote a major analysis to it, but all we know about Weber's intellectual biography shows the same preoccupation. There are many points in his work where the references to problems of socialism are very clear. Still, I would contend that compared to the intellectual world of Marx, the world I dealt with was a new world.

It wasn't just a continuation of Marxian thought. If you take only the economic side of it, the theory of marginal utility had not yet appeared on the scene in Marx's day. It had become the theoretical center of what came to be called neoclassical economics and Marshall was one of four, I believe, independent discoverers of the principle of marginal utility, which Marx did not know. Now whether

Marx would have held to the labor theory of value if he had understood the marginal principle, I don't know. But most of Marx's technical economics is wrong largely for that reason. He didn't understand this very vital part of modern economic theory, and most of the neo-Marxists carefully avoid the subject They never discuss Marx as an economic theorist. That wasn't Marx's conception of himself at all—his economic theory was at the very center of his thought. But if you're a New Leftist you carefully avoid Marxian economic theory.

Question (Graduate Student): How is your rejection of positivism related to your own views on socialism in the period we are considering, and has there been a change in your views?

PARSONS: That's not a terribly easy question to answer. I was enormously interested in the socialist movement: the Russian Revolution occurred shortly before I went to college, Lenin died during my senior year, I got enormously interested in the British labor movement. Incidentally, I was in England when the first Labor government came into office under Ramsay MacDonald, and naturally I was following this closely. I never converted to what my friend Robert Bellah would call this particular version of the "civil religion," and I do think that essentially Marxism is a secular religion in its basic symbolic structure and so on. It's a theory of salvation by proletarian revolution, which has striking parallels to the Christian idea of salvation, but the symbols are at a different level.

In my other capacity—not as a technical, hopefully somewhat systematic, theorist, but as an interpreter of the social scene—an awful lot has happened since 1924, when I graduated from college. Among the things that have happened have been very complex vicissitudes of the socialist movement. It gained political ascendency in Eastern Europe—in the Soviet Union of course, which was economically a relatively backward, underdeveloped country at the time. Marx himself and many after Marx expected the revolution to come in the industrially most advanced country. I'm pretty sure it's true that Lenin thought in 1917 that he was engaged in a holding operation, that the real revolution was going to come in Germany in the very near future.

It didn't. It certainly didn't come in Great Britain. That sort of phenomenon has given me very much food for reflection.

Why didn't this happen? The Chinese revolution wasn't even a proletarian revolution. The recent discord between the Russians and the Chinese goes a long way back. Stalin backed Chiang Kai-shek and tried to get the Maoist movement liquidated. Stalin! Not the bourgeois agents, unless you consider Stalin to have been a bourgeois agent. The history of the thing is shot through with apparent anomalies of that sort. It did not unfold according to the original scenario at all. Of course, the United States is "the most advanced capitalist country in the world" and it's never been anywhere close to a proletarian revolution—not simply because of the powerful repressive capacities of bourgeois-dominated government. Relatively speaking, ours hasn't been more repressive or more powerful than those of Germany, France, and Britain where Marx fully expected the revolution to win in spite of the bourgeoisie. It didn't win there and it hasn't won here.

I've had a continuing intellectual interest in these problems. Why have things gone the way they have? We have had, of course, another tremendous revival of socialism in the so-called third world. All the Arab countries and most of the African regimes call themselves socialist. How authentically socialist they are is a rather complicated question, but socialism has become a major salient symbol all over that part of the world.

Question (Ray Goldstein): Following this up on your view of Marxism and what it turned out to be, would the inequality in America give you food for thought also on how capitalism as a system works, just as what has happened with Marxism?

PARSONS: As part of an answer to that question I think it's appropriate to refer to Tocqueville. It was more than a century ago that Tocqueville observed American society, but he was impressed from a European background with the egalitarianism of this country, not with its inequality. I don't think that American society of the 1830s was (in the sense that most of the "left" would think ethically acceptable) a very egalitarian society. I don't think it was very much more egalitarian than the society has been in its more recent phase. To be sure, there weren't very large industrial corporations in Tocqueville's day; even railway building had barely begun. I think myself, by most comparative standards, it is a relatively egalitarian society and in this respect it hasn't changed terribly much over a long time. It comes awfully close to being as egalitarian as that of the Soviet Union, in a great many respects.

Question (Mr. Rueschemeyer): Karl Mannheim has developed a concept of political generation or intellectual generation, that is, a generation shaped by crucial experiences that result in a generational imprint. Could you say a few words about how you see your generation and your place in it and what specific political and social developments crystallized and shaped your theoretical thought?

PARSONS: It's been a dramatic period. I came to what you might call some kind of an intellectual self-awareness just about the time of the First World War and its early aftermath. The First World War was not just a simple little event that didn't have much of an impact on the culture and intellectual tone of its time. It was one of the major events of modern history. My interest in it was one of the motives that impelled me to accept the opportunity to go to Germany. I was one of the type of young intellectuals who could hardly accept the violently anti-German stereotype that was so common in this country during the war. I didn't go as far as Malinowski. He was a Polish national, originally, but there he was with an academic post in Great Britain, and he was continually saying: "Oh, the Germans are so much better than the British! The British are backwards, stupid, nasty, and the Germans, those are real people." He used to say this to his classes, everywhere, all the time. He wouldn't travel on a British ship, he always traveled on a German ship . . . things like that. I didn't go quite that far.

There had been the Russian Revolution, which certainly made a great impact on my generation. We found it very difficult to believe the atrocities of Stalin. There may be really loyal Soviet-type communists in this room who believe that there weren't any atrocities in the Stalinist regime—it was all made up by the bourgeois enemies of the revolution. I don't think that's true, personally. Of course, I formed some pretty strong emotional attachments to the liberal Germany, having been a student there, and the phenomenon of Nazism was pretty darned appalling. Again, it was really only after Hitler's defeat that it came to be widely appreciated how bad it was. You remember that in the 30s Nazism and, still more, Italian fascism, which was very much milder, had quite a good press in this country. They all said, "Mussolini makes the trains run on time (the old Italian regime could never do that); Mussolini must be pretty good." There was a certain disposition to say the same about Hitler, although German trains had always run on time, in the Weimar period and in the days of what when I was a student there I came to call the reign of Wilhelm der Letsda. I was in Germany from June 1925, with an interval back here, till the end of the summer of '27. The great inflation had only been brought under control about a year before I got there. The inflation was a matter of very serious social disorganization, not just economic dislocation but social disorganization. I happened to be there in a very brief good period, the best period of the Weimar regime.

Most of you are not old enough to remember the "little yellow bastards," which was the vernacular term for Japanese. It was not a very friendly attitude and this was before Pearl Harbor. That brings us to 1944, essentially the fall of Hitler—less than 30 years ago. The explicitness of drama hasn't been as great since then.

Well, it's been a very very turbulent period in world history through that time. I certainly would have been a different person if I had not been intellectually inclined and intellectually and emotionally involved in all these complicated events. Had it been something like the Victorian period I have no idea what difference it would have made. I'm a kind of optimist but I hope not a just plain, Pangloss, naive kind of optimist who doesn't believe there's any real tragedy in human affairs. I've been accused of not believing in the reality of conflict. I don't think one could be very acutely aware of the Nazi movement and not believe in the reality of conflict. There are people who assert: "Here's a guy who doesn't even know conflict really exists." I just don't see how they arrive at that conclusion.

Martel: I think this begins to give us some understanding of how a young, respectable economist went so wrong, and I think our time is running out and we shall adjourn now for lunch. . . .

SEMINAR PART II

Afternoon Session

Birth of the Social Relations Department 1945–1951

Martel: This morning you were telling us about developments in your work and your career about up to the time of World War II. I wonder if you would pick up the story. You were talking about how you got into the study of professions and how this led you to a whole different direction, and how a sociologist rather than an economist went wrong.

PARSONS: Well, this led away from economics, of course. But just about the time I came to be quite closely associated with a psychologically minded group of people. I suppose the most important person, and the one closest to me, was Clyde Kluckhohn the anthropologist. He was a very close friend of Henry Murray who was director of a clinic and a professional psychologist; and we used to see quite a lot of each other. And in the early part of the war (even a little past Pearl Harbor), I remember we not only had a discussion-group devoted to "shop talk" as well as intellectual matters but we began to get interested in more practical organizational questions. And really the idea of what became the Department of Social Relations was born in some of those discussions (bringing the three fields of anthropology, psychology, and sociology together).

I won't take time here to recount the full story but the venture came to a head in the first full academic year after the war (1945–6); and the Department of Social Relations actually opened in the fall of '46. Now Kluckhohn and Murray, who I mentioned, were very key people in it. Gordon Alport, the social psychologist, was another; and in this connection there was an opening which brought Samuel Stouffer there. Actually, during this early Social Relations period, the informal self-appointed "executive committee" members were

Stouffer, Kluckhohn, and myself. Stouffer was director of the research organization (which was called the Laboratory of Social Relations). I was chairman of the department, and Kluckhohn was the senior anthropologist. So I think we came honestly by our membership in a kind of an executive committee. Among the key psychologists, Alport and Murray were most central. But Murray less so only because he was not administratively minded. He really didn't care very much about that side of things. Alport was the main one who represented the psychological group and was most active administratively.

Well, we were very lucky in one respect. Because the war had produced a backlog of students who had left the university for various kinds of war service, and they all came flocking back when they were demobilized. Those who came were a very exceptional student group, including a fair number who wouldn't have been able to do so financially except for the GI Bill, which operated very much in our favor. Quite a number of these early students have very much made their mark subsequently. (The creation of this rather unusual interdisciplinary department had an important *intellectual* influence on all of its members.)

One aspect that particularly affected my own work was that we were approached by the Carnegie people who had given our laboratory a substantial free research fund. (They also, incidentally, had initially financed the Russian Research Center of which Kluckhohn became the first director.) The Carnegie group suggested some kind of a theoretical stock taking, and I was then the freest of the senior people in the department who also was strongly theoretically minded. [So it happened that] I took over the sort of chairmanship of this stock-taking project.

We had money from the Carnegie people so we brought F. C. Coleman (the Berkeley psychologist) and Edward Shills from Chicago to Harvard for a semester, and I had leave from teaching for that semester. (So there were the three of us for a start.) We also had a somewhat larger group that met once a week, and this whole group became the author of the volume, *Toward a General Theory of Action* (published in 1951). That's how that volume originated. It may be of interest to mention that I had met Shills in 1937 when I was a visiting teacher at Chicago for the summer quarter. Shills at that time was a graduate student, and he with Herbert Goldheim organized an informal seminar that summer. [For almost 10 years after that] I'd hardly seen Shills, although I'd heard about his activities, especially in England. But then we were very closely associated in this *General Theory* project. And this collaboration continued, with Robert F. Bales also joining us in a couple of years. Bales and I started the detail work on the *Working Papers in the General Theory of Action* (published in 1953); and we were able to bring Shills in for a summer toward the end of that project. [I might mention here that recently] I've been seeing Shills again. We two, and Joseph Ben-David, gave a joint seminar in Chicago last fall on the sociology of higher education.

The Pattern Variables

[Going back to the Carnegie project], the contact with Edward Tolman, the psychologist, was exceedingly valuable to us, and initiated a good many intellectual things. One of them was the so-called pattern-variable scheme. This had begun earlier, partly as a critique of Ferdinand Tönnies' idea of "*Gemeinschaft* and *Gesellschaft*," and had figured a good deal in my study of the professions. But Shills and I now carried the scheme much further in connection with *Toward a General Theory of Action*. And in the *Working Papers* sequel two years later (with Bales as a third partner), the pattern variables turned out to be the seedbed for the "*four-function*" scheme with which I've been working ever since. And the core ideas really broke in the course of working with *Toward a General Theory of Action*.

The "Four Functions" and a Return to Economy and Society

This [the four-function scheme] was very important from one point of view because without it I would never have made the new step, [returning to] the relations of economics and sociology. I'll say something about that next. This new step eventuated in the little book to which Neil Smelser and I gave the grandiose title of *Economy and Society*. Lest we be accused of immodesty, you might read our preface, which said we were well aware that this was a translation of Max Weber's famous work, *Wirtschaft und Gesellschaft*, and we were duly humbled. But there was no prospect at that time of a full edition of Weber's book in English. And we thought we were justified in using the title (with the qualifications given). Now that the full translation is out, [I guess we can say that] there's the "big" *Economy and Society* and the little one.

Well, Mr. Martel suggested that I draw a four-function paradigm on the board. Is this a good time to do it?

Well, it can very simply be drawn like this, working (to begin with) at the four-cell level. As you may know, [the scheme has been developed in some detail on the 16-cell level, and occasionally we have ventured to the 64-cell level, which brings it closer to specific content problems]. We also have developed it both on (1) the level of the organization of *social systems*, as well as (2) for the *general action system* (which includes the additional systems of culture, personality, and the behavioral organism, plus the social system). But I'll discuss

Figure 1

The "Four-Functions" Scheme: Functional Imperatives and Major
Subsystems of Advanced Societies

Fiduciary System	Societal-Community	
L *Pattern maintenance*	*Integration function* I	
Economy	Polity	
A *Adaptation function*	*Goal attainment* G	

it here mainly on [the highest level of social systems, which can be called "society"].

There are various arbitrary matters about the placement of the four basic cells (and how they are best labeled). But let's put the "L" and "I" cells at the top, and the "A" and "G" on the bottom row. It's the simplest possible diagramming convention. By the way, I was introduced to the idea of the four-fold table, believe it or not, by Paul Lazarsfeld himself.

But the letters (A-G-I-L) are, of course, simply abbreviative designations for the four functional categories, which [might more fully be termed] "Adaptation," "Goal Attainment," "Integration" and, for the fourth, Bales introduced the very long and cumbersome term, "*Latent pattern maintenance & tension management.*" (The "L" stands for "latency.") In our own earlier uses we would refer to it by that whole clumsy phrase, but it is usually shortened to "pattern maintenance." The "latency" idea corresponds very closely to latent functions in Merton's sense, but we dropped the extra wordage. (I know the terms are a little awkward, and they always need explanation.) Well now, *these* designations [apply to the functional systems when they are applied] to the broad, *general-action* level.

When the scheme is applied to the *organization of society*, a [different], more appropriate terminology is needed. In recent years I've been referring to these as:

1. The *fiduciary* system for the pattern-maintenance aspect (Figure 1).
2. The *societal community*, as a useful designation for the "integrative" system. This is what Durkheim essentially referred to as the aspect in which society is a moral community.
3. The *economy* [is the term applied to the] lower left side, or the "adaptation" system of society, as a result of the analysis [Smelser and I developed] in the "little" *Economy and Society* book. And
4. The term *polity* [seems to be appropriate for the lower-right, or "goal-attainment" cell], as a word nearly parallel to economy. In other words, there is "political primacy" here, functionally speaking, in a way that is analytically parallel to the "economic primacy" suggested for the adaptive system.

[The point of this is] the idea that all organized systems of *action* must have some distinguishable subsystems which give primacy to each of the four basic functions in the paradigm. This seems to be true for organized societies as well as all other organized action systems. And on a very broad level, it seems important that *economic and political* systems, in something like the usual sense that economists and political analysts conceive of these, have the primary functions of "adaptation" and "goal attainment" respectively. While economists and political scientists usually treat these two systems as if they were each mainly *closed* and relatively discrete, this approach regards them as subsystems of the larger organization of societies. As subsystems, they are partly interlinked, so each affects the function of the other in part. They also are importantly linked to the two higher-order systems of the "societal community" and the "fiduciary." But each has its own partly independent sphere of functioning as a subsystem in its own right. To look at it in this way, then, calls attention to theoretical problems of *both* how each system functions internally, as a partly autonomous subsphere, [and also how it is interlinked to the others]. We have run through the implications of this notion in a great many ways, and it has proved extraordinarily useful.

Now, you might say: "Isn't this oversimple?" Sure it is. But it's overly simple in the same sense that the core ideas of any theoretical science are. You may recall the famous quote of Whitehead, for example, that the framework of classical mechanics is a terrible oversimplification of reality. *But if you don't simplify in an analytical sense, you never get anywhere (in science).* And the complications should be introduced by combinations, and not by a primary ground scheme that is very complicated. That, in any event, is my own view on the matter.

Well, to return to [the earlier crystallization of this approach in *Economy and Society*], at a rather strategic moment I was invited to a visiting professorship at the University of Cambridge in England, for the year 1953–1954. As part of this invitation (but not an integral part), I was invited to give the Marshall Lectures, which is a series of three public lectures named in honor of the economist, Alfred Marshall, who was the first professor of economics at Cambridge. And I was asked to give them on the topic of "The Relations Between Economic Theory and Sociological Theory." So I had to revisit the whole topic which was so important in (my prewar book), *The Structure of Social Action*. In preparing these lectures, while I didn't have too much time since they had to be delivered in November, I did reread a good deal of Marshall. For the first time I also then thoroughly read John Maynard Keynes' famous general theory. This was published, by the way, after his writings published in 1936, when my own work on *The Structure of Social Action* was already done.

And I had a sudden hunch. You may remember that the classical economists used the classification of three (basic) factors of production: land, labor, and capital. To these Marshall added a fourth: organization. Schumpeter also had used something similar to that. Well, I said to myself: "Four factors of production with corresponding shares of income—and four functions. Is there a fifth?" Well, we pursued the idea of a fifth and it worked.

Now, I had that partly worked out at the time of the oral delivery of the Marshall Lectures, but there was another very fortunate circumstance—[the presence of Neil Smelser in England]. I had known Smelser as an undergraduate at Harvard, where he was very much of an undergraduate leader; and he was then in the second year of a Rhodes Scholarship at Oxford. He was taking the "PPE Course" there (philosophy, politics, and economics), concentrating on economics. So I thought he'd be a good person to talk to, and I sent him a manuscript of these lectures. He came back with excellent, penetrating, and detailed comments. And while we were both in England we had two or three face-to-face meetings and long discussions over these problems.

Well, Smelser came back to Harvard the following fall and I was also back by that time. On top of his Oxford B.A., he enrolled for a Ph.D. at Harvard, and some people said that Smelser sounded too good to be true. (You see, he graduated from Harvard College with a *summa*, and he graduated from Oxford with a "first." Now, there aren't that many people who have both. And he also was a member of the Society of Fellows at Harvard after he came back from Oxford, and that's a very special honor—especially for a sociologist because they didn't, on the whole, like sociologists.) He really had quite a record of being on the very top of any list.

But when we settled down at Cambridge [USA], Smelser and I decided to build this Marshall Lecture thing into a small book, and that's how *Economy and Society* happened. By the way, our collaboration on this book [in 1953] was before he wrote his dissertation: his [well-known] book on the Industrial Revolution.

Further Developments: The "Media of Interchange"
(Money, Power, Influence, and Value Commitments)

Well, this collaboration started an awful lot of things. It not only gave a surprising application of the four-fold paradigm, but it led into many other developments. Probably the most important among them was the idea—to cite the whole cumbersome phrase—of the "generalized symbolic media of interaction." This notion started with a consideration of some aspects of what you might call the "sociology of money" as a "medium of exchange." [As a background point], what we had done in the little book *Economy of Society* gave an excellent starting point [for the "media" conception]. But we didn't really get into money in that book. However, along the line it occurred to me that money simply could not logically stand by itself, as most economists (and most other social scientists) had assumed. That is *the general assumption was that* it was a totally unique phenomenon. But it seemed increasingly clear that money must be a member of a larger family of meaning.

On this point I remember being very much stimulated in that idea by another former student, James Olds, who went off in a very different direction. Olds now is one of the leading people in the country in some areas of brain research. And [at that time] he had very recently discovered the so-called *reward center* of the brain, the "lax brain." This was the first phase of his career along these lines, and he was then working at McGill University. The striking thing about this discovery was that Olds found you could put a rat through all the paces of the classical learning experiments and never have to give any "reward" (in the sense of Clark Hull's then influential learning theory). Well, this just blew Clark Hull sky-high! Hull claimed [that if a rat] was to become experimentally conditioned, you have to give it food (or get him very thirsty and give him water to drink or something like that), some form of *external* reward. But Olds did it with electrical stimulation of the brain: that is, with *rewards given directly* in the brain. Now, the inference was that learning experience was not necessarily generated by external reward but, rather, could be internal to the processes of the central nervous system.

So here I was, thinking hard [about the links between] money and meaning, and it struck me that what Olds called "pleasure" was probably a generalized meaning in this sense. The first time I broached it to him, he said: "Well, this is crazy, there's nothing in that." But a few months later I saw him again (by which time he'd moved to California) and we spent a whole day on the problem. This time I think he was getting convinced that it really worked at that infra-social level [of action].

But then I went off on another tack, and explored the idea that there were several other media [in this sense] that operated within the *social* system. The first of these *other media* that I happened to tackle, besides money, was *political power*, and if I do say so, I think it worked. It's even been taken up a bit by some political scientists. And it isn't simply laughed out of court. But to work through this parallel, you have to modify the political science conception of power much more drastically than I had to modify the economist's notions of money. The reason for this is that, even though the way economists use the concept of "money" is partly along the same lines in which most political scientists use the word "power," the latter really is very much broader. Often, it's not really theoretically specific at all. Power is essentially anything that is effective in getting the power-holders (or users) sway, even against opposition. This is very close to the definition of power given by Max Weber, so in this respect I'm not a Weberian.

But [to explore the parallels] you have to be theoretically more specific; you have to introduce some narrowing assumptions. And this, of course, is a risky business in the face of the predominant opinion of the whole profession [of political science]. But there's a long essay on record ["On the Concept of Political Power," 1963], and there have been some fruitful applications.

Moving on, then, from the treatment of power as a "generalized medium," the notion was further applied to the concepts of "influence" and to "value commitments." (This still was at the social-system level, not the general-action level.) And Gerald Platt and I have very recently worked out a much more elaborate formulation of the media conceptions, both on the social-system and general-action levels, in the course of an analysis of higher education in America that will be available soon in a new book, still in press. The title of the book will be *The American University*, and it's quite a fat volume (giving our most detailed statement to date).[2] In this work we used the [third and fourth media concepts] of influence and of value commitments quite extensively; insisting throughout on a [strong] distinction between "influence" and "power." As you may know, this distinction was proposed (in a sketchier way) in one or two earlier articles, but it is presented much more thoroughly and systematically in the new book. And it turns out to be a simply indispensable line of theoretical distinction. (There are some precedents for making such a contrast, in the field of political theory.) However, most political scientists include much of what we call "influence" within their definitions of power. Well, I won't stop to go into the precise distinctions right now.

[In addition to the elaboration of the four media model on the social-system level], in the new book Platt, some others, and I also have tried to extend the generalized-media idea on the analytic level of the general system of action. To do this, we've introduced a four-member set [of more generalized media conceptions]. These are called "intelligence," "performance capacity," "affect," and—borrowing a phrase from W. I. Thomas—the "definition of a situation." And we have tried to use the same fundamental paradigm consistently in our analysis. Well, that's a long and complicated story, and some of those most closely involved have not been able to reach full agreement on some important points. But we've at least taken this idea of "generalized symbolic media" very seriously, and I think it's borne quite a lot of fruit. [For the social-system part of it], if it holds up and is better verified, I think it will prove that the same kind of analytical strength that economic theories [of monetary exchange] have achieved are attainable in sociology.

Just this one point. Platt and I took the concepts of "inflation" and "deflation"—not of money, but of influence and value commitments—and used them by partial analogy very extensively in our book. We're very anxious to see how this analogy is received. I'm sure we'll get snide reviews from some people who will say: "Why, these guys are really just plain crazy, they don't have a leg to stand on." Some also may say: "This suggested analogy is pure speculation. It has nothing to do with science." I'm sure we'll get some reviews like that. But *The Structure of Social Action* in 1937 had a number of reviews more or less in this vein, and it's still paying royalties.

Questions about "Power" and Other Media

Question (Mr. Goldsteen): Mr. Parsons. In your three main papers on stratification theory [1940, 1953, and 1970], the first two really didn't have much to say on power. In the third there is more attention, but I really didn't understand how you saw where power came from.

PARSONS: Well, the first two papers were written some years before the development of the concept of power as a "generalized medium," and I was much more conventional in using the term at that time. That's one part of the difference. By the last of the three [in *Sociological Inquiry*, 1970], the media paradigm was used quite explicitly.

Martel: Could you elaborate on that for us a bit?

PARSONS: Well, the essential point (to me) is building stratification as the hierarchical dimension of social structure: locating it—in terms of *this* paradigm—in the first instance within the societal community. [The "I" cell in Figure 1, on the level of society.] Now, of course, many people will say: "Oh, but that's nonsense. The real locus of stratification is probably in the economy. It basically concerns inequalities of wealth and income." Well, I simply dispute that! By contrast, [my own emphasis] has been on *prestige* as a central factor in terms of the media paradigm, rather than wealth and power. Prestige, then, is placed [between the "L" and "I" cells of the figure] as concerning the *value* basis of the medium of influence. (Note this is said in terms of the technical meanings of "money," "power," "influence," and "value commitments" within the paradigm where the notions are somewhat different from their more familiar meanings.) And it's very hard to get yourself into the habit of viewing influence, or power for that matter, in this new perspective.

Remember here the point of view of the classical economist, that *money has value in exchange, but has no value in use.* (This view goes back quite a way. I'm pretty sure it's basically found in Adam Smith, and it certainly is in Ricardo.) Money just is not a commodity which is "consumable" in the economist's sense of consumption. It has other functions, [most notably] as a medium of exchange, as they sometimes put it. John Stuart Mill gave an admirable clarification when he said that it operates as a *measure* of value (in an economic sense), and also as a *store* of value. The last is one of its most important properties. In other words, apart from runaway inflation, money does not deteriorate over time in the sense that most physical commodities do, unless they happen to be "antiques." (Mill had an interesting discussion of *that* case.) Still another example is wine that's in the process of "maturing." Up to a point, the older it is, the better it is. But this isn't true of most foodstuffs, at least without refrigeration (or other preservative methods like canning).

Now, it's hard to think of *influence* as having no "intrinsic" basis of effectiveness. So we found in our early discussions of this approach that we were continually falling back on the idea that transmission of information is a way of exerting influence. But that violates the ["nonuse"] condition because information—specific information—is something that you *can* use, in a sense that you can't use money *except in exchange!* [Now, it took us some time], but I think we finally got the idea through our thick heads, to the point of taking habitual account of this complication.

[As I said], I think of "prestige" as the value ground of the *capacity to influence*, in the same way that I think of "authority" as the value ground of the *capacity to use power*, and "property" as the groundwork for *money.* Authority isn't power because authority is not a circulating medium like money is, and property is not a circulating medium either. [In using the paradigm] you have to make all sorts of subtle distinctions and be consistent in adhering to them. That's awfully hard. But we can then say that prestige is a property of statuses in a social system, which carries over to the incumbents of those statuses. By virtue of this the incumbents are able to persuade others to follow certain desired lines of action without having to exert realistic pressures (i.e., without threatening coercion, or without offering specific rewards). In other words, if I say I'd like to have you do so and so, and if you do a handsome honorarium will appear, that isn't using influence. That's buying compliance. It becomes an economic transaction, which sociologically is a very different kind of exchange.

That's illustrative of the kind of problem we have been trying to work through [in developing the media paradigm]. Now, in the case of the academic fields which Platt and I have been studying, we have tried to make an empirical discrimination between influence and power using survey research methods. (This part of the study has not yet been published.) We tried this by using questions such as the following, addressed to members of university faculties included in a national sample: "Would you rather be chairman of your department, or an influential senior member without any formal office?" And we obtained the interesting finding that the higher the prestige of an institution, the larger the proportion who would prefer to be the "senior member with influence" rather than hold the chairman's power. I think this is a very interesting finding, which runs contrary to much of the common sense of academic professionals. Many people would say: "Professors are very power-hungry people, and if they have a chance to get into a specific position of power they'll grab it, and the hell with being an influential person; otherwise, you haven't got the basis on which to act, and to quash opposition." But this turns out not to work, at least it isn't consistent with our data. Of course, there are such people [in academic life], but statistically— with various things controlled—they are distinctly a minority in our sample. Well, this is an example of how we really have been trying to operationalize some of these ideas, and I think with some modest success.

Question (Mr. Martel): Is "charisma," in Max Weber's sense, a special test case here?

PARSONS: I think it comes pretty close to being that, yes. At least it's in that universe. There are some special problems raised [by this notion], partly because there are some major ambiguities in the use of the term. But I must say we haven't tackled them as systematically yet as we ought to.

Question (Mr. Williamson): How does this concept of power relate to your criticisms of C. Wright Mills and David Reisman on the distribution of power in the United States?

PARSONS: Well, I was just beginning this kind of analysis of power [in the late 1950s] when I wrote a review article on Mills' *The Power Elite* to which you may be referring. At that time, I didn't use very much of the technical terminology. But I did go down very strongly then on one very major point, using the terminology the "theory of games." That is, it's perfectly clear that Mills, like many others, treated power as a zero-sum phenomena. In other words, power is seen as a fixed quantity which has to be allocated; and the more power one set of units in a social system have, the less there is [available for] others. Now, this is not true of money, as anyone with even the [background of] an elementary economics course ought to know. For money is a phenomenon of credit creation, by virtue of which an increased amount of money can be put into circulation without anything but purely monetary operations. That is, it can grow without any increase in the production of goods, services, etc. Banks do it as a routine operation [when they make loans], and there are many other similar mechanisms.

What happens in such cases is that, quote, "dollars do double duty." They function both as the "same dollars" and [as the additional supply that can be loaned]. Well, the question now is, what does it mean when you say "the same dollars"? It means they are the same quantities, under the same order of control. But dollars have no individuality whatever: one dollar is exactly like every other dollar. In their function as bank deposits, their control is never abandoned by the depositors who retain the basic right to withdraw their deposits, at will and on demand. But borrowers who make loans also are simultaneously in possession of the recipient loans from the bank. So where does this added money come from? Of course, the source is the depositors' money. There's no other source for loans. So part of the same money which is at the disposal of the bank's depositors is also at the disposal of the recipients of loans. And the extra part is a net addition to the total amount of money in circulation.

Now, when the recipient of a loan uses it, let's say, in a business investment to buy materials (or to pay labor, or something like that), he doesn't very carefully say to the supplying firm: "Be careful my friend. This money belongs to the depositors of such and such a bank." Or he doesn't say to the workers he hires: "This really isn't my money. It belongs to the depositors, and they might come around and take it back from you." That just isn't the way it works!

Well, now, there obviously are certain conditions under which this extension [of the money supply] can work, and one of them is that the average depositor must keep a positive balance in his account. You have the famous phenomenon of the "run on the bank" when too many people demand immediate repayment of too large a proportion of their deposits.

To put it a little different way, any bank that is really doing its job is technically insolvent. That's supposed to be very, very wicked indeed. And power has analogous properties (and involves the use of analogous mechanisms).

Question (Mr. Marsh): May I ask you to go on, in as much detail as possible, to the "power" side of the analogy, because some people really have questions about how far the analogy carries.

PARSONS: There is one general matter of principle here, which Smelser and I have tried to make clear. It is that the escape from the zero-sum *vicious circle always is dependent on support at the next higher-up cybernetic level.* (An increase in money, then, depends on potential support from the power system, which in turn depends on the influence system. And the last in turn depends on support through value commitments.) Going back to the *case of money* again, the problem of credit creation by banks [can serve to illustrate first]. Here the loan recipient is protected by contractual agreement (which sets the basic terms). In a simple case where a borrower receives a 90-day loan from a bank—which does not yet raise the complications of amortization schedules and so forth—the bank can demand repayment when the period expires, but the borrower has free use during the interim. [On both sides], the terms of the contract serve to guarantee possession at any point in time. The contract is potentially enforceable by law, that is, ultimately by the powers of the state (at the next-higher cybernetic level). To resort to this would be to call upon *power* as a medium to guarantee possession of the newly banked money. And there are many other supportive governmental mechanisms of this kind, like Federal Deposit Insurance and so on, [to protect the credit system]. But [to resort to a higher level is fairly extreme and disruptive]. Generally speaking, the depositor's first line of defense [is his confidence in] the discretion with which the bank manages its funds. In other words, that they don't go out on a limb by lending out too large a proportion of their deposits. (The extension depends on a balance between double-extension and reserve.) But, of course, under panic conditions, no bank can be safe without outside support.

In the case of *power* as a medium, the next higher level would be *influence*. And essentially the same principle applies. The way we might put it is this. Especially in a democratic system, influence is mobilized largely through the party system, and through leadership. An influential political leader—especially if he's backed by a strong party organization (and note that parties as such don't have coercive power)—can give a guarantee of the effective use of the *extensions* of power. There also are many other political mechanisms for accomplishing this. For example, it may be done through legislation. But [to further illustrate with the proverbial American situation, although the point is still clearer in a parliamentary system like that of Britain or Canada], a president also can have pretty strong influence on what Congress does. A strong president, then, can make commitments to the public which *go beyond* the actual resources [he has] in hand at the time these commitments are made.

Now, a president may be *un*successful in carrying out such commitments. This means his position of influence isn't strong enough, and he can't mobilize the needed support. But if the president is to be successful in his efforts, the people whose cooperation he needs must *trust* his capacity to influence. And if he appears to fail in backing up his promises, such support may then evaporate. . . . The supporter, of course, always judges this on the basis of his information, . . . and this may be insufficient or incorrect. . . . He has to *trust* him before he will cooperate, and he may not be getting the specific dope.

Question (Mr. Dupree): How is the range of information needed connected with the range of influence?

PARSONS: . . . the range here . . . is the case of the influence range. All [the] "ego" has to give the alter with whom he is interacting is the specific information, and he will draw his own conclusions. Alter doesn't have to tell him everything.

Question (Mr. Martel): I wonder if we could come back to power?

PARSONS: Well, are you more or less satisfied with the "non-zero-sum" idea?

Question:

PARSONS: Well, I'd say first that the actual use of power as a medium should be presumed to involve the command of coercive resources. [These] always operate conditionally, you know, and only under *failure* of the attempt to have an effect on the other's actions. There's a very important *asymmetry* between money and power in that respect, [and] this is one reason why the similarities are a little hard to see. Namely, if an agent makes an offer of money, and this offer is accepted by alter, then ego (the agent) has to pay. But if an attempt on ego's part to get alter to do something *succeeds*—and this is made under the explicit or implicit threat that if alter doesn't do it, negative sanctions will be applied—*if alter goes ahead and does it the negative sanctions aren't applied.*

[For example], when I take the risks and chances of driving from Providence to Boston, there's always a chance that I'll be stopped by a cop, who'll give me a ticket for something or other. But if I succeed in getting through (as I did this morning), and no cop interferes with me in any way, this doesn't mean at all that police authority was suspended. It just means that the occasion didn't arise to use it. At least no cop patrolling the road (on my route) came to the conclusion that I was violating some rule, and pulled me in. Well, this is a very important asymmetry. On the other hand, if I want gas I drive into a station; and when I say, "Fill it with regular," I am implicitly offering to pay. And I can't drive out of that station without either paying cash or submitting a credit card. I have to pay money. The flow of monetary transactions on an economic level, therefore, is not parallel to the flow of the actual use of coercive sanctions in a power system. The question is whether they are adequately in reserve.

One measure of the effectiveness [of coercive sanctions] is that they don't have to be used. The more effective they are, the less they are actually used. It seems paradoxical.

Some of you may remember Durkheim's famous essay on the two laws of punishment. One of them calls attention to the symbolic significance of punishment. This is a way of asserting to possible violators that those who say violation will be punished *really mean it!* We know plenty of cases from our experience where dire threats are made: "If you do so and so, you'll really get hell!" But alter goes ahead and does it, and nothing happens. Durkheim would say here— I think quite correctly—[that the failure to back up such threats] undermines confidence in the rules of the system.

[*Inflation* also is an important factor in the implementation of power.] In the case of power, "inflation" is the tendency to expand the number, the range, and the seriousness of making commitments to action, on the presumption that these commitments will be backed by coercive sanctions, if necessary. But when the expansion of such commitments reaches a point where the capacity to come through with the [threatened] sanctions, if need be, becomes progressively less, the commitment *depreciates* in value from the standpoint of its probability of fulfillment. Now, very generally there are time lags between the time of making such commitments and the occasion for having to prove that you can meet them. Therefore, it's easy for *over commitments* to develop. And this would be an inflation of power [to the extent] the fulfilment involves the capacity to use negative sanctions: either to ensure fulfillment, or to properly punish in cases of nonfulfillment. It's that kind of thing. I think we could point to many cases in national or international affairs where that kind of thing has seemed to happen. Of course, we also want to remember *the reciprocal escalation of expectations*, which can always happen, and how raising certain questions may be a deflationary thing. Take the recent business at Harvard of the radical economists. Well, I'm not sufficiently familiar with the facts of that particular case. But in the early days of the Conant administration [in the 1930s], there was a case of two radical economists not being promoted: the famous "Walt Sweezy" case of which you may have heard. They weren't fired. They just weren't promoted. One part of the situation there was that the former Harvard president [President Lowell] had been guilty earlier of *an inflation* of promises and expectations. He had created an atmosphere where there was an expectation of nearly automatic promotion. And Conant came [after him] right in the middle of the Depression. When he had learned enough about the state of university finances, he found that many of these inflationary expectations— which at least had been condoned by Lowell—simply could not be fulfilled, for reasons of financial strains. Now, in one of Conant's early years it happened that the Economics Department had seven assistant professors whose terms all expired in the same year. And the central administration had decided that only one [of the seven] could be promoted in that year. And of the seven, two were "radicals" and the other five were not. (A very close friend of mine was one of the other five, and one of four of them who didn't get promoted.) Of course, there was a terrible cry about the two radicals. "Political discrimination." "When there's only one slot, you should promote both of them." You go to the administration and tell them they've got to give you another slot!" Whereas, there was no outcry at all about the other four who weren't promoted. And the people who made the outcry, by and large, were not competent judges of the relative qualifications of [these men] as economists. Now, this was a *deflationary* episode with respect to the power to promote, and [the response] was a common thing.

Question (Mr. Dupree): It seems to me that one of the main themes running through this discussion is to somehow or other set social theory on a cybernetic base.

PARSONS: Very definitely.

Dupree: When you are talking here about moving from money to power to influence, aren't they somehow crucially connected by a common information system?

PARSONS: Right!

Dupree: Well, I wonder if you'd comment a bit more in depth on the cybernetic side of your theory, and how that got into the picture?

PARSONS: This has been very important indeed to me personally. For one thing, like practically everyone else who tried to think through the question about the relations between [symbolic, material, and other factors in human action], I've found it awfully hard to avoid getting caught up in a "vicious circle." (It really isn't a chicken-and-egg question.) But it is the question of which, among certain groups of factors, is more important. In the older German traditions [at the turn of the century]—in which Weber figures so centrally—the Germans had a pair of terms that were widely used [in discussing the issues]: namely, "*realfactorem*"—which meant economic and political factors; and "*idealfactorem*"—by which they meant sorts of things like influence, values, and so on. And the pendulum swang back and forth. "Oh, the *realfactorem* are really the important things," and "Oh, the *idealfactorem* are really the important things." And there seemed to be no way to resolve this. Except Weber [began to clarify the issue] by bringing in certain qualifications; although his position sometimes is misunderstood. You may remember that at the very end of *The Protestant Ethic and the Spirit of Capitalism*, he says: "It is not my intention to substitute an idealistic account of these events for a materialistic account." But this has persistently been ignored, and many say Weber had [offered] an idealistic explanation [for the rise of capitalism]. This is simply a bad interpretation of Weber, who was very, very careful on these issues.

Well now, the advent of *cybernetic* thinking [as a general conception]—and not simply the very specific mode of it introduced by Norbert Weiner—changed [the whole issue of the relation between ideal and "real" factors] in the determination of human events enormously. Before that [most thinkers] couldn't see a way of doing justice to [the very complex relations involved]. Now, in cybernetic terms, it seems to me the basic distinction is between [two kinds of systems]: those which are high in energy, and those which are high in information. (The "realfactorem" can be viewed as the former, and the "idealfactorem" as the latter. And we can begin to say more precisely how both considerations are involved. And this doesn't mean that, for rigorous scientific purposes, we have to say that "ideas" are either irrelevant or always secondary.) Remember the famous question attributed to Stalin at the Yalta conference? "The Pope? How many divisions does he have?" It could be inferred, then, that since the Pope didn't have any divisions, you could safely and totally ignore him. Which I would say is a monumental *nonsequitur.*

Question (Mr. Dupree): I think the chart over there (if the camera can get it) has the contrast between high-information and high energy systems [Figure 2 below].

PARSONS: Well, [if we follow the hierarchy of the major subsystems of the general-action system on the chart (Column A in Figure 2)], the *cultural* system is the system highest in *information,* and the *organism*—at the bottom—would be highest in energy. The other two systems—that is, the *social* system and then *personality*—fall in between, and in that order. The core idea is that each organizational system in higher position is higher in the overall hierarchy of cybernetic control. And each higher-placed system also is higher in *information.* So the "emergentist" formula of earlier traditions now can be effectively restated as: symbolic, or ideal, factors become partly autonomous and determining systems, through mechanisms which permit systems high in energy to partly gain organizational "com-

Figure 2

Cybernetic Hierarchy of Action Systems*

(A) Subsystem of General-Action System	Primary Functions of Subsystems	(B) Subsystems of Organized Society (and "Media")
Culture ↓ Social System ↓ Personality ↓ Organism	(L) Latent Pattern Maintenance (I) Integration (G) Goal Attainment (A) Adaptation	Fiduciary (value commitments) ↓ Societal-Community (influence) ↓ Polity ("power") ↓ Economy (money)

*This figure is a simplification of two charts used at the March 10 session.

mand" of other systems which are higher in energy but *lower* in their informational capacities. This must be said with the qualification that the *lower-order systems* always set the terms under which the higher-placed systems can function at all. So there is a *conditions hierarchy* which runs the other way, from the "bottom-up" as it were. And the higher-placed information system, of course, only can maintain itself if its control over the lower-placed systems it depends on is secure. But with this qualification, we can say fairly clearly that "ideal factors" (those high on information) can, albeit conditionally, exert significant and partly independent influence on human events. And the cybernetic framework makes it possible to say this in a way that is both logically and empirically explicit.

I've become imbued with this mode of thinking, which has become very prominent in [many different scientific fields]. It has had an important role [in recent work] in the field of *linguistics*, which many would say is the most empirically precise of the social-behavioral sciences. And it also has turned up in the field of *genetics* in a most interesting way. What this shows to me is that [emergentist] viewpoints can be used in a very rigorous way, and that to hold to them does not, in itself, [mean that one is "soft-headed," scientifically speaking]. You know, some of my critics have [said] that I belong to the "soft school" [in giving due weight to "idealfactorem"]. To be "hard," and really scientific, they say "you must put emphasis on high-energy" (or "material") factors, and say that the high-information systems don't count. Well, [I think some critics have been as mistaken on this point] as when they say that I must believe everything is static, or everything is harmonious, or that I have no appreciation of conflict. (My point here is that high-information systems *do* count.)

As one instance of [the importance of high-information systems], I regularly use in my class the example of the *thermostat*; and if they think a minute, most students will know what a thermostat is, and how it applies. And it's perfectly clear that my thermostat does not heat my house. The oil that is burned and manipulated by an oil-burning mechanism is what heats the house. But we [can't deny] that the thermostat controls the oil-burner in a certain sense. And the amount of energy the thermostat uses is negligible compared to what the furnace consumes. It's a *tiny* bit of electrical current.

Question (Mr. Dupree): But being tiny, and being negligible, are two different things?

PARSONS: Oh yes. I had a Japanese friend back in my youth, who was very short in stature. And you know he was very sensitive about it, especially in an Anglo-Saxon environment where most males were a good foot taller than he. When he felt [put out] about this, his rejoinder used to be: "Well, Napoleon was only five feet tall!"—which I believe is quite true But Napoleon had quite an impact on the world; certainly more, say, than Gorgeous George, the wrestler.

Question (Mr. Martel): Would you apply this to societies?

PARSONS: Yes, I think I can. In my little book with the title *Societies* (1966), I had a special chapter on what I called "seedbed societies," which dealt with ancient Israel and ancient Greece. Now, in the power system of the time they both were virtually negligible, compared to Egypt and the Babylonian Empire, or compared to what Rome became as an imperial power. Athens, with its 150,000 *total* inhabitants and only 30,000 citizens. It was very small potatoes. But Athens has had a profound effect on the history of civilization. I don't think anybody can dispute that. They always choose cases that are favorable to them.

Well now, one of the most sensational developments [relating to cybernetics] is the appearance of this kind of thinking in *microbiology*. It simply didn't exist at the time when my ideas were forming. And even so tough-minded a geneticist as J. B. Watson asserts unequivocally (speaking of DNA), that it represents a cybernetic type of control. It isn't that DNA is the equivalent of powerful muscles, you see, in determining what's going to happen to an organism. It's that *DNA carries information.* In other words, it's kind of a book! So from one point of view this development has been an enormous boost to a theorist working along my lines

Values, Value Commitments, and Cultural Change

Do you want me to say a little something about value commitments here? [All concur.] Well, the way I interpret the concept of values— and my prime teacher here was Max Weber—they constitute a low-energy component of the social system which has very important cybernetic significance. As a most convenient point of reference, I have tended to take Clyde Kluckhohn's *definition* of values—from the article he wrote for our *Toward a General Theory of Action* volume (1951). His operative phrase is that values are *conceptions of the desirable*, and we must be very careful to note that the desirable and the "desired" are not the same. Kluckhohn also introduces some further considerations of importance: like the distinctions between "explicit and implicit" values, and also between the values of individuals and groups.

[As I see it], values are an *interstitial* element between the social-system level and the cultural level. If they were purely social structure, the word "conception" would be inappropriate. They are, I would take it, *patterned conceptions* of the *desirable directionality in action.* We must distinguish values very carefully from *goals* [in two respects], since goals are situational and they are also "relative." That is, goals are oriented to specific situations (and their changing exigencies) while values decidedly, in this use, are not.

That is, let's say you value academic freedom. Well, academic freedom isn't any particular mode of academic organization. However, we'll say that for a department of sociology to turn out (in its graduate operations) well-trained sociologists is an instance of a goal—a collective goal. As such, it would not be a value in the sense that academic freedom is, although [the goal takes its meaning in part from a variety of value criteria or value standards that provide general criteria of goal attainment]. The levels of values and of situational goals are often confused.

[Actually, the terminology here often is a problem, and there are many ambiguities.] I like to compare what's happened to the term *value* with what happened to the term *instinct.* [The latter] ran into the ground, becoming virtually a label for a type of behavior of animals. Some would say: "Humans are acquisitive." You then ask: "What makes them acquisitive?" And the answer is: "Well, they have an 'instinct' of acquisition." This is no more than another way of saying that you can observe acquisitive behavior. *It doesn't explain a damn thing!* It only labels.

[Similarly, in some uses of the term "value"] almost any change in behavior is said to be a change in values. "How do you know it's a change in values?" Well, because people behave differently. [That doesn't explain much either.]

To see the significance of the notion, theoretically speaking, we have to pay attention to *value systems,* not only to isolated values. A value system is a very complex cultural entity, and [over time] parts of it can change while other parts of it remain quite unchanged. Also, different parts [of such systems] can change in different ways, so the common assertions that you hear about changes in values—if it's only that [which is being said]—may be quite theoretically meaningless. And you run into claims about value changes very frequently.

Now [given the importance of the value concept to me in a more technical, theoretical sense], the sort of intellectual position noted really puts me on the defensive. And so—in any specific instance where people say: "Oh, the values have changed"—I'm continually asking the following questions:

1. First, what do you mean by value change?
2. What parts of a value system have changed?
3. Has everything changed in exactly the same way, or have some parts changed while others have not?
4. Have different parts changed in different ways?

And the average person who uses expressions like, "The values have changed" can't easily answer these questions. I submit that if you impute value change and can't answer these questions, you haven't achieved anything scientifically.

QUESTION (Mr. Rafferty): Professor Parsons. It might help to introduce a partly theoretical and partly historical question on values. In your 1952 article on the teaching of religion (in Fairchild) you said that our basic values were laid down essentially about the fifth century B.C., concurrently with the rise of the great religious traditions, and really haven't changed very much. Since then, I think the main notion you have used to characterize major shifts that have occured is *value generalization*. You did mention that their social situation then was much like ours, in that there was broad chaos in the whole world. Would you please comment on this comparison in terms of: (1) How did these basic values start, or originate; and (2) What is the comparison between the situation in their time and ours?

PARSONS: The first question [on origination] is an exceedingly difficult one, and I think one can draw a biological analogy. You're talking about long-term and major processes of change, and getting over into the area of *evolutionary* thinking. For one thing, I don't think very useful theories of genetic change in biological species or populations could have developed without very detailed factual knowledge of the actual zoological world, the history of the distributions of different species, and so on—which is at the core of

Darwin's work. Without this, you couldn't jump directly to the question of "how do species change?"

I have a very favorite quotation from Darwin on this point, which appears at the head of one of my books, which I don't see on the table: the book *Theories of Society* (1961). I know it's a big book, and probably no one was strong enough to carry it. But Darwin says to start with that "I do *not* believe in natural selection because I can actually prove that it has caused the transformation of one species into another!" Now, most people wouldn't think that sounded like Darwin; because [his notion of] natural selection has been conceived as a kind of magical entity that does anything that you want.

But Darwin actually is very cautious in his claim. And he goes on to say that [the principle] "is essentially useful because it orders a vast body of knowledge or data." He then enumerates about six or seven fields of zoology. Note that he says—*orders them!* The notion isn't asserted in a simple sense as a "causal" principle at all, you see. I think in the social sciences that we are often in a comparable kind of situation. Even Weber's famous concept of "charisma" is more of a label than an explanation for problems of value change.

[Returning to value change] now, here we do know a good deal about certain processes of change in *value systems*; and I happen to think that the kind of process I've been calling "value generalization" is one of the most important phenomena. I think this process can be pinned down in terms of very specific historical changes in many different times and places. Of course, this concept cannot stand on its own. It's related to such categories as *differentiation* and *specification*—among others.

Now, you quoted a paper which I wrote [on religion and value change] in 1952. About 15 years later, I wrote an article on Christianity (which you also may know), for the *International Encyclopedia of Social Sciences* (1968). And I would say that the underlying view in this later article still argues for the [position you rightly attributed to me]—that in certain respects the most general value patterns of the Western world have remained unchanged since the early Christian period, and this [does not ignore] cases of secularization.

Incidentally, I'd say that the fundamental differences between

Marxist views on this issue and (quote) "Weber's Protestant Ethic" does not lie primarily on this level of basic value patterns. Now, I'm sure a Marxist would be enraged by such a statement. He might say: "The real truth (in history) has nothing to do with Christianity!" "It's in conflict with everything that's Christian." But this is only one level of discourse, you see.

[But I think we have to say that in the development of the West during this entire period, there have been important levels of continuity as well as change in values. A "balanced account" would have to give due consideration to each.] As for the continuities, even the major contrast with which Weber started—between ascetic Protestantism and Catholicism—is only a *relative* contrast, not a total difference. And Weber himself wouldn't ever have claimed that it was anything else. But it's still a very important difference of emphasis. (And we have to keep both sides in mind.)

To see the other side [of discontinuity], I think the "Reformation" was an important evolutionary step because it *brought in a new conception of secular society*. The new view brought in two previously separate components, which—in Catholicism—had previously been allocated to "church," on the one side, and to "state" on the other. And it combined them in a quite unprecedented way. As an example [of the magnitude of the change] Weber quotes a not terribly well-known German historian (of the Reformation, I think—a man named Frank) as saying the new idea meant "that every man, in principle, became a monk!" Now, the Protestant movement, of course, repudiated and destroyed the monastic orders. *But the ideal* of ascetic behavior, the attitude, this was not destroyed. It's that sort of thing.

And *the change here is importantly one of "value generalization,"* [in that the ascetic ideal then was extended to broader spheres]. Before, the ideal said that ascetic behavior was found mainly in segregated monastic orders withdrawn from secular society. But after, you could have ascetic behavior within secular society as well. [So the value ideal was generalized or extended.] That sort of conception.

Or take it the other way around, in terms of changing [notions of] *celibacy*. It had been decreed—although, to be sure, not from the beginning—that celibacy (in the Christian view) was superior to marriage. Luther, you recall, as an extremely deliberate act, got married. Remember that for many years he had been a monk under vows of celibacy. Now, Luther wasn't simply saying: "These vows are unreasonable restrictions and, you see, I'm going to be really modern and defy them, and I'm going to live the hedonistic life!" Luther was saying that it is religiously *legitimate* even for a priest of God's religion to be married; and if you don't believe it, I'm going to set an example. Which he did, and by the way he married a former nun.

Question (Mr. Rafferty): Could I take this opportunity to press you on the hardest question of all on values. In the article on "Culture and Social Systems" in *Theories of Society* (1961), you have a statement which has become one of my favorite quotes. It's that "*values are somehow constrained, or limited, by the fundamental exigencies of our existence.*" And that for our moral notions to be intelligible to us, they must be responsive to these exigencies—which you say is the problem of meaning.

Could you take the idea of fundamental exigencies, and that creativity occurs especially in times of chaos, and perhaps speculate on present-day values, and our present situation?

PARSONS: Well, one common theme in all the separate theoretical traditions that I dealt with in *The Structure of Social Action* (1937) is clearly the "*problem of order*" as I called it. And this is a way of naming and locating a whole set of these exigencies. [Note that in these traditions the problem is crucially seen as an *empirical* problem]: it isn't only an abstract "moral or ethical" problem of whether order—in certain forms, or on certain levels—is or is not judged to be desirable on the basis of certain [*a priori*] value positions. Rather, it is a question of the empirically demonstrable *consequences* of the breakdown (or the maintenance) of a given order.

Now, Weber was acutely conscious of the problem [and gave one plausible approach]. We might take as a case in point, thinking of the Reformation period [we were discussing], the case of the Anabaptists in the early Reformation. You may argue that, in terms of their ideals, that [by one's standards] the Anabaptists deserve the highest religious admiration. But I think that Weber—who of course was a student of the Reformation—would say that the way of life of the Anabaptists cannot be [a sufficient basis for] a stable society. *They don't accept certain of the essential exigencies of social life*, and they tried to live as if these didn't exist.

Well, some "vulgar Freudians" take the view that "the only mentally healthy way to live is to act out all your fantasies"—a view that most definitely was not shared by Sigmund Freud himself. Since Freud himself laid a very special stress on the Oedipal fantasy, you might argue [in this vein] that all sons should kill their fathers! Because *they obviously hate their fathers enough to kill them!* So if they want to kill them, why not go ahead and do it? Yet, what would happen to *society* if this became the norm of behavior?

Or, one could think of many other alternatives which would be equally [unviable]. As another example, instead of "female infanticide" (which is known to have been practiced under very special conditions), you might instead have *male* infanticide. After all, any man who fathered a child might say. "Well, in due course he's going to murder me, so I'd better get rid of him before he has the chance." That's one possible reaction. And the exponent of the libertarian ethic is going to say that, for the sake of his own mental health, the son should murder his father or *vice versa*. Well, confessedly these are very extreme cases, but they illustrate a point. [In terms of the exigencies, and the "problem of order," there always is the empirical question of how far certain ideals of conduct are viable over time in the real social world of actors.]

Question (Mr. Martel): How far would you say that technology can significantly or fundamentally change the exigencies? For example, recent movements toward genetic control, famine reduction, psychological drugs, and things like that?

PARSONS: Well, it can considerably change some of them [up to a point]. I think it's a very subtle and difficult question to ask what the limits here might be. We're all well aware of the fact, for example, that the past century—in spite of major wars—has seen the doubling of life-expectancy at birth. Now this surely is a profound change in the human situation. (And it has important implications for ideologies and values.) For example, the slogan "Never trust anyone over 30" might have been a fairly reasonable slogan when the average person didn't live beyond age 35; but what about when he lives to be 70? One way I like to put it is to say: "If you really take that slogan seriously, and *you don't commit suicide*, you face on the average 40 years of life when you're not to be trusted—by your own definition! This to me is a rather horrendous prospect!"

Question (Mr. Wolf): To carry this line of questioning just one step further: in your two recent books [*On Societies*, 1966; and *The System of Modern Societies*, 1971]—you have traced the development of societies up to the present. Would you be willing to speculate a little on the *postmodern* stage of social development?

PARSONS: Well, I don't particularly like the term "postmodern society," and I've tended toward a different view. I'm quite willing to accept Daniel Bell's alternative term—"postindustrial"—although it needs further explanation.

I very recently completed a piece for Dan Bell's project on the future, to go into a volume on the year 2000. This led me to reconsider the problem of prognostication of the future and some of its limits. I think we have very thin bases for future predictions. But I also think [to begin with] that we can say something about certain *constancies*. Well, let's put it this way. Language is a very ancient human phenomenon, but modernization doesn't involve the abolition of language and its replacement by something totally different.

Is our time nearly up?

I would argue that the development of what we tend to call "modern" society is a very long process of development and that its development is far from complete as yet. [I suspect] that the year 2000 will not see a basically different kind of society from ours. But, again, I think we have very thin bases for predicting what many of its specific characteristics will be like.

Question (Mr Dupree): Talcott, we are getting quite close to the end, and we've been talking most of the day about social theory. Now that we have got you in a predicting mood, would you give us a brief prediction as to where you think social theory is going to go between now and the year 2000, and beyond?

PARSONS: Well, I think that's very difficult to say. Maybe it's as much a matter of personal faith as anything else. But if the story of the so-called natural sciences (and of economics and linguistics, as the most advanced behavioral sciences) provides any guide, I would expect a *decline* in the prevalence, and the passionate insistence, on a nontheoretical kind of "empiricism." I would expect this rather than an increase. In this regard, I think we're in the middle of something of a new wave right now, [a backswing against the anti-theoretical "negativism" of the late 1960s, which partly came from the New Left with its often narrow] concept of "relevance." But there are other sources as well. In this country, if you read a sheet like *Science* (or a number of other things), you find that many people in the sciences are very much worried about [fund cuts], including the tendency in recent years for both government and foundations to cut down support for so-called basic science. They only support things that have prospects of fairly quick and practical payoffs. Now, on this point the budget officers of the Nixon Administration and the New Left are in the same camp, which we don't expect to find too often. [Both contributed to the emphasis on short-run results, with its negative attitude toward more basic and more theoretical efforts.] They both like to see abstract, general theorizing cut way back, if not eliminated, and with really practical stuff put in its place. Their ideal scientist would be a Pasteur, who was a very great man. But if medicine had had to depend only on Pasteur-type clinical research, I don't think it would have advanced nearly as much as it has. And so on.

[But, as I was saying, there are some signs of a new wave, or a backswing within the physical and behavioral sciences against the empiricism of the late 1960s.] And my guess is that the pendulum will swing back, but on how long this would take, who knows?

I also happen to think that, *for the social sciences, the biological models are considerably closer than the physical models.* Physics has tended to be our ideal-type of a theoretical science; and the logical structure of biological theory is quite different. In the volume to which Hunter Dupree and I are fellow contributors [Gerald Holton, *Twentieth-Century Science*, 1972], there's a very notable article by Kurt Stern of Berkeley—one of the senior citizens of genetics.

Stern makes it very clear indeed that the logical structure of genetic theory from Mendel on—and this includes current micro-genetics—is very different from the analytic use of the differential calculus in classical mechanics, and also in mathematical economics. It's much more a shuffling and reshuffling of indivisible units, rather than a logic of infinitesimal variation along linear continua.

My guess is that most of sociology, when it gets to be more theoretically systematized and formalized, will look much more like genetics than like classical mechanics. I think that's going to happen, although the timing again is questionable. And there may be parallels to the loss of Mendel's work for a generation in biology. In other words, people don't bother about theory for a generation or two, and then suddenly it will begin to revive again. I think theory is too much in the cards for it simply to be forgotten indefinitely, but I'm sure a lot of my sociological colleagues will not share this view.

Question (Mr. Martel): Are you optimistic about the future?

PARSONS: In that respect, yes; the long future. Oh, I think I'm basically optimistic about the human prospects in the long run. We have a great deal of abject pessimism about it. (And it looks by the clock like we'd better stop.) But perhaps one closing point. I was a student in Germany just at the height of the vogue of Oswald Spengler, author of *The Decline of the West* [*Der Untergang des Abenlandes*, 1918] and he didn't give the West 50 more years of continuing vitality after the time in which he wrote. He gave it much shorter shrift. In fact, he said that for all practical purposes it already was over and that its last culturally significant event was the break between Wagner and Nietzsche. Well, it's more than 50 years later now, and I don't think the West has just simply declined. He was wrong in thinking it was the end.

Question (Mr. Dupree): Did we close the tape with the words, "the end"?

PARSONS: (Chuckling.) Oh. That's very interesting.

Martel: We in the seminar thank you very much.

[End of transcript of the March 10, 1973 Seminar]

Notes

1. On the Meiklejohn affair see Rutherford Malcolm. 2003. "On the Economic Frontier: Walton Hamilton, Institutional Economics, and Education." *History of Political Economy*. 35 (Winter): 611–653.

2. Parsons, Talcott and Gerald M. Platt. 1973. *The American University*. Cambridge, MA: Harvard University Press.

CONTEMPORARY RESPONSES

Power

A Note on Talcott Parsons and the Brown University Conversations

By ROBERT HOLTON*

ABSTRACT. Professor Holton offers his impressions of the recently discovered transcriptions of the seminar Parsons participated in at Brown University on March 10, 1973.

In one sense, the Brown University conversations see Parsons reflecting in a fairly predictable way on the major preoccupations of his intellectual life. The consistent drive to map the social through general theory building is well represented here, as are the polemical foils of utilitarianism and economistic theories of rational self-interest. Parsons's cybernetic and evolutionary emphases of the 1960s and 1970s are also prominent. While some of this may seem dated, there is nonetheless an engaging reflexivity and gentle irony in his presentation, together with a rehearsal of the reasoning that persuaded Parsons of the coherence and robustness of his theoretical schema. This is perhaps most evident when he is questioned on his controversial discussion of the place of power in social life.

The immediacy, accessibility, and even modesty of Parsons's manner of exposition is a striking feature of these conversations. This is worthy of note because it contrasts so markedly with the superficial way in which the Parsons's theoretical legacy has been formalized by sociological textbooks into the arid dogmas of structural-functionalism. It is hard to recognize these textbook caricatures in the intellectual milieux in Europe and the United States that Parsons evokes in these conversations and within which he defines the trajectories of his thought. What he portrays here as exploratory theoretical lines of argument, subject to constant refinement and

*The author is at Trinity College, Dublin.

American Journal of Economics and Sociology, Vol. 65, No. 1 (January 2006).

elaboration, as reflected in work on the generalized media of exchange, somehow became hypostasized by critics into a theoretical edifice of axiomatic certainty and dogmatic aspiration. *The American Journal of Economics and Sociology* has therefore done scholarship a significant service in publishing this transcription. It helps shed light on a legacy that still has the capacity to enrich debate rather than become consigned to the museum of lost sociological causes.

Parsons was, of course, a formalist in the way he conducted general theory building, as the four-function AGIL paradigm and its subdivision into 16 (4 × 4) and even 64 (4 × 4 × 4) conceptual boxes indicates. This mode of proceeding, together with the particularly dense abstraction of *The Social System* (1951), may have made it easier for formalistic textbook caricatures to become plausible. Parsons's negative reputation nonetheless also draws on widespread intellectual and political skepticism as to his capacity to recognize and analyze power, inequality, and conflict in the social world, leading to his reputation as a conservative apologist for social order and Western modernity. The Brown conversations, however, help to make clear a view recognized in specialist literature (e.g., Holton and Turner 1986) that Parsons *was* politically engaged with world crises of his epoch. He was also well able to position himself and his work, in a reflexive manner, within the narratives of social change in which he was implicated and within which he took a self-confessedly optimistic liberal-democratic position.

What implications does all this have for the ways in which he approached the analysis of power?

Aspects of Parsons's comparative political sociology of power, inequality, and stratification are rehearsed at a number of points in this transcription. They engage with formative world events in his lifetime such as the two world wars, the Russian revolution, and the rise of Hitler. In response to the widespread failure of proletarian revolution, he is particularly scathing about the analytical capacities of Marxist traditions—old or new—to analyze world trends and social change. Themes in this critique include the failure of Marxist economics to come to terms with marginalism, and excessive reliance on ideas of power domination, including recourse to "the powerful repressive capacities of bourgeois-dominated government." What Parsons does not explain here is how a knowledge of marginalism might assist the analysis of capitalism. And while it may come as news to some readers that Parsons accepted that bourgeois governments exerted a powerful repressive effect, he shows little interest here in broader arguments about social control, whether Marx's emphasis on "the dull compulsion of economic circumstance" or the major foray of critical theory into the analysis of ideological repression and co-option.

Parsons's interlocutors at Brown pushed him repeatedly on the problem of power, but the oblique ways in which he responded suggest, if not a dialogue of the deaf, then perhaps something closer to a "ships passing in the night" effect. Parsons certainly makes some effort to bridge the gap between the two, arguing that power conflicts are not a zero-sum game. We are dealing, rather, with a generalized medium of exchange that circulates between actors, which is enabling as well as constraining. Ironically perhaps, this brings him closer, on certain levels, to Foucault, who also emphasized the efficacy of power and its capillary-like circulation. Parsons and Foucault seem both to reject the zero-sum game assumption, arguing that power is endemic in social life. Having said this, Parsons continued to think of power as a matter of sovereignty, rather than developing an interest in exploring discursive power as Foucault was later to do. Second, while Parsons did develop some important innovations in the sociology of the body, around the notion of the sick role, these were developed through the analysis of norms, rather than in the direction of a microphysics of power.

So instead of engaging with the problem of power as advanced in questions from the floor, his alternative moves are twofold. One is to emphasize prestige rather than power as the basis for much social stratification and hence inequality. This pits the status order against economic interest as alternative explanations of social order, restating a classic standoff between two types of sociology, neither of which has much interest in pursuing any kind of synthetic resolution (Lockwood 1992 being a notable exception). Parsons's second move is to compare the nature and impact of different generalized media of exchange.

While this is a conceptual domain with an architecture that few sociologists feel any strong rapport with, Parsons does make some interesting points that are worth retrieving. One is the centrality of money as a medium of exchange grounded in property. Much that critics might expect to be located in the area of power is redistributed in this architecture under the heading of money, replicating, in a sense, the analytical distinction between adaptive (economic) and goal-attaining (political) system features. Another is the emphasis on influence as a further analytically distinct element in exchange alongside money and power.

Conclusion

ENGAGEMENT WITH PARSONS'S WORK seems to induce a contradictory set of responses, including fascination and horror, frustration and enlightenment. The present transcript assists a more positive though still critical engagement with his legacy in several ways. It breaks down textbook stereotypes by allowing access to a theorist thinking aloud. It shows Parsons's own estimation of the priorities, continuities, and contrasts in his work. There is also a very strong sense of the profound interdisciplinarity of Parsons's approach, a quality somewhat diminished with the consolidation of sociology as a free-standing self-subsistent discipline. The transcripts also link the personal and political with the intellectual, reminding us that reflexivity is not something invented in the last decade or so by a new cadre of epistemologically privileged theorists.

Finally, applying Parsonian analysis to Parsons himself, the discussion suggests how grand theorists, whatever their merits, are always faced with residual problems that remain inadequately treated in the main corpus of work. The problem of power is a leading contender for Parsons's most insistent residual. Eventually, the weight of residuals breaks apart the theoretical core. It is hard to be confident that this has finally happened to Parsons. This is partly because he is still a major reference point in general theory (see, for example, Habermas 1984–1987) and partly because the research agenda emanating from his work is not exhausted. To dispose of his approach to power, for example, would require a more systematic critique of his discussions of prestige, influence, and money, not simply a selective focus on those parts of the corpus explicitly devoted to power. For the moment, it is arguable that engagement with Parsons remains indispensable in any attempt to map the social.

References

Habermas, J. (1984–1987). *The Theory of Communicative Action*. London: Heinemann.

Holton, R., and B. Turner. (1986). *Talcott Parsons on Economy and Society*. London: Routledge.

Lockwood, D. (1992). *Solidarity and Schism*. Oxford: Clarendon Press.

Parsons, T. (1951). *The Social System*. London: Routledge.

A Comment on Talcott Parsons
at Brown University

By Giuseppe Sciortino*

Abstract.   Professor Sciortino offers his impressions of the recently discovered transcriptions of the seminar Parsons participated in at Brown University on March 10, 1973.

The publishing of the transcript of the 1973 seminar with Talcott Parsons at Brown University is a lucky event: it provides a fascinating glimpse into Parsons's biography and ideas in one of the lesser known and less-investigated phases of his career; it highlights some features of his intellectual education that are often overlooked in the folklore of the social sciences; and, aided by the informal environment of a seminar with a sympathetic audience, it provides a clear-cut discussion on some aspects of his theory. I will try to provide some brief comment on each of these aspects.

Parsons's work during the last decade of his life is often neglected. Not surprisingly, texbooks usually prefer to focus on the ascending phase of his popularity and influence. Most scholars identify Parsons with his works from the 1930s to the mid 1950s, from *The Structure of Social Action* to *Economy and Society.* The few exceptions enlarge their focus at best to Parsons's evolutionary work, culminating in his 1971 *System of Modern Societies.* Only the very few people who actively specialize in Parsons's action theory are aware that the late 1960s and the 1970s were quite productive periods for Parsons, with the introduction of many conceptual innovations and a steady flow of activities and projects. In the first category deserve to be mentioned the vast and far-reaching analysis of generalized symbolic media, starting with the seminal papers on power and influence in 1963 (Parsons 1963a, 1963b) and the related attempts to formulate a theory of the general system of action and, ultimately, of the whole human condition (Parsons 1978). In the second category, it is enough to mention

*The author is a Professor of Sociology at the Dipartimento di sociologia, Universita' di Trento, Via Verdi 26, 38100, Trento, Italy; e-mail: giuseppe.sciortino@unitn.it.

American Journal of Economics and Sociology, Vol. 65, No. 1 (January 2006).

the long and complex study of the academic complex in American society (Parsons and Platt 1973) and his extensive study of the U.S. societal community (Parsons 2006).

The neglect of the later phase of Parsons's thinking is easy to understand. From one view, the intellectual and political climate of the late 1960s did not provide much incentive to read Parsons beyond a superficial glance at his books, which were predigested and molded by critics into the convenient strawman of the archconservative, theoretically dry, empirically empty sociologist. From the other, Parsons's late essays and books tend to be highly formalized and based on a labyrinth of quite specific conceptual references, and thus have a very limited appeal for large sectors of the audience. The fact that such neglect is easy to understand does not imply it is less wrong. As the readers of the transcript will see for themselves, Parsons in the 1970s was not merely repackaging old wines in new bottles, nor was he a bitter old man unable to accept that his time had passed. He was the same theorist as ever, genuinely trying to advance the sociological understanding and, as Jurgen Habermas once said, looking for solutions to problems other theorists could not even see. He was willing, moreover, to revise his conceptual scheme whenever he realized it was necessary in order to gain an adequate understanding of the issues involved. The transcript documents how many of Parsons's analyses in the last phase are controversial. Quite a number may trigger doubts and sustained criticism. But none of them may be dismissed as trivial or irrelevant.

A second line of interest concerns Parsons's intellectual biography as outlined in the first section of the interview. To be sure, Parsons himself had been willing to release biographical information at several stages in his career (Parsons 1959, 1970, 1978, 1980, 1981), and the interview does not contain any radical break with what is already known. At the same time, however, the interview here published is likely to be the best text for getting the "flavor" of Parsons's intellectual formation. It surely triggers curiosity about a time in which Weber's and Durkheim's ideas were new, hot stuff for graduate students. But it has also a contemporary relevance when the international, cosmopolitan profile of the young Parsons is contrasted with the current state of graduate education in the social sciences. The experiences he describes show how important it was for his own intellectual development to be able to read Weber and Durkheim in the original, to attend classes in other countries and in other disciplines, to experience—with a certain degree of serendipity—different research traditions.[1] When Parsons stresses with dismay that faculties have been forced to relax or drop the language requirements for graduate students and that most of his students take for granted that reading translations is more than enough, an implicit comparison with his own formative experiences is hard to miss. We have never talked much of globalization providing an astonishingly provincial training to our new cohorts.

Last but not least, the interview here published provides the reader with an effective introduction to the basic tenets of Parsons's work at a time of both consolidation and restructuring. If read carefully, the interview reveals a strong continuity of Parsons's heritage, which may be described as inspired by both a strong respect for economics (as an analytical discipline) and a strong opposition to "economic ideology," a category that in Parsons's definition includes both neoclassical "economic imperialists" and the various varieties of Marxists. Such concern is particularly visible in Parsons's discussion of generalized symbolic media—power, influence, and value commitment— treated conceptually as analogous to money in the economic sphere but never assumed as similar, or reducible, to it. In his view, an adequate analysis of these media should provide the other social sciences with the same kind of analytical strength that economic theories of monetary exchange already provide to economic theory. But, at the same time, such a goal may be achieved only if the analyst does not forget that these media are *not* money and that their analysis is not simply the transfer of money-related properties to other fields. Moreover, generalized symbolic media have the theoretical advantage of being at the same time an interactional resource and a mediator of social systemic interchanges. This gives Parsons a powerful vocabulary for dealing with the dynamics of social systems and for adequately differentiating between structural change and variations in the stock of available social resources.

Not surprisingly, Parsons's definition of generalized symbolic media is the main focus of the seminar. There is, however, a second important dimension of the debate, concerning social values and cultural change. Parsons is quite effective in his criticism of those who claim to have discovered radical changes in the social values of contemporary societies. He argues that the most general value patterns of the Western world have a history of more than 2,000 years and that they may be appreciated only by taking this into account. He claims that there are important cultural continuities between modern societies and their predecessors (Parsons 2006). In a period in which dramatic changes in social values are announced, claimed, or blamed on a daily basis, his argument deserve at least some consideration. At the same time, Parsons is very careful to stress that such continuity does not mean absence of change. On the contrary, the continuity of some key value elements is contingent upon difficult and complex processes of value generalization, differentiation, and specification able to mediate the constant tensions between the definitions of the desirable (i.e., values) and the situational constraints of human life. Again, such a view may be challenged on various grounds. But it deserve consideration and debate, rather than being ignored.

Note

1. In another seminar held previously at Brown (Parsons 1976), Parsons wondered if he could have taken a quantitative methods specialization had regression analysis been available during his graduate years.

References

Parsons, T. (1959). "A Short Account of My Intellectual Development." *Alpha Kappa Deltan* 29: 3–72.
——. (1963a). "On the Concept of Influence." *Public Opinion Quarterly* 27: 232–262.
——. (1963b). "On the Concept of Political Power." *Proceedings of the American Philosophical Society* 107(3): 232–262.
——. (1970). "On Building Social Systems Theory: A Personal History." *Deadalus* 99: 826–881.
——. (1976). "Dialogues with Parsons (1973–1974)." *Indian Journal of Social Research* 17: 1–33.
——. (1978). "A 1974 Retrospective Perspective." In *The Theory of Social Action: The Correspondence of Alfred Schutz and Talcott Parsons*. Ed. R. Grathoff. Bloomington, IN: Indiana University Press.

———. (1978). *Action Theory and the Human Condition*. New York: Free Press.

———. (1980). "The Circumstances of My Encounter with Max Weber." In *Sociological Traditions from Generation to Generation*. Eds. R. K. Merton and M. W. Riley. Norwood, NJ: Ablex.

———. (1981). "Revisiting the Classics Throughout a Long Career." In *The Future of Sociological Classics*. Ed. R. Budford. Boston, MA: Allen & Unwin.

———. (2006). *American Society: A Theory of the Societal Community*. Boulder, CO: Paradigm Publishers.

Parsons, T., and G. M. Platt. (1973). *The American University*. Cambridge: Harvard University Press.

On Teasing Out Sociology from Economics

A Brief Note on Parsons and Schumpeter

By RICHARD SWEDBERG*

ABSTRACT. Of the many interesting pieces of information that can be found in Parsons's March 10, 1973 seminar at Brown University, one concerns his relationship to Schumpeter, and it is to this that this brief note is devoted. Parsons and Schumpeter knew each other for some 20 years, and one of the many things that Schumpeter taught Parsons was that one can read the texts of economists for the sociological insights that they contain. In Parsons's formulation from the seminar: "economists must have some sociological ideas."

At several points in his 1973 Brown Seminar, Parsons mentions events and people that may help us to get a better understanding of his life and work. This is also true, on a minor scale, for his relationship to Joseph Schumpeter, his colleague and (distant) friend at Harvard for some 20 years. One of Parsons's comments on Schumpeter has a broader bearing for economic sociology; and this is another reason for this brief comment.

Let me begin by telling what sources other than the Brown Seminar tell us about the relationship between Parsons and Schumpeter. Parsons was an instructor at the Economics Department at Harvard when Schumpeter first arrived. The meeting with the Austrian economist was of great importance to Parsons's intellectual development:

> In the first year I was at Harvard [1927] Joseph Schumpeter was there as a visiting professor. I sat in on his course on "General Economics", and it was here that I first began to get a clear conception of what a theoretical system was. (Parsons 1959: 6)

"For some years," Parsons also confirmed in a letter, "I stood rather close to the conception of pure economics which I first learned from Schumpeter" (Parsons 1941).

*The author is at Cornell University, e-mail: rs328@cornell.edu.

American Journal of Economics and Sociology, Vol. 65, No. 1 (January 2006).

Schumpeter was one of the original reviewers of Parsons's famous work *The Structure of Social Action* (1937). In his report to the Committee on Research in the Social Sciences, which had funded part of Parsons's research, Schumpeter wrote, tongue in cheek: "The author has in fact so deeply penetrated into the German thicket as to lose in some places the faculty of writing clearly in English about it, and some turns of phrase become fully understandable only if translated into German" (Swedberg 1991: 221).

There were at least two more points at which Parsons and Schumpeter intersected. The first of these was at a seminar on rationality that Schumpeter organized at Harvard in 1939–1940; and the second was in 1948, when Schumpeter was the president of the American Economic Association.

The story of Schumpeter's seminar on rationality at Harvard, in which Parsons participated, still remains to be written (e.g., Swedberg 1991: 279; Schumpeter 2000: 324). In the meantime, the following can be said. Schumpeter's decision to have a Seminar on Rationality in the Social Sciences (as it was called) was triggered in 1939 by a paper on rationality by Chester Barnard. The participants came primarily from different departments at Harvard, and it is clear that Schumpeter wanted an interdisciplinary group. The members included Parsons, Wilbert E. Moore (sociology), David McGrannahan (psychology), Gottfried Haberler (economics), Wassily Leontief (economics), and Paul Sweezy (economics). There were about 10 meetings, starting in October 1939 and ending in April 1940.

An attempt to put together a book from the papers that were presented at the seminar failed, partly because Parsons, who had been appointed co-editor by Schumpeter, lost interest. "In fact I let it die," he later would put it (Parsons 1970: 834). Schumpeter's paper from the seminar, it may be added, was many years later published as "The Meaning of Rationality in the Social Sciences" (Schumpeter 1991: 316–338). Parsons's paper, on the other hand, remains unpublished as far as I know. It was entitled "An Approach to the Analysis of the Role of Rationality in Social Action" and was nine pages long.

The last scholarly interaction between Parsons and Schumpeter probably took place in 1948, when Schumpeter was president of the American Economic Association. Schumpeter was very interested in improving the relationship between economics and the other social sciences, including sociology. The result was a number of joint sessions at the annual meeting that took place in December 1948 in Cleveland, Ohio. There was, for example, a roundtable in commemoration of the centenary of the Communist Manifesto ("The Sociology and Economics of Class Struggle"), in which Parsons participated (e.g., Swedberg 1991: 279; Schumpeter 2000: 365–366).

After having summarized what other sources tell us about the relationship of Parsons and Schumpeter, let me now turn to the Brown Seminar and what it adds to our knowledge. Parsons says at one point: "I was fortunate enough that Schumpeter was here [Harvard] on a visiting basis that year [in 1927]." He also notes that whatever distant (and frosty?) relationship he entertained with most of the members of the Department of Economics, where he worked at this point in his career, "I was befriended by people like Taussig and Gay and Schumpeter." This was the time, in brief, before Parsons made the decision to become a sociologist and move to the Department of Sociology at Harvard.

The Brown Seminar confirms what we know about Schumpeter and his view of the relationship of psychology to economics, namely, that economics should not rest on psychology or be an empirical science. According to Parsons:

> The famous Wesley Mitchell wrote a very interesting article [on the problem of the rational pursuit of self-interest] just about that time [in the late 1920s], in which he went off on what I am sure was a wild goose chase. He said that economics ought to absorb the psychology of the non-rational and be a kind of applied psychology which abandoned the postulate of rationality. Schumpeter would have none of that—I remember talking to him about the problem—he'd have none of it and Schumpeter, I think, was right. If it had gone that way economics would have had to become primarily empirical, not a theoretical, discipline.

The most significant (and novel) piece of information about the relationship of Schumpeter and Parsons from the Brown Seminar, however, deals with another issue, namely, that one may make a *sociological* reading of the works by economists. This may seem like an easy and trivial idea, but like everything new it was initially difficult to think of—and it was Schumpeter who pioneered it and was then followed by Parsons. The relevant section reads:

At least two-thirds of the fall semester [of 1927?] Taussig devoted to Alfred Marshall's *Principles of Economics* and I really got to know Marshall. As a matter of fact, before that I'd never even read Marshall at all. It was that that gave me an idea, following up my discussion with Richard Meriam, namely: economists must have some sociological ideas.

I was sensitized to that idea by Schumpeter, to a very considerable degree. Schumpeter was a strict constructionist about economic theory and he wanted to define it technically and relatively narrow. But he knew that there were a lot of other things; he himself wrote a number of essays on sociological topics, for example, a notable one on social stratification.

Parsons used the technique of how to tease out sociology from economics primarily for his project of constructing a general sociological theory, which resulted in *The Structure of Social Action*. But the technique itself can also be used for other purposes, not least for economic sociology, something that Parsons showed many years later in *Economy and Society* (1956). Parsons, in brief, made good use of what he had learned from Schumpeter in this respect.

By way of concluding this brief note, I want to emphasize that the technique of teasing out sociology, and especially economic sociology, from texts by economists has many advantages. The most important is perhaps that the sociologist gets to work very closely with major economists and learn from them, at the same time as he or she may discover new and inspiring *sociological* ideas about economic phenomena.

References

Parsons, T. (1941, January 27). Letter to Adolf Löwe. Harvard University Archives.

———. (1959). "A Short Account of My Intellectual Development." *Alpha Kappa Deltan* 29(1): 3–12.

———. (1970). "On Building Social Systems Theory." *Daedalus* 99: 826–881.

Schumpeter, J. (1991). *The Economics and Sociology of Capitalism*. Ed. R. Swedberg. Princeton: Princeton University Press.

———. (2000). *Briefe/Letters*. Eds. U. Hedtke and R. Swedberg. Tübingen: Mohr.

Swedberg, R. (1991). *Schumpeter—A Biography*. Princeton: Princeton University Press.

Parsonian Economic Sociology

Bridges to Contemporary Economics

By MILAN ZAFIROVSKI[*]

ABSTRACT. This article focuses on Parsonian economic sociology and its actual or potential bridges and contributions to contemporary economics. These bridges are methodological or epistemological and theoretical or substantive ones. A relevant instance of the methodological bridges is socioeconomic holism, epitomized in the systems approach to economy and society. An important case of the theoretical bridges is sociological institutionalism. The holistic systems approach is a pertinent methodological bridge in that it treats the economy as an integral element of society as a larger system, and consequently treats economics as part of the complex of social sciences. Sociological institutionalism is an important theoretical bridge to (especially institutional) economics by virtue of its emphasis on social institutions and their economic significance. Some other methodological and theoretical bridges of Parsonian economic sociology to contemporary economics are also identified and discussed.

Parsons conceives of economic sociology in terms of a sociological analysis of the economy, including markets, which has become a standard definition of the field (Smelser and Swedberg 1994; Swedberg 2003). In general, his economic sociology is an analysis of the relations between economy and society (as the title of his main work in the field suggests), especially of the impact of the latter on the former. Adopting socioeconomic holism exemplified in a systems approach to these relations, the hallmark of Parsonian economic sociology is treating the economy as a particular social system in relation to the other, noneconomic subsystems of a society.

*Direct correspondence to Milan Zafirovski, Department of Sociology, University of North Texas, Denton, TX 76203; e-mail: zafirovski@unt.edu.

American Journal of Economics and Sociology, Vol. 65, No. 1 (January 2006).

Curiously, Parsons rarely uses the term *economic sociology* and seldom explicitly defines its subject and scope, usually defining it by implication. Thus, he implicitly defines economic sociology by reference to its Weberian formulations. For instance, in his introduction[1] to the English translation of (the first volume of) Weber's *Economy and Society*, Parsons comments that Weberian economic sociology is characterized by "two deep underlying convictions" that differ from the "dominant tone" of orthodox economics: first, the "fundamental variability" of social institutions; second, the "inherent instability" of social structures. In particular, Parsons notes that in (Weberian) economic sociology, the concrete association of economic rationality with—more precisely, its dependence on—"settled routine" social conditions indicates a special link between "institutional patterns, backed by moral sentiments, and the 'self-interest'" (Parsons 1947: 53). His implied case in point is the Weberian historical interconnection or "elective affinity" between the ethic of ascetic Protestantism (Calvinism) and the emergence of the "spirit and structure" of modern capitalism. Like Weber's (and, for that matter, Marx's) early formulation, Parsons's is mostly an economic sociology of modern capitalism, a sociological conception and analysis of the social, notably institutional and cultural, conditions of the capitalist economy.

As known, Parsons's first academic work (his doctoral dissertation) is devoted to the "concept of capitalism" (in the German literature, e.g., Marx, Weber, Sombart), which continues to occupy a prominent place in his later works in the field of economic sociology. Thus, in his 1937 magnum opus *The Structure of Social Action*, referring to Weber's investigation of the "relations of Protestantism and capitalism," he implies that economic sociology represents an examination of the principal social or noneconomic features of the "modern economic order" or capitalism, also termed "free enterprise" or "economic individualism." These features, inter alia, include an integral system of cultural values, an institutional structure, and an economic-political ideology. Specifically, Parsons remarks that a "single, relatively well-integrated system" of cultural values (or value attitudes) is epitomized in Weber's notion of the spirit of modern capitalism. Moreover, Parsons generalizes and reinforces Weber's connection of Protestantism and capitalism by arguing (also) à la Durkheim that such an integration between cultural values and economic structures, including markets, is "one reason why Marxian [pessimistic] predictions about the 'capitalistic' economy have not materialized" (Parsons and Smelser 1956: 160–161). Also, Parsons emphasizes the institutional structure of modern capitalism, as manifest in what he calls the "institutionalization of self-interest," a social process that helps explain the observed "acquisitiveness" or "possessive individualism" of capitalist society. He identifies still another social feature of modern capitalist society as an ideological one consisting in the concept of capitalism (just as socialism), deemed an instance of "political and economic ideologies" (Parsons and Shills 1951: 169–170). While Parsons's first two social features of modern capitalism deliberately evoke Weber as well as Durkheim, the third feature is somewhat unwittingly reminiscent of Marx (and Mannheim), thus creating a curious mixture of Weberian-Durkheimian and Marxian elements.[2]

Parsons's economic sociology contains certain relevant elements that can serve as methodological and/or theoretical contributions and connections—that is, simply bridges—to contemporary economics. The methodological bridges are represented in socioeconomic holism or a holistic systems approach to economy/economics and society/sociology, and the theoretical in sociological institutionalism or a focus on social institutions, discussed in this order next.

I

Socioeconomic Holism: Systems Approach to Economy and Society

AN ESSENTIAL ELEMENT AND CONTRIBUTION of Parsons's economic sociology is what can be described as socioeconomic holism, specified and implemented in the form of a holistic systems approach to economy and society. In this respect, Parsons's economic sociology is redefined as the holistic or systems analysis of the relations between economy and society as systemic categories and consequently those between economics and sociology as social sciences.

In retrospect, Parsonian socioeconomic holism or systems approach to economy and society follows and builds on early holistic[3] or systemic sociologists/economists like Durkheim, Pareto, and in part Comte and Spencer (Lechner 2000), as well as, though less obviously, Weber, seen by Parsons as eventually overcoming the methodological individualism characteristic of orthodox economics and utilitarianism.[4] (Recall, Parsons apparently borrowed the title *Economy and Society* for his major systematic work in economic sociology from that of Weber's sociological tour de force.) In this respect, an essential element of what Parsons famously (and controversially) identifies and argues as the convergence by sociologists Durkheim, Pareto, and Weber, plus economist Marshall, on a normative-institutional ("voluntaristic") theory of human action and social structure is socioeconomic holism, including a systems approach to economy and society. Parsons finds this systems approach explicit and elaborate in Durkheim and Pareto, and implied or derivable in Weber, usually perceived as a nonholist or methodological individualist[5] (Swedberg 1998). For illustration, Durkheim, elaborating on Comte's insight into the "laws of action and reaction of different parts of the social system," describes economies, like noneconomic phenomena, as "systems of values" and so integral elements of society as a whole (Durkheim 1974: 97). Likewise, Pareto treats the economy in systemic terms and characterizes the economic system as a special case of what he calls the "sociological system," described as "much more complicated" (Pareto 1963: 1440). Also, Weber implicitly conceives the (capitalist) economy as an "organized system of continuous economic action," including (rational orientations to) a "system of values" almost à la Durkheim, and as existing within and influenced by the "autonomous structure of social action" or society (Weber 1968: 341). In addition to continuing and elaborating the theoretical tradition of socioeconomic holism from classical sociology, Parsons's approach is linked with the general systems theory as emerging and becoming prominent during the 1950s to 1960s. While in order to understand the theoretical-methodological background of Parsons's own systems approach to economy and society one needs to take into account its origins or elements in both of these traditions, socioeconomic holism is more relevant, at least for our purpose. If so, this approach is better described or more important as a continuation and elaboration of the classical holistic conception of economy and society in sociology and economics than as a special application of general systems theory (e.g., from cybernetics, biology, etc.) to the relations between economic and social phenomena.

A. Economy as a Social System

Parsonian (and neo-Parsonian) socioeconomic holism in the form of a systems approach conceives of the relations between economy and society as those between a part and a whole or a smaller and a larger type of system. Notably, it postulates or implies that the "whole [society] is more than the sum of its parts [economy plus others]" (Luhmann 1995: 5). Particularly, economy-society relations are conceptualized as those between a partial and a total social system, which is the hallmark of the systems approach in economic sociology. This indicates that a key argument of Parsonian (and neo- or post-Parsonian) economic sociology is that economy constitutes a certain social system, just as does society as a whole. Arguably, the economy is a social system in the sense of a "set of relations of units of social interaction [if] their interaction determines prices, quantities, and methods of production" (Parsons and Smelser 1956: 15). More precisely, the economy is better described as a partial or smaller social system in relation to society as a total or larger one. Thus understood, the economy represents an integral element of society or a subsystem of the total social system. As Parsons (1951: 175) states, the "allocation of facilities and rewards," as the defining and constitutive element of the economy, is "part of the structure" of society as a whole, which indicates socioeconomic holism. In systemic terms, he describes the economy as constituting a "subsystem" of society as a larger or total social system and as differentiated from its other subsystems like polity, culture, and societal community (Parsons and Smelser 1956: 6–46).

The Parsonian basis for differentiation of the economy from these other social subsystems is functional, that is, the specific function it performs within a society, which apparently adopts and blends socioeconomic functionalism with systems analysis, thus following and developing Durkheim's ideas. This Durkheimian fusion of functionalist and systems analyses is apparent in the proposition that "as a social sub-system, the economy is differentiated on the basis of functions of the society" (Parsons and Smelser 1956: 15). As known, elaborating on Durkheim et al. (e.g., Malinowski), Parsons specifies these societal functions or functional imperatives (prerequisites, requirements) as Adaptation, Goal attainment, Integration, and Latent-pattern maintenance and tension management (the AGIL model), each fulfilled by a definite partial social system within a society. Specifically, the economy fulfills the function of adaptation, the polity that of goal attainment, societal community (or civil society) that of integration, and culture (or cultural-motivational systems) that of latent-pattern maintenance and tension management (Parsons 1967: 261).

The preceding results in the integrated systems-functionalist definition of the economy as that "sub-system of a society which is differentiated with primary reference to the adaptive function of the society as a whole," thus representing a functional subsystem of the total social system (Parsons and Smelser 1956: 20). The general functionalist (Durkheimian) assumption that the function or goal of any differentiated social subsystem is to contribute toward the survival and functioning of its total system leads to specifying the systemic contribution of the economy as its "specialization in the solution of the adaptive problem" of a society. Specifically, the economy provides a "solution of the adaptive problem" of a society through optimizing the "economic value of the total available means to want satisfaction" or simply "maximizing utility" as its concrete system goal, function, or contribution within the larger social system (Parsons and Smelser 1956: 20).

The above indicates that within the Parsonian functionalist-systems framework, first, adaptation signifies, involves, or presupposes basic economic processes like the production, distribution, exchange, and consumption of wealth; second, the economy fulfills this adaptive function within and *for* a larger social system or society as a whole. In brief, the primary (adaptive) function or goal of the economy, as a social subsystem, is wealth production and accumulation on "behalf of the society as a system" (Parsons and Smelser 1956: 29). In this view, the economy's purpose is less general than societal systemic purposes on the grounds that wealth production and accumulation is sensible "only as a contribution to the functioning of some larger social system," which is another illustration of socioeconomic holism à la Durkheim and Pareto (Parsons and Smelser 1956: 297). Parsons simply proposes that the economy exists and functions both within and (as Durkheim et al. would put it) for the sake of human society, not conversely[6] (as often assumed or implied in orthodox economics and its modern rational-choice extensions in other social sciences, including sociology and political science). Such a proposition thus reestablishes or reinforces the noneconomic, social-systemic rationale for economic processes by fusing functionalist and systems approaches to economy and society. Curiously, neoclassical economists such as Lionel Robbins (1932: 145) implicitly adumbrate or admit such a rationale by stating that "there are no economic ends" but only economic and noneconomic means or ways for attaining "given ends" or, rather, socially conditioned (Hodgson 1999) human goals in society.

B. Economic and Other Social Systems

To summarize the aforesaid, in the Parsonian framework, far from being a self-contained entity, the economy constitutes just one of the four major social subsystems alongside polity, culture, and societal community, each existing and fulfilling a specific function within and for society as a total system. Consequently, a major concern of this framework (especially the AGIL model) is the issue of relations or what Parsons calls interchanges between the economy thus understood and the other three social subsystems, and so their corresponding functions, within society as a whole. In this respect, Parsons et al. essentially adopt, elaborate, and specify Comte's classic statement concerning the "laws of action and reaction of different parts of the social system" (Comte 1983: 224) as the subject matter of what he probably first calls *social statics*, incidentally a term that, along with *dynamics*, John Stuart Mill borrowed from him and introduced to economics (Hayek 1950: 17). Namely, they propose that "just as the economic variant of instrumental orientation must be placed relative to other types—so must the empirical [economic] processes be placed in terms of their relations to those other aspects of the total social system which are not susceptible of analysis in terms of economic theory" (Parsons and Shills 1951: 28).

The first part of the above proposition evokes and is likely influenced by Weber's suggestion that "we shall not consider every instrumental [rational] action as economic" (Weber 1968: 339), in an apparent critique of their perceived equation in orthodox economics (and a sort of prophetic warning to modern rational choice theory with its standard equivalence of the two). The second part is in a sense a reformulation and specification of Comte's "laws of action and reaction of different parts of the social system" in the form of interpenetration or interchanges between the economy and noneconomic systems, in addition to casting doubt on the theoretical validity of an analysis of these systems "in terms of economic theory" as the defining mark of rational choice (including especially public choice) models. In Parsonian terms, polity (goal-attainment system), societal community (integrative system), and culture (pattern-maintenance and tension-management systems) specifically form the "primary social situation" for the economy as the adaptive subsystem of society. In short, they constitute the Durkheimian noneconomic, notably political and institutional-cultural, milieu, environment, structure, or boundary of the economy. A Parsonian-Durkheimian exemplar of these interchanges between the economy and noneconomic systems is what is identified as certain correspondence between "economic differentiations and those of social structure"[7] (Parsons and Smelser 1956: 52). As known, this correspondence is epitomized in the association, as first analyzed by Durkheim and then embraced by Parsons et al., between the increased division of labor and a new type of social solidarity (organic-contractual) in modern society.

Generally, what Parsonians call, à la Durkheim, the "phenomenon of interpenetration" between economic and other social systems precludes that an economy dominated by monetary factors ("money talks") be "strictly segregated from a contiguous sector of the society which excludes [such] considerations entirely" (Parsons and Smelser 1956: 142). (The second part of this statement is probably dubious to most economists, especially rational choice theorists.) Alternatively, this contiguous sector incorporates and focuses on nonmonetary factors, such as power or authority in polity, solidarity or integration in societal community, and respect or prestige in culture, in contrast to money or wealth in the economy. In Parsons's terms, money and power as well as solidarity and respect represent special cases of a "generalized capacity to control" regulating the relations, or simply "generalized symbolic media" mediating[8] the interchanges between the economy and noneconomic social systems within society. More-over, arguably, the "primary interchange processes" whereby eco-nomic and noneconomic subsystems are integrated within the total social system operate via "generalized symbolic media of the type of money and power" as well as solidarity and respect. In particular, Parsons describes power as a generalized symbolic medium that is involved in the "political interaction process" and is "in a sense parallel" to money or wealth as the corresponding medium of the economy. Also, solidarity or integration, as the concrete "output" of societal community or the integrative social subsystem to society as a whole, is described as "another generalized capacity to control behavior analogous to wealth and power." Still another generalized capacity or symbolic medium "analogous to wealth and power" is considered respect or prestige—understood as a "reward for con-formity with a set of values"—as the respective "output" of culture to society (Parsons 1967: 364–367). (In his later writing, Parsons also introduces the concept of influence as a generalized symbolic medium or a "means of persuasion" and sort of substitute for respect and the "extension of claims to authoritative decisions" or of authority and power.)

Though these analogies between money or wealth and power, solidarity and respect or influence, just as overall the AGIL model of economy and society, often seem "too abstract and artificial" (Swedberg 1987: 106), the aforesaid suggests fruitful substantive insights or (as Parsons liked to say) working hypotheses. These are, first, that the economy and the "contiguous sector" of a society are linked with each other via such generalized media; second, that economic and noneconomic subsystems are governed by different, monetary and nonmonetary, types of considerations, respectively. The first is an evident expression of socioeconomic holism and a further application of the systems approach, while the second preempts the analytical reduction of society to "economy" and thus provides ontological-empirical grounds for justifying and making soci-ology and other social sciences not reducible or subservient to eco-nomics and its approach (i.e., against rational choice academic "imperialism").

In historical terms, Parsons et al. imply that the Durkheimian phenomenon of interpenetration between economy and society is particularly salient in traditional or precapitalist societies, thus echoing to some degree Polanyi. In this view, in simple societies the economy is "fused" with other social systems, notably culture, and exists and functions within a "single multifunctional structural matrix" (Parsons and Smelser 1956: 283). The latter appears to be essentially equivalent to what Polanyi identifies in traditional nonmarket societies as the "sociological compass" or the "cultural matrix" constituted of customs, law, religion and magic, etc., in which the economy exists and is "embedded" (the formulation of the embeddedness conception). Yet, unlike Polanyi lamenting that the matrix of modern, as opposed to premodern, societies is a "self-regulating," socially disembedded market so that "instead of the economy being embedded in social relations, social relations are embedded in the economic system" (Polanyi 1944: 3–4), Parsons et al. imply that in contemporary capitalism the fusion between these systems is not entirely absent but only less complete and manifest than in what Weber denotes as economic traditionalism. In the Parsonian framework, the difference between simple and complex societies in the integration between the economy and other social systems—that is, the embeddedness or entanglement of the former in the latter—is one of degree or transparence rather than of kind or substance (as Polanyi assumes, implausibly to contemporary economic sociologists or socioeconomists). This is also indicated by the observation that the "relative importance of noneconomic parts of the theory of social systems for the empirically 'economic' problem areas increases until, in the case of 'primitive' economies, it becomes overwhelmingly great" (Parsons and Smelser 1956: 84).

If the above interpretation is correct, the statement that, since the economy is the "primary adaptive sub-system of the society, it should interchange with three other cognate sub-systems [with] each differentiated according to the appropriate system exigency" (Parsons and Smelser 1956: 297)—in other words, goal attainment, integration, and latency—applies to both traditional and modern societies, though probably in varying degrees. So does the proposition that economic processes are "always conditioned by noneconomic factors" manifest and operating in the "parametric characteristics of the noneconomic sub-systems" of a society (Parsons and Smelser 1956: 306). Likely influenced by and evoking Weber's insight that the economy is "usually also influenced by the autonomous structure of social action within which it exists" (Weber 1968: 341), in this proposition "always" evidently includes or signifies simple and complex, traditional and modern, nonmarket and market societies. An expected, theoretical implication of this empirical conditioning of the economy by society is the Parsonian suggestion that the analysis of economic processes "always must rest on noneconomic assumptions." Alternatively, it is suggested that treating social noneconomic conditions "merely as given data is scientifically unsatisfactory," in an apparent reference to the "orthodox economics" approach, on empirical grounds that institutional change in an economy is pervasive and salient, and consequently the "primary factors involved cannot be economic" (Parsons and Smelser 1956: 308). This suggestion is also probably inspired by and evocative of Weber's classic admonition that "phenomena that must be treated as constants in economic analysis are very often compatible with significant structural variations—from a sociological point of view" (Weber 1968: 341) adopted by economic sociology. A case in point is the differing treatment of economic rationality: as a parameter, axiom, or assumption in orthodox economics and its rational choice extensions versus a variable, social construct or institutional-cultural phenomenon in economic sociology (Smelser and Swedberg 1994; Swedberg 2003). In turn, the observation that the "contiguous" societal sector excludes monetary considerations logically leads to the methodological warning that other social systems cannot be treated "as if they were economies; they clearly are not" (Parsons and Smelser 1956: 308), a variation on the overarching theme that society is simply not (exhausted by) the economy as its integral part. In retrospect, this warning concerns orthodox economics and is reminiscent or perhaps inspired by Weber's contention that "forms of social action follow laws of their own" as well as that they "may always be co-determined by other than economic causes" (Weber 1968: 341). In prospect, it anticipates the frequent critique of rational choice theory as the (overly) comprehensive economic approach to noneconomic phenomena and systems.

Within the Parsonian systems approach, the economy as a special case of a social system is also itself subject to functional differentiation and thus differentiated into definite elements or economic subsystems, just as is society as a whole. Specifically, the "primary functional bases of differentiation" of the economy as a social system are classified into four categories: economic commitments, the production and distribution of wealth, provision of capital or investment, and entrepreneurship or organization (Parsons and Smelser 1956: 43). Consequently, the economy is reconstituted as a system composed of four units or subsystems representing concrete "solutions" for its systemic problems and maintaining "boundaries" to each other. Formally, the AGIL model of four functional prerequisites/systems—adaptation, goal attainment, integration, and latency—is thereby also applied to the economy, just as to society as a whole. In this application, the economy is endowed with all the standard attributes and elements of a social system, for example, a "common value system; institutional structure; adaptive, goal-attainment, integrative and pattern-maintenance processes, etc." (Parsons and Smelser 1956: 306). So is even the firm by treating economic organization (e.g., a plant) as a "concrete social system in itself" notably an institution. While seemingly a "too abstract and artificial" if not trivial, application of the systems approach, specifically the AGIL model, to the economy and its elements, this anticipates or approximates contemporary institutional economists' treatment of firms as complex institutions or governance structures rather than mere production functions as technological constructions (Williamson 1998: 75–77). In this sense, treating business enterprises as social systems or institutional structures is an instance of Parsonian economic sociology's bridges or links to contemporary, including the new institutional, economics.

C. *Economic and Social Equilibrium*

Predictably, Parsons's systems approach to economy and society adopts and operates with the notion of system equilibrium, just as does conventional economics. This is predictable since (or insofar as) Parsons et al., like neoclassical economists and even some classical sociologists (e.g., Comte, Durkheim), endow a "boundary-maintaining" social system with an inherent property of or tendency to equilibrium. The latter is, however, seen as a "theoretical assumption" or "first approximation" resembling Weber's ideal types rather than an empirical generalization or actual state (as sometimes naively understood both by equilibrium theorists and their critics).

Thus, Parsons (1947: 15, 1951: 323) suggests that sociologists should adopt the concept of a social system as a "balance of forces in equilibrium, of relative degrees of integration and disorganization," and even as an "optimum balance." Generally, he remarks that "both economic theory and the general theory of social interaction [and systems] make important use of the concept of equilibrium"[9] (Parsons and Smelser 1956: 247) and consequently (or implicitly) that of optimum, in accordance with the standard (Walrasian) equivalence theorem of equilibria and optima (Allais 1997). In particular, the Parsonian systems approach to economy and society shows "strong resemblance" (Piore 1996) to what economists call general equilibrium analysis particularly characteristic of or culminating in neoclassical (excepting Austrian) economics or marginalism. The obvious difference is that the relevant concept in neoclassical economics is that of market-economic equilibrium and in the general theory of social systems that of societal or cultural equilibrium. Within this theory, the second is a general (or in Parsons's words) "total equilibrium" (Parsons 1951: 6) of social systems,[10] especially societies, in contrast to the first as by implication a partial one, consonant with treating society and economy as a whole and a part, respectively. Apparently, in the general theory of social systems, the terms *partial* and *general* or *total equilibrium* have meanings different from those conventionally established in economics (e.g., Marshallian and Walrasian equilibria referring to a certain market and the entire economy, respectively). Thus, market-economic equilibrium can be general (Walrasian) in terms of the economy, and yet partial in the sense of society as a whole. This is another, Parsonian, way to say what Durkheim argued and in part demonstrated: reaching, tending to, or approximating general economic equilibrium (e.g., prosperity as an indicator or proxy) is not always a sufficient condition for societal equilibrium but can also lead or relate to disequilibrium in this sense (e.g., moral crisis or anomie, etc.). To paraphrase Keynes and Schumpeter, Say's law of self-equilibrating markets, Bastiat's self-established economic harmonies, and Walrasian pseudo-automatic general market equilibrium do not necessarily mean Dukheimian-Parsonian social integration or harmony—in other words, simply, the economy's homeostasis or nirvana (if ever) is not simply or invariably society's. If so, building on or evoking Durkheimian sociological holism, the Parsonian concept of a "total equilibrium" of social systems casts doubt on the fallacy of economic determinism claiming precisely the opposite ("it is the economy") and, curiously, shared (as Durkheim himself noticed) by such otherwise different and hostile schools as Marxian and rational choice economics, including the Chicago School (thus converging on "rational choice Marxism").

On the other hand, it might seem that Parsons et al. simply transplanted the concept of equilibrium from economics to economic sociology, a procedure adopted with even greater theoretical ambitions and more methodological rigor by modern rational choice theorists (e.g., Coleman 1990), but that both pure economists and especially sociologists may find "too abstract and artificial" or unproductive and unoriginal. While this impression is present and probably in part grounded, it is also likely that in so doing Parsons et al. simply continued and elaborated on a sociological tradition of socioeconomic holism, notably a systems method, of which the concept of equilibrium is an integral though somewhat latent component. To recall, inspired from physics and biology rather than economics, Comte effectively introduced the concept of equilibrium and implicitly of optimum, in conjunction with those of social statics and dynamics (subsequently adopted in economics), to sociology, with early sociologists such as Spencer and especially Durkheim adopting and further developing the concept. In particular, Parsons's use of the concept seems influenced by or evokes that of Durkheim, who (following Comte) posits a "law of social equilibrium" in the sense that society tends to attain and maintain this as by assumption an optimal state, describing that of small stationary societies as "necessarily stable" in contrast to its instability in their large dynamic counterparts.

Thus, a variation on Durkheim's law of social equilibrium cum optimum is the Parsonian argument (formalized by the AGIL model) that any social system is "subject to four independent functional imperatives or 'problems' which must be adequately met if equilibrium and/or continuing existence of the system is to be maintained" (Parsons and Smelser 1956: 16). Arguably, a social system, including a society, tends to attain and maintain equilibrium insofar as it satisfies its specific functional imperatives or problems of adaptation, goal attainment, integration, and latent-pattern maintenance and tension management via its differentiated subsystems, that is, economy, polity, societal community, and culture, respectively. Reminiscent of Durkheim as well as of some neoclassical economists (e.g., Knight, Schumpeter), this societal equilibrium is considered to be not only stable, stationary, or static, as in the case of Durkheimian traditional small communities, but also unstable, dynamic, or moving, especially in reference to modern large and complex societies. In this view, it can also assume the form of "a moving, not a static, equilibrium" by virtue of involving "certain orderly processes of change" (Parsons and Smelser 1956: 481–492). This highlights Parsons's characterization of a social system in terms of a balance of "relative degrees of integration and disorganization" (Parsons 1947: 15), a mix or transition between static and moving equilibrium. The Parsonian notion of moving or unstable equilibrium admits of or implies the possibility of system disequilibrium as some degree, form, or symptom of societal disorganization or what Durkheim calls a "disturbance" of social equilibrium in the form of normative-moral crisis (anomie). Admittedly, moving equilibrium or the "transition between two structurally different equilibrium states involves periods of disequilibrium and/or unstable equilibrium" (Parsons and Smelser 1956: 248). While, as Durkheim puts it, "every breach of social equilibrium takes time to produce its consequences" (Durkheim 1966a: 47) for society, in the Parsonian systems approach these periods of disequilibrium, disorganization, strain, or crisis are mostly exceptional and transient in relation to a "balance of forces," integration and order underscored by common values/norms institutionalized at the macrosystemic level and internalized on the personal level.

The last point leads to identifying the specific conditions for attaining and maintaining social equilibrium, thus by implication a societal optimum[11] ("optimum balance"), in a Parsonian systems framework. Thus, Parsons (1937: 707) considers the "value element" (including both ultimate values and "value attitudes") common to the members of a society "one of the essential conditions" of equilibrium in social systems. In this connection, he formulates à la Durkheim two "fundamental conditions" for maintenance (and alteration) of societal equilibrium: first, the process of socialization providing actors with the "orientations necessary to the performance" of roles in the social system and, second, "mechanisms of social control" seeking a "balance between the generation of motivations to deviant behavior and counterbalancing motivations to restoration of the stabilized interactive process" (Parsons 1951: 482). These conditions of systemic equilibrium, as "empirically observed pattern-constancies of a boundary-maintaining system" (Parsons 1951: 483–484) presuppose, involve, or facilitate the micro-internalization of social values and norms by individuals and their macro-institutionalization by society, respectively—that is, simply, socialized persons and legitimate institutions (including government). The second process appears particularly relevant in this respect, as the Parsonian-specific application of the concept of equilibrium to society and its integral social systems becomes "one aspect of the phenomenon of institutionalization" in respect of these values and norms. Alternatively, for Parsons (1951: 491–492), in virtue of (or if) impinging on or interfering with these "institutional patterns," a change in social equilibrium is "never just alteration of pattern, but alteration by overcoming of resistance," especially the "resistance of vested interests."

The aforesaid also holds true of market-economic equilibrium as a special case, phase, or dimension of societal equilibrium. In general, an integral assumption of the Parsonian systems approach to economy and society is that economic equilibrium is determined by exogenous social, especially institutional and cultural, conditions, not only by endogenous market factors as usually assumed in neoclassical economics. In particular, the equilibrium of an economic system undergoing a process of institutional changes (e.g., growth) is assumed to be determined by the "balancing of forces outside as well as within the economy" (Parsons and Smelser 1956: 277–278), that is, social institutions and market transactions, respectively. These institutional changes imply and correspond to moving or unstable rather than static or stable economic equilibrium that is in turn conditional on two differentiated, though entwined, sets of factors emanating from the economy and society alike. This can be described as the social-institutional co-determination of moving market-economic equilibrium, a variation on the theme (to paraphrase Weber) that the economy, in virtue of being an integral part of society, "may always be codetermined by other than economic causes." Since various social conditions govern economic equilibrium, this leads to the methodological suggestion that "it is necessary to inquire into certain noneconomic relations" between its variables (e.g., growth factors), including those between the "conditions of an equilibrium rate of growth and the process of structural differentiation" (Parsons and Smelser 1956: 277–278). More precisely, in a Parsonian framework, an equilibrium rate of growth represents a particular form, stage, or effect of the process of structural-functional differentiation à la Durkheim, notably institutional change, as well as Weberian societal rationalization. Hence, these intertwined (or twin) processes of structural-functional differentiation and societal rationalization in modern society epitomize the social co-determination of economic equilibrium in a capitalist economy.

To summarize, though sometimes "too abstract and artificial," Parsons's systems approach to economy and society, as a reflection, specification, or implementation of socioeconomic holism, can serve as a potential bridge or connection with economics in the following respects. The first is reaffirming, reinforcing, and formalizing the relatively noncontroversial idea (even for most economists) of the economy as a social phenomenon through the systemic concept of it as a particular societal system. The second is reestablishing and elaborating the related holistic notion of the economy as an integral element of society by treating the economic system as a differentiated subsystem of the total social system. The third is emphasizing and illustrating the interdependence between the economy and the other parts of society in the form of fusion or interchanges between economic and noneconomic social systems, including polity, culture, and community. The fourth is conceiving the economy as featuring systemic differentiation within itself as a system and so differentiated into its own units or subsystems that are themselves also subject to this process (e.g., firms as peculiar microsocial systems). The fifth is specifying the relations between market-economic and social equilibrium by treating the first as partial in relation to the second as general or total, thus giving a different novel meaning to the standard conception and classification of (Marshallian and Walrasian) equilibria in economics. And the last is the assumption of co-determination of market-economic equilibrium (and behavior) by exogenous social, especially institutional and cultural, factors, as well as by those endogenous to the economy and markets. Generally, the systems approach to economy and society posits and predicts that economic processes and behaviors "will inevitably involve interdependence with noneconomic variables" (Parsons 1966: 236), including social institutions, as discussed next.

II

Sociological Institutionalism

IF THE SYSTEMS APPROACH IS Parsonian economic sociology's major methodological bridge and potential contribution to contemporary economics, then sociological institutionalism is the main substantive or theoretical one. Parsons's version essentially builds on and develops Durkheim's sociological "classical institutionalism" (Merton 1998: xii), which suggests that a fuller understanding of the first and its possible bridge and contribution to economics presupposes some familiarity with the second. Durkheim is often considered the "father" of sociological institutionalism and even of economic sociology as a discipline (e.g., Piore 1996), perhaps on account of his definition of (general) sociology as the "science of institutions, of their genesis and functioning," including the suggestion that its purpose is to help "understand present-day [capitalist] social institutions" (Durkheim 1966b: lvii). Consequently, he defines economic sociology in institutional terms, stating that its subject matter incorporates socioeconomic institutions such as "institutions relating to the production of wealth," "institutions relating to exchange," and "institutions relating to distribution." So implicitly does Parsons by using the expression the "institutional structure of the economy" (Parsons and Smelser 1956: 102), which indicates Durkheimian sociological institutionalism in respect to economic processes and behaviors. In short, Parsonian sociological institutionalism posits and emphasizes the role of social institutions in the economy, including markets.

As Parsons (1966: 236) proposes, the economy, specifically the "optimum utilization of resources and cost," necessitates a "distinctive institutional structure" as well as the "organization of motives" around certain types of ends. In turn, such an "organization of motives" presupposes or involves the institutionalization of economic values and motivations, including the profit motive or self-interest, as seen below. Generally, Parsonian economic sociology assumes, in a characteristic functionalist manner à la Durkheim, that social institutions function to "integrate action within the economy itself" (Parsons and Smelser 1956: 102). In systems-functionalist terms, then, the economic function of institutions is the integration (and so legitimation) of a capitalist (or other) economy as a differentiated social system endowed, like society as a whole, with definite functional imperatives (e.g., the AGIL model).

Parsons's institutional structure of the economy involves noneconomic as well as economic institutions, described as a "set of structural features" of social systems arising from the advanced division of labor and its consequences for society, with contract cited as a case in point, which apparently follows on or evokes Durkheim. In particular, by characterizing contract as the "central economic institution," Parsons et al. essentially adopt Durkheim's famous argument, also embraced by early (e.g., Commons) as well as contemporary institutionalist economists (Hodgson 1999), that in market contracts "not everything is contractual" but that they also contain various noncontractual or social-institutional elements. Thus, this characterization implies what Durkheim states explicitly, that "a contract is not sufficient unto itself, but is possible only thanks to a regulation of the contract which is essentially social" (Durkheim 1965: 215), notably institutional-normative, including not only formal legal norms but also, and even more crucially in some views (Hodgson 1999), an informal "body of moral rules." Another related instance of socioeconomic institutions is property or ownership, described as the "institutionalization of rights in objects of possession or non-social objects" (Parsons and Smelser 1956: 123–131) involving contractual relations (including a "contract of investment") between the property rights holder and the institutional structure of society (e.g., an organization). This leads to the proposition that capital or investment as a factor of production, just as labor, has to be reproduced via "institutionalized processes" (mostly) within noneconomic social systems, especially polity and culture. Consequently, so-called boundary zones between the economy of which capital or wealth is a generalized symbolic medium and the other social subsystems with different media (power, solidarity, influence), but where the first is seen as "relative effective,"[12] become the "foci of some degree of institutionalization" (Parsons and Smelser 1956: 142).

A salient aspect of the social-institutional structure of the economy is that of markets and competition. In Parsonian economic sociology, particularly its systems approach, the market is "considered as a social system" (Parsons and Smelser 1956: 174), which implies or leads to a consideration of markets as institutions. This redefines the market, just as the entire economy, in terms of an "institutionalized system of exchange relations." Noting that a "central problem area" of conventional economics is the "structure of markets," including market (im)perfection, Parsons et al. imply that the focus of economic sociology by contrast is their social-institutional structure. In turn, this contrast is a variation on the broader theme that, as Schumpeter suggests (influenced by Weber and Durkheim), pure economics treats markets as economics mechanisms à la Walras's mechanism of self-regulating free competition, while economic sociology conceives of them as Durkheimian social institutions.

Predictably, the Parsonian application of the systems approach or the AGIL model to the market as a social system yields four particular markets assumed to connect the "different subsystems" of the economy. Specifically, these markets are the labor market and the market for consumer goods located at the economy's goal-attainment boundary or subsystem, as well as the capital funds market and the market for "control of productivity" at the adaptive boundary or subsystem. These four markets are described as not merely "imperfect in degree" of competition, but as displaying "different qualitative types of imperfection," which both echoes and goes beyond Robinson-Chamberlin's imperfect/monopolistic competition theory of market structure or industrial organization. This is more clearly indicated by the argument that market structures, like perfect competition, monopoly-oligopoly, and imperfect competition, "differ in sociological type, not merely along some dimension of competitiveness" (Parsons and Smelser 1956: 173). Arguably, markets' imperfection "differs not only in degree" of control over output and prices by par-

ticular firms or simply competitiveness—a key premise of monopolistic competition theory—"but in sociological type," specifically
social-institutional structure. The above signifies that perfect or pure
competition, monopoly, oligopoly, and imperfect or monopolistic
competition are not only different market structures or alternative
forms of industrial organization (as seen in conventional economics)
but also varying social systems, notably institutional arrangements,
from the prism of Parsons's (and Durkheim's or Schumpeter's)
economic sociology. In turn, this yields the suggestion that a better
understanding of market structures and their imperfections "can be
attained only by supplementing economic theory with other elements
of the general theory of social systems" (Parsons and Smelser 1956:
84).

A second related dimension of the social-institutional structure of
the economy is what Parsons describes as the process of institutionalization of economic values and motivations. Notably, such a process
involves and makes economic rationality an institutional attribute
within the economy, including markets, as a social system (Luhmann
1995: 462), an analogue to what some Parsonians call instituuonal-
ized (as oposed to atomistic) individualism (Bourricaud 1981: 15).
Consequently, from the stance of the economy as a social system,
market-economic rationality is "not a postulate, but a primary empirical feature of the system itself" (Parsons and Smelser 1956: 102)—
that is, not a constant, but a variable subject to institutional and
historical variation (Smelser and Swedberg 1994; Swedberg 2003).
Traditionally, the first treatment has been characteristic (with some
exceptions) of orthodox economics and its rational choice expansions
into other social sciences, the second of economic sociology and its
proxies (e.g., social economy, Veblenian institutional economics).
Thus, in a retrospective critique of orthodox economists and a
prospective admonition to rational choice theorists, a sociological-
institutional argument is made that a society's values "never can be
defined in terms of economic rationality," but the societal value
system determines the "relative importance of economic functions
(and hence of economic rationality) in the hierarchy of functions on
behalf of the society" (Parsons and Smelser 1956: 175). This argument
therefore means that society is not only (or mostly) an economy,
including a "great marketplace" (Bastiat), a "catallactic [exchange]"

system (Wicksteed, Mises) as in orthodox economics, or a sum of economic and social "markets" (Becker and Murphy 2000: 5) in modern rational choice theory. Alternatively, the relative importance of economic functions and rationality in the "hierarchy" of social functions and values clearly suggests a respective variability or relativity in social-institutional and historic terms, that is, that rational behavior in the economy (and beyond) "varies greatly" across societies and their institutions as well as over time. The variability of economic rationality has thus two entwined dimensions: the first dimension consists in the "degree of differentiation between the economy and other social subsystems" in historical or evolutionary terms, the second in the "strength of economic values in society relative to other value systems" (Parsons and Smelser 1956: 178). Specifically, the structural differentiation between the economy and other social systems reportedly reaches a high degree "only at an 'advanced' level of economic development" such as modern capitalism, and so does by implication the "strength of economic values in society relative to other value systems" (both specifications echoing in part Weber and Polanyi).

Predictably, Parsons identifies a concrete form of the institutionalization of economic motivation and rationality in that of the profit motive or self-interest overall. In this regard, he describes the orthodox economic theory that individual behavior in a market economy is exclusively or mainly motivated by the profit motive or rational pursuit of self-interest as "partly wrong" and as partly hiding a "complexity of elements and their relationships" (Parsons 1940: 64). Alternatively, he argues that the institutionalization and thus legitimization of the profit motive or self-interest explains "one very important element" of economic motivation and rationality, specifically the perceived "acquisitiveness" (Tawney 1920) or "possessive individualism" (McPherson 1962) of modern capitalist society. A particular and salient historical facet of such institutionalization and legitimization is what heterodox contemporary economists detect as "political arguments for capitalism before its triumph" (Hirschman 1977). The above, conjoined with what Parsons (1951: 551) describes à la Pareto and Freud as the "non-rational and irrational mechanisms of the functioning of personality,"[13] provides, as he puts it, the "fundamental reason" why economic sociology should not follow pure economics (or utilitarianism) in explaining "motivational forces" in economic and other "institutional behavior."

Negatively, Parsons contends that an "adequate theory of institutional motivation does not rest on a theory of human nature"—as a venerable favorite resort of orthodox economists and rational choice theorists in some variant of *homo economicus*—a theory he sees as yet unavailable or incorrect. A main reason why Parsons regards a *homo economicus* theory of human nature as incorrect is probably implied in Weber's observation that "a man does not 'by nature' wish to earn more and more money, but simply to live as he is accustomed to live and earn as much as necessary for that purpose." This observation implies that the "isolated economic man" à la Robinson Crusoe is a conceptual abstraction not observed in reality and, alternatively, the presence and salience of institutionalized economic motivation or money seeking through conventions, customs, and other institutions. Essentially, Parsons and Weber agree that, while one does not know yet what human nature exactly *is*, it is not definitely *homo economicus*, as well as being preceded and shaped by social institutions[14] and relations or society, contrary to the Hobbesian idea of the antisocial state of nature (as Durkheim also emphasized). Instead, Parsons argues that an adequate theory should take into account that the fundamentals of institutional economic (and other) motivation are "learned in the course of social experience" rather than being inborn in the form of Adam Smith's "propensity" for exchange or the "selfish genes" of contemporary sociobiologists and economists. This suggests that the institutionalization and legitimization of economic motivation, including money seeking, at the macro level of social structure corresponds to its internalization via socialization on the micro level of individuals.

Further, following Weber, Parsons suggests that an "adequate theory" of institutional motivation in the economy and beyond should be pluralist or multidimensional rather than monist or one-dimensional on the grounds that economic motivations are "complex," not simple. In this view, the "central fallacy in much of economic thought is to postulate some single motivational entity as an explanation of all economic behavior," that is, the profit motive, the instinct of acquisition, the rational pursuit of self-interest as an "inborn propensity of human nature" (Parsons and Smelser 1956: 184–185). Such a postulate is implicitly treated as the variation on the familiar "fallacy of misplaced concreteness" or a single-factor explanation in the realm of economic motivation. In particular, this fallacy is detected in the orthodox economics theory of motivation in consumption on the grounds that an assumption of inborn human propensities or psychological forces in consumer behavior with no reference to institutional-social structure is "unsatisfactory,"[15] apparently evoking the Weberian theory of status groups defined by certain lifestyles or consumptive patterns as well as the Veblenian explanation of its conspicuous type.

The above objection echoes, if not replicates, Weber's identification of "naturalistic monism in economics," epitomized in its assumption ("fantastic claim") about the "operation of one psychic motive" in the economy in the belief that economic behavior is "unambiguously determined" through the "psychological isolation of a specific impulse, the acquisitive impulse [or] economic principle." Weber's (and Durkheim's) implied alternative to such "naturalistic monism" is institutional pluralism in economic motivation, as indicated by his proposition that individuals in their actions (even) in a market economy are motivated by "ideal or material interests"—not only the latter as assumed in the "psychological isolation of a specific impulse." Parsons et al. make explicit this Weberian-Durkheimian motivational institutional pluralism and complexity. Specifically, a Parsonian satisfactory theory of institutionalized motivation in the economy and beyond incorporates these explanatory factors: the "relevant internalized value system" of economic actors, "facilities available" to them in given situations, the "immediate reward sanctions" for their activities, and the "diffuse symbolic reward meanings of success" (Parsons and Smelser 1956: 184–185). The first factor involves the process of socialization, diffusion, or learning of economic (and other) motivation on the part of individuals, conjoined with its institutionalization; the second the distribution of resources or prior endowments ("budget constraints") within the "logic of the situation"; the third Weber's material interests (profit); and the fourth ideal interests (e.g., religious salvation in early Protestant capitalism). This leads to the inference that economic rationality is a function of the degree to which human action is, first, "oriented to a central function" in the economy; second, "in accordance with an appropriate institutionalized and internalized value system" of the latter; and third, "integrated within itself as a system" in relation to rationalist values (Parsons and Smelser 1956: 184–185).

In sum, Parsonian sociological institutionalism can serve as a bridge or contribution to contemporary economics in several ways. A general way consists in identifying and emphasizing the institutional structure of the economy, which anticipates the analytical rediscovery of the importance of social institutions in contemporary economics as well as economic sociology during recent times. A particular way in this respect is by means of stressing the institutional structure of markets and thus treating them, from perfect competition to pure monopoly, as social institutions (or as differing in "sociological type"), a treatment that has become increasingly adopted in much of contemporary economics, including the theory of industrial organization. Still another particular way whereby sociological institutionalism can serve as a bridge or contribution in the above sense is through considering business organizations as institutional arrangements (or social systems), thus adumbrating and converging with their consideration as governance structures in the new institutional economics. An additional way is by positing and demonstrating the institutionalization of economic motivation and behavior, including the institutional origin and attribute of rationality, as well as institutionalized individualism, in the economy and beyond, which, apart from continuing the sociological tradition, links or contributes to the reaffirmation of the motivational and behavioral significance of social institutions in much of contemporary economics.

III

Conclusions

THIS ARTICLE HAS FOCUSED ON Parsonian economic sociology and its bridges or contributions to contemporary economics. Of these bridges, for the sake of illustration, it has identified and discussed one methodological or epistemological and one theoretical or substantive bridge of economic sociology to economics. The methodological bridge is the systems approach to economy and society expressive of socioeconomic holism, and the theoretical sociological institutionalism, as characteristic elements of Parsonian economic sociology.

As elaborated, the holistic systems approach provides a methodological bridge or contribution to economics by situating and embedding the economy in the larger society and, by extension, economic science within the social sciences. Specifically, it does so, first, by conceiving the economy as a social system; second, by considering it a differentiated subsystem of society as the total system; third, by stressing the interdependence between economic and other subsystems; fourth, by analyzing the economy's operation and structure in terms of internal systemic differentiation; fifth, by treating economic equilibria as special cases of societal equilibrium; and sixth, by positing that economic equilibrium is co-determined by exogenous variables such as institutions in combination with endogenous forces like market processes.

In turn, sociological institutionalism represents a theoretical or substantive bridge and potential contribution to contemporary economics by its focus on the "genesis and functioning" of social institutions, including their constitutive role in the economy as the major theme of Parsonian (and Durkheimian) economic sociology just as the old and (in part) new institutional economics. Thus, sociological institutionalism is pertinent or interesting for contemporary economics, notably its institutionalist or socio version, in, first, stressing the economy's institutional structure and thus contributing to the recent conceptual reaffirmation of the relevance of social institutions by economists; second, by treating markets as institutions by virtue of their institutional features and influences; third, by conceiving business organizations as institutional-governance structures; and fourth, by reconsidering economic motivation and conduct, including rationality and individualism, as institutionalized variables subject to variation across societies and over the course of history.

Of course, these are not the only potential or actual methodological and theoretical bridges and contributions of Parsonian economic sociology to contemporary economics. But they are probably the most pertinent and indicative and to some extent comprise or condense many others. Thus, the holistic systems approach to economy and society as a subsystem and a system, respectively, comprises or implies a corresponding specification of the relations between economics and sociology or social science as a whole. For example, Parsons states that economics is the "relevant subsystem" or the "most closely articulated analytical system" of the general science of social systems and action, thus based on the fundamentals of this theory (e.g., instrumental orientation), just as is the economy in relation to society.[16] In this view, historically, economics has had its "conceptual foundation" in the general theory of social action and systems and only becomes its "distinct subtheory" at a "more elaborate level of differentiation." Consequently, economics becomes a "special branch of the theory of the social system" and so "does not stand alone," as the latter is a "general conceptual scheme" of which the former is a "special case" and from which it can be derived by making "appropriate logical restrictions." Specifically, Parsons describes economics as one of the "three analytical social sciences of organized action systems," the other two being sociology and politics. Notably, the relationship between economics and sociology as social sciences is described as one of "intrinsic intimacy," though often (especially since the 1930s) concealed by different intellectual traditions and separate institutional arrangements. Thus understood, economics' subject matter is implicitly identified in the "economic aspect" of "empirical action systems"—more precisely, of instrumental orientation in Weber's sense of aim-rational (*zweckrational*) action—or the allocative process[17] (apparently adopting or echoing Robbins's definition). This specification is premised on the (strong) view that, since economics is a "special case" of the general theory of social action and systems, "no specifically economic variables" exist other than those of this theory, which is another way to restate that the economy is an embedded subsystem of society rather than an independent, self-contained entity. Alternatively, Parsons et al. argue that economics "cannot be the theory of processes in a total society, but only those of a differentiated sub-system of a society," thus implicitly considering rational choice theory[18] or a comprehensive economic approach to all human behavior a sort of a nonsequitur.

In turn, Parsonian sociological institutionalism entails or leads to a sociology of development in the sense of a social-institutional conception of economic change in general and of growth in particular. Such a conception suggests redefining structural economic (and other social) changes as a "problem of institutional change" in the specific form of Spencerian-Durkheimian structural differentiation/reintegration and/or Weberian societal rationalization.[19] For instance, economic change has an institutional character and basis in that it presupposes what Parsons et al. describe as the "complex of value attitudes" exemplified in the Weberian ethic of ascetic Protestantism (as well as Marshall's category of activities analyzed in the *Structure of Social Action*). In systemic terms, structural change in the economy as a social system is linked with institutional changes in the noneconomic systems of a society, thus changing "in each of these sub-systems."

Another element of the Parsonian sociology of development is what is described as a sociological model of economic growth that situates the latter in the "framework of social-process dynamics." In essence, this model conceptualizes and explains economic growth in institutional terms by establishing a link between "an equilibrium rate of growth and the process of structural differentiation" or rationalization. Specifically, in this model economic growth (in qualitative terms as development) "constitutes one aspect" of structural differentiation and/or rationalization[20] as institutional social processes. This signifies that economic growth (or "adaptive mobilization" in the economy) presupposes and occurs within, just as it subsequently affects, the institutional framework or structure of a society. Moreover, arguably, in the long term, economic growth "merges" with changes in this institutional structure, which in turn are seen as "neither purely economic nor quantitative." More precisely, it merges with or presupposes "specific noneconomic processes of institutionalization" at the following three levels: first, the level of organization, entrepreneurship, and invention in the economy; second, in the noneconomic subsystems of a society; and third, in their "boundary relations" or interchanges. The above suggests that sociological institutionalism is not necessarily static or negligent of economic and other change, as its Durkheimian-Parsonian variant is often criticized, but also dynamic by taking into account and providing institutional explanations of changes in economy and society.

Notes

1. According to Swedberg (1998: 217), Parsons's 1947 introduction to Weber's *Theory of Economic and Social Organization* (the translated first volume of *Economy and Society*) is the "most important commentary" on Weberian economic sociology.

2. At this juncture, Parsons (1965: 172) comments that "primarily historical in orientation, Marx's formulation was essentialy a theory of capitalism as a concrete historical system. Weber was a true 'historicist' [i.e.,] he called [modern society] capitalism, thus following [Marx's] terminology and in part sharing [his] negative evaluation."

3. At one occasion, Parsons (1961: 360–362) states that "neither old-style 'atomism' nor old-style idealism is tenable any more." He also identifies three major cases of atomism: (a) "economic individualism," including its generalized form in Spencer's "individualistic rationalism"; (b) "personality-focused individualism" suspecting any "independent integrative significance attributed to society or culture"; and (c) behavioristic atomism à la the stimulus-response mechanism. The above statement may be plausibly interpreted as indicating that Parsons rejects both atomistic individualism (nominalism) and idealistic holism (realism), but at least his systems approach indicates that he essentially adopts Durkheim-Pareto's holistic or systemic methodology in analyzing the relations between the economy and society, especially in his writings since the 1950s (e.g., the *Social System, Economy and Society*).

4. In the view of Parsons (1965: 173–174), Weber "overcame the methodological individualism inherent" in orthodox economic theory (and utilitarianism) through his "insistence on the importance of 'understanding' subjectively held meanings and values" in a sharp contrast with economics' treating of individuals' wants or preferences as "given." This (perhaps controversial) interpretation of Weber reveals Parsons's negative preference for methodological individualism and by implication a positive one for its alternative in structural-functionalist holism à la Durkheim or, minimally, institutional individualism.

5. Swedberg (1998: 164) remarks that Weber's methodological individualism was of a "social rather than an atomistic nature as in [orthodox] economic theory."

6. The frequent saying that normal humans (should) "work to live" rather than "live to work" (e.g., Weber's early Protestants or American "workaholics") can be deemed some sort of lay or commonsense, micro level variation on the Durkheimian-Parsonian functionalist-systemic macro argument that the economy as a social subsystem exists and functions within and for human society or the total social system, not conversely.

7. Parsons and Smelser (1956: 52) add that the Durkheimian "scheme of functional differentiation is grounded in the general theory of social systems

and therefore applies to the economy and to its cognate sub-systems in society."

8. Parsons and Smelser (1956: 269) remark that the modern large economic organization (corporation) "stands at the centre of a complex of organizations mediating between it and the noneconomic societal sub-systems."

9. Parsons and Smelser (1956: 247) define the concept of equilibrium in the sense that "relatively small changes tend to be 'counteracted' by the effects of their repercussions on other parts of the system, in such a way that the original state tends to be restored." As it stands, this definition seems to mirror those in neoclassical economics as well as physics and biology. So does Parsons's (1951: 251) "fundamental paradigm" that a "stably established interactive process, i.e., one in equilibrium, tends to continue unchanged." This paradigm generates a principle of societal inertia in the sense that a social system in a state of equilibrium "tends to remain in that state unless 'disturbed' from outside" (Parsons and Smelser 1956: 256). In addition to a dubious analogy from physics, critics may object that such a paradigm of stability and principle of inertia somewhat contradict the concept of moving, unstable, or dynamic equilibrium that Parsons et al. adopt, just as do neoclassical economists like Schumpeter, Robbins, Knight, and so forth.

10. Parsons (1951: 125) states that wealth or money ("economic power") represents a linear-quantitative variable in the "total equilibrium of social systems" in contrast to (political) power or influence as a nonlinear and qualitative variable.

11. Parsons and Smelser (1956: 30) propose that the welfare of a community is the "problem of the social optimum" and thus of total-system equilibrium as its equivalent, apparently echoing Pareto et al. (neoclassical welfare economics).

12. Stating that "generalized purchasing power is relatively effective" in some noneconomic subsystems stands uneasily with Parsons's quoted statement that an "economy where 'money talks,' cannot be strictly segregated from a contiguous sector of the society which excluded monetary considerations entirely."

13. His full statement is that the importance of internalized values via socialization to the determination of social, including economic, action is not via the "mechanisms of instrumental rationality but through the non-rational and irrational mechanisms of the functioning of personality" (Parsons 1951: 551). Besides displaying late Freudian influences, this statement provides a sort of preemptive critique of modern rational choice theory, especially its instrumentalist, cost-benefit explanation of socialization (e.g., Coleman 1990).

14. Following Durkheim, Parsons (1966: 231) argues that institutional patterns, including institutionalized roles, represent the "mechanism by which varied potentialities of 'human nature' become integrated" and reject what he calls "anti-intellectualistic theories of human nature." In passing, even

putative hard-line individualists like Popper (1973: 94) admit à la Durkheim (and *contra* Hobbes et al.) that "social institutions and, with them, typical social regularities or sociological laws, must have existed prior to what some people are pleased to call *human nature*."

15. Also, Parsons and Smelser (1956: 233–236) comment that, like consumers, investors are also "partially governed by certain noneconomic exigencies or constraints" and consequently that the capital market involves a "great deal of psychological confusion and strain." In their view, owing to its "institutionalized uncertainty," "manifestations of strain appear prominent in the capital market, especially waves of anxiety and of unrealistic optimism, the former tending to culminate in panic conditions, the latter in speculative 'bubbles'" (Parsons and Smelser 1956: 263), which evokes Keynes et al. as well as early sociologists like Tarde and Le Bon with their social contagion or imitation theories.

16. Parsons (1937: 766–777) says that the concept of an economy "makes sense only for systems of action" (though applicable to the system of action of a particular individual—'Crusoe economics')."

17. Parsons (1951: 551) adds that economics as "a social science is concerned with the phenomenon of rational decision-making and the consequences of these decisions within an institutionalized system of exchange relations."

18. As a historical curiosity, Parsons (1937: 60) is among the first sociologists and other social scientists to use the very term "rational choice" (of means) in contrast with what he detects as the assumed "randomness" of (given) ends in utilitarianism and its ramification in orthodox economics.

19. Parsons sometimes defines Weberian societal rationalization in strikingly Durkheimian terms, for instance, as the "tendency of social systems to develop progressively higher levels of structural differentiation under the pressure of adaptive exigencies."

20. Parsons and Smelser (1956: 288–289) add that in a process involving "both large-scale quantitative growth and structural differentiation," any two "differentiated substructures" of society like economy and state are likely to both experience "continuing growth" that is "not incompatible with continuing differentiation from each other." Hence, they infer that the "development of 'big government' is by no means incompatible in principle with the continuing growth of a [capitalist] economy," as economic and political differentiation alike are "destined" to move toward "bureaucratization" as well as "differentiation" between economy and polity.

References

Allais, Maurice. (1997). "An Outline of My Main Contribution to Economic Science." *American Economic Review* 87 (Supplement): S3–S12.

Becker, Gary, and Kevin Murphy. (2000). *Social Economics.* Cambridge: Harvard University Press.

Bourricaud, Francois. (1981). *The Sociology of Talcott Parsons.* Chicago: University of Chicago Press.

Coleman, James. (1990). *Foundations of Social Theory.* Cambridge: Harvard University Press.

Comte, Auguste. (1983). *Auguste Comte and Positivism.* Chicago: University of Chicago Press.

Durkheim, Emile. (1965). *The Division of Labor in Society.* New York: Free Press.

——. (1966a). *Suicide.* New York: Free Press.

——. (1966b). *The Rules of Sociological Method.* New York: Free Press.

——. (1974). *Sociology and Philosophy.* New York: Free Press.

Hayek, Friedrich. (1950). *The Pure Theory of Capital.* Chicago: University of Chicago Press.

Hirschman, Albert. (1977). *The Passions and the Interests.* Princeton: Princeton University Press.

Hodgson, Geoffrey. (1999). *Economics and Utopia.* New York: Routledge.

Lechner, Frank. (2000). "Systems Theory and Functionalism." In *The Blackwell Companion to Social Theory.* Ed. Bryan S. Turner. Malden, MA: Blackwell Publishers.

Luhmann, Niklas. (1995). *Social Systems.* Stanford: Stanford University Press.

McPherson, C. B. (1962). *The Political Theory of Possessive Individualism.* Oxford: Oxford University Press.

Merton, Robert. (1998). "Foreword." In *The New Institutionalism in Sociology.* Eds. Mary Brinton and Victor Nee. New York: Russell Sage Foundation.

Pareto, Vilfredo. (1963). *The Mind and Society.* New York: Dover Publications.

Parsons, Talcott. (1937). *The Structure of Social Action.* New York: Free Press.

——. (1940). "The Motivation of Economic Activities." *Canadian Journal of Economics and Political Science* 6: 187–203.

——. (1947). "Introduction." In Max Weber, *The Theory of Social and Economic Organization.* New York: Free Press.

——. (1951). *The Social System.* New York: Free Press.

——. (1961). "The Point of View of the Author." In *The Social Theories of Talcott Parsons.* Ed. Max Black. Englewood Cliffs, NJ: Prentice Hall.

——. (1966). *Essays in Sociological Theory.* New York: Free Press.

——. (1967). *Sociological Theory and Modern Society.* New York: Free Press.

Parsons, Talcott, and Edward Shills (Eds.). (1951). *Toward a General Theory of Action.* Cambridge: Harvard University Press.

Parsons, Talcott, and Neil Smelser. (1956). *Economy and Society.* New York: Free Press.

Piore, Michael. (1996). "Review of the *Handbook of Economic Sociology.*" *Journal of Economic Literature* 34: 741–754.

Polanyi, Karl. (1944). *The Great Transformation.* New York: Farrar & Rinehart.

Popper, Karl. (1973). *The Open Society and Its Enemies.* Princeton: Princeton University Press.

Robbins, Lionel. (1932). *An Essay on the Nature and Significance of Economic Science.* London: Macmillan.

Smelser, Neil, and Richard Swedberg. (1994). "The Sociological Perspective on the Economy." In *The Handbook of Economic Sociology.* Eds. Neil Smelser and Richard Swedberg. Princeton: Princeton University Press.

Swedberg, Richard. (1987). "Economic Sociology: Past and Present." *Current Sociology* 35: 1–215.

———. (1998). *Max Weber and the Idea of Economic Sociology.* Princeton: Princeton University Press.

———. (2003). *Principles of Economic Sociology.* Princeton: Princeton University Press.

Tawney, R. H. (1920). *The Acquisitive Society.* New York: Harcourt, Brace and Company.

Weber, Max. (1968). *Economy and Society.* New York: Bedminster Press.

Williamson, Oliver. (1998). "The Institutions of Governance." *American Economic Review* 88: 75–79.

Pareto, Parsons, and the Boundary Between Economics and Sociology

By PAUL DALZIEL and JANE HIGGINS*

ABSTRACT. Recent discussions of the separation between economics and sociology in the United States highlight the way Talcott Parsons used Vilfredo Pareto's *Trattato di Sociologia Generale* to propose that economics study logical actions and sociology study nonlogical actions. This article argues instead that in Pareto's treatise: (1) sociology is a synthetic discipline concerned with the study of human society in general; (2) human behavior is nearly always logical from a subjective point of view; and (3) sociology studies both logical and nonlogical behavior judged from an objective viewpoint. Thus, Pareto is an important intellectual ancestor for economic sociology.

I

Introduction

DURING THE LAST 15 YEARS, SCHOLARS HAVE BEGUN DISCUSSING the personalities and ideas that produced an almost complete separation between economics and sociology for a significant part of last century,

*Paul Dalziel is Professor of Economics at Lincoln University, P.O. Box 84, Lincoln University Post Office, Canterbury, New Zealand; e-mail: dalzielp@lincoln.ac.nz. Jane Higgins is Senior Research Fellow of the AERU Research Unit at Lincoln University; e-mail:higginj2@lincoln.ac.nz.
The research for this paper was undertaken while the authors were Visiting Scholars at Wolfson College, Cambridge, UK. They are grateful to Geoff Harcourt for generous hospitality and many stimulating discussions on economics and sociology, to Geoff Hodgson for providing a copy of his (2001) chapter on Talcott Parsons in advance of publication, and to Patrick Aspers for helpful suggestions. Earlier drafts were improved by comments received at a sociology seminar of the University of Canterbury (March 15, 2002), at the annual conference of the New Zealand Association of Economists (June 26–28, 2002), at the annual conference of the History of Economic Thought Society of Australia (July 17–19, 2002), and at the annual conference of the European Society for the History of Economic Thought (June 9–12, 2005). Finally, the authors thank an anonymous referee and the editor.

American Journal of Economics and Sociology, Vol. 65, No. 1 (January 2006).

particularly in the United States (Camic 1987; Swedberg 1987, 1990: 13; Friedland and Robertson 1990; Granovetter 1990; Subrahmanyam 1992; Swedberg and Granovetter 1992; Smelser and Swedberg 1994; Davern and Eitzen 1995; Ingham 1996). The account typically focuses on the conjunction of two events at Harvard University in the 1930s. The first was the foundation of a separate Department of Sociology in 1931 after decades during which sociology had been taught within the Department of Economics, by Edward Cummings from 1893 to 1902 and then by Thomas Nixon Carver (Sorokin 1963; Mason 1982; Homans 1984; Johnston 1986). The second event was the organization by Lawrence Henderson of a seminar group that met between 1932 and 1934 to study the sociological thought of Vilfredo Pareto, the Italian successor to Léon Walras as Professor of Economics at Lausanne University (Homans and Curtis 1934; Henderson 1935; Heyl 1968; Weintraub 1991: 62–66). Common to both events was Talcott Parsons, who was to become "widely regarded as the most significant and influential twentieth-century American sociologist" (Robertson and Turner 1991: 1). Parsons had been in Harvard's Economics Department for more than three years in 1931, but his prospects for tenure were not bright since he was not interested in the more technical developments in economics emerging at that time. He therefore became a charter member of the new Department of Sociology, and was also a member of Henderson's seminar studying Pareto's (1916) *Trattato di Sociologia Generale* in its (1917) French edition.

At the time, Parsons was already engaged in studying the relationship between economic and sociological theory in the works of Werner Sombart, Max Weber, and Alfred Marshall (Parsons 1928, 1929, 1931, 1932). This research took on additional importance as he sought to legitimize his move from economics to the lower-status field of sociology (Camic 1987, 1991; Hodgson 2001: ch. 13). Pareto's *Trattato* was very useful for this purpose since "Pareto had been an eminent economic theorist [who] had attempted the formulation of a more comprehensive system of sociological theory" (Parsons 1970: 828). Parsons began writing articles on Pareto (Parsons 1933, 1935a, 1935b, 1936), and devoted three chapters of his (1937) book *The Structure of Social Action* to Pareto's sociology and its implications.

This book was very influential. As Camic (1989: 39) observes, "no sociological work from the period has been so widely discussed, and few theoretical developments in the discipline over the past half century have been launched without an engagement with Talcott Parsons' towering first book."

According to Parsons, Pareto rigidly restricted the discipline of economics to the study of logical or rational behavior: "action is economically explicable only in so far as it is logical; hence all factors responsible for deviation from the norm of intrinsic rationality may be ruled out as non-economic" (Parsons 1949: 265).[1] These nonrational, noneconomic elements were the proper focus of study for analytical sociology. This interpretation of Pareto came to be widely accepted, in economics as well as sociology. Paul Samuelson, for example, who was in the Department of Economics at Harvard from 1935 to 1940, wrote in his famous graduate textbook that "many economists, well within the academic fold, would separate economics from sociology upon the basis of rational or irrational behavior" (1947: 90), a remark that he later agreed did trace to Pareto (Swedberg 1990: 3, fn. 4). This view is still widely accepted, as the following recent statements illustrate: "[Pareto's] basic premise was that economics studies rational action, and sociology studies nonrational action" (Swedberg 1990: 11); "One way of doing this, suggested by the Italian social scientist, Vilfredo Pareto, is to institute a division of labor between the rational and nonrational aspects of social life" (Holton 1992: 14); "Like Pareto, [Parsons] accepted the rational action postulate for economic analysis, but argued that sociology addressed a set of problems left open by economics that required attention to nonrational elements" (Coleman and Fararo 1992: xvii); "Vilfredo Pareto, the only figure who deeply influenced both disciplines, held that economics was the study of rational behavior and sociology the study of nonrational behavior" (Baron and Hannan 1994: 1116); "Economics, Pareto argued, should only deal with 'logical action' and sociology with 'nonlogical action'" (Smelser and Swedberg 1994: 20, fn. 5).

More recently, three contributors to the *American Journal of Economics and Sociology* have offered an alternative interpretation of Pareto's work. In their review of economic sociology, Milan Zafirovski and Barry Levine (1997: 269–270) suggest that Pareto broadened the scope of sociology to include *both* economic and noneconomic phenomena, and hence *both* logical-rational and nonlogical actions (see also Zafirovski 1999: 585–586). Patrick Aspers (2001) takes this idea still further, devoting a full article to arguing that Pareto crossed the boundaries of economics and sociology. In particular, Aspers (2001: 532–533) observes that "Pareto integrates interests and sentiments in his analysis of economic phenomena," giving rise to what may be labeled as "economic sociology" studying "nonlogical actions that take place in, and affect, the economic sphere." Aspers acknowledges that Pareto did not use the specific term "economic sociology" but argues that it can be inferred from his text (2001: 527). In particular, Pareto recognized that "economic issues are not separated from sociological issues [but] are intertwined, and a complete analysis of an economic phenomenon must face this" (2001: 528).[2]

If Zafirovski, Levine, and Aspers are correct (and we think they are), Pareto should be restored as an important intellectual ancestor in the history of economic sociology. But what then of the widely accepted interpretation of Pareto introduced by Talcott Parsons? The purpose of this article is to argue that in fact Parsons read too much of his own early views into Pareto's text.[3] Our analysis is presented in three parts. First, we contrast Parsons's claim that Pareto explicitly refused to define sociology rigorously with the definition given in the opening paragraph of the *Trattato*. Second, we show that Parsons's description of Pareto's distinction between logical and nonlogical action involved a change of emphasis that lost an important aspect of what Pareto wrote about the subjective and objective points of view. Third, we explain that Parsons's identification of economics with logical action and sociology with nonlogical action is not supported by Pareto's text. Of course, Parsons himself did not maintain a sharp division between economics and sociology after his Marshall Lectures in 1953 (Parsons [1953] 1991; Parsons and Smelser 1956). This article corrects the myth that Pareto would have disagreed with that development, and so concludes that Pareto's writings are indeed an important founding contribution to both "old" and "new" economic sociology (see Swedberg 1997: 163 for an explanation of this distinction).

II

Pareto's Definition of Sociology

PARSONS PUBLISHED A NUMBER OF PAPERS ON PARETO IN THE MID-1930S but his fullest treatment is found in *The Structure of Social Action*. There Parsons argued that Pareto adopted a two-fold approach to sociology:

> The only other social science [Pareto] mentions is sociology, which, though he explicitly refused to define it rigorously, appears to include two aspects. One is an analytical aspect, the analysis of the nonlogical elements of action, the other a synthetic, the total account of concrete action generally, including the economic element. It is clear that sociology for Pareto must be considered, in the analytical sense, a residual science since it is concerned with a residual category of action elements. (Parsons 1949: 766)

In contrast to Parsons's claim that Pareto explicitly refused to define sociology rigorously, consider the following passage, which is the opening paragraph of *Trattato*:

> Human society is the subject of many researches. Some of them constitute specialized disciplines: law, political economy, political history, the history of religions, and the like. Others have not yet been distinguished by special names. To the synthesis of them all, which aims at studying human society in general, we may give the name of sociology. (Pareto 1935: 3)

Thus, Pareto did give a rigorous definition of sociology—the study of human society in general—that is consistent with what Parsons termed its synthetic aspect. At the very least, Parsons appears to be guilty of what he himself called a violation of "the canons of careful textual criticism by ignoring the author's own definition of one of his leading concepts" (1949: 200, fn. 4), an action that appears particularly hard to justify given the prominent placement of this definition at the beginning of Pareto's work.[4] Other references in *Trattato* also reflect Pareto's view that sociology is broader than economics rather than being a sibling discipline; for example: "Economics is a small part of sociology, and pure economics is a small part of economics" (1935: 1194, fn. 5); and "The results that [pure economics] achieves form an integral and not unimportant part of sociology, but only a part" (1935: 1408).

The main source for Parsons's discernment of an "analytical" sociology in Pareto's thought comes from a *Trattato* diagram reproduced below as Figure 1 (see Parsons 1949: 183). Pareto's associated text made the following comments:

> **33.** . . . Let *O* in Figure 1 stand for a concrete situation. By analysis we distinguish within it a number of facts: *c, e, g*. . . . The fact *c* and others like it, *a, b*. . . are brought together under a certain theory, under a general principle, *P*. In the same way, *e* and facts like *e* (*d, f*. . .) yield another theory *Q*; and the facts *g, l, m, n*. . . still another theory, *R*, and so on. These theories are worked out separately; then, to determine the concrete situation *O* the results (*c, e, g*. . .) of the various theories are taken together. After analysis comes synthesis.

> **34.** *Example*: Let *Q* stand for the theory of political economy. A concrete situation *O* presents not only an economic aspect, *e*, but the further aspects *c, g*. . . of a sociological character. It is a mistake to include, as many have included, the sociological elements *c, g*. . . under political economy. The only sound conclusion to be drawn from the facts is that the economic theory which accounts for *e* must be supplemented (*supplemented*, not replaced) by other theories which account for *c, g*. . . . (Pareto 1935: 19–20)

The first point to note about Figure 1 is that Pareto's purpose was *not* to define the noneconomic theories such as *P* and *R*, but rather to defend the validity of pure economic theory, *Q*, despite its apparent inability to explain concrete facts. In particular, the core predic-

Figure 1

Pareto's Theory of Analysis and Synthesis

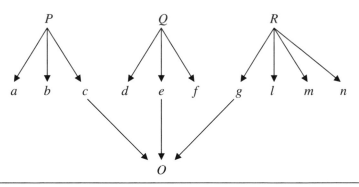

Source: Pareto (1935: 19).

tion of economic theory that restrictions on free trade would harm prosperity was not supported by experience at the time of Pareto, who commented that "nobody understands why English prosperity has increased under free trade, while German prosperity has increased under protection" (Pareto 1935: 1409). Pareto argued that observations such as this did not mean the economic theories were wrong, but that they had to be supplemented from other sources. Hence in the next paragraph after the two cited above (i.e., paragraph 35), Pareto cites his (1906) *Manuale di Economia Politica* to argue that "in political economy itself, the theories of pure or mathematical economics have to be supplemented—not replaced—by the theories of applied economics" (Pareto 1935: 20; see also Steiner 1995).

Further, the components of Figure 1 termed "sociological" by Pareto are not the *theories* (*P* and *R*), but are the *facts* (*a*, *b*, *c*, and *g*, *l*, *m*, *n*). This is entirely consistent with the opening paragraph cited above that expected the theories to come from the specialized disciplines of law, political economy, political history, religious studies, and other disciplines not yet distinguished by special names. Sociology was not included in the named list. This is not surprising since, as Tarascio (1968: 74) points out, "during Pareto's time such modern specialized disciplines as social psychology, political science, physical and cultural anthropology, and sociology did not exist."

It would, of course, have been a legitimate extension of Pareto's ideas for Parsons to suggest that among the not-yet-named disciplines might be one to be called analytical sociology. It would also have been reasonable for Parsons to suggest that all the noneconomic theories in Figure 1 might be grouped together under the generic heading of analytical sociology. There is no evidence in the *Trattato*, however, that Pareto took either of these steps himself.

III

Logical and Nonlogical Actions

THE DISTINCTION BETWEEN LOGICAL AND NONLOGICAL ACTION was an important one for Pareto, and he devoted Chapter 2 of the *Trattato* to this topic. According to Pareto, the logic of a person's behavior had to be considered from two aspects: subjectively, from the point of view of the person performing the action; and objectively, from the perspective of a scientifically educated observer. This is expressed in paragraph 150:

> From the subjective point of view nearly all human actions belong to the logical class. In the eyes of the Greek mariners sacrifices to Poseidon and rowing with oars were equally logical means of navigation. . . . Suppose we apply the term *logical actions* to actions that logically conjoin means to ends not only from the standpoint of the subject performing them, but from the standpoint of other persons who have a more extensive knowledge—in other words, to actions that are logical both subjectively and objectively in the sense just explained. Other actions we shall call *nonlogical* (by no means the same as "illogical"). (Pareto 1935: 77)

Note how Pareto assumes people typically see themselves as acting logically even when the outcomes they anticipate from their actions are not supported by objective scientific knowledge. Parsons (1949: 187) quotes from the above paragraph, but then provides his own interpretation a few pages later:

> All that it is possible to know is the objective end or the outcome of the action. But this must, in the nature of the case, always be the "logical" outcome of the operations actually performed. For in so far as a course of events is scientifically understandable in any sense its later phases must always be, in the sense in which Pareto means it, "logically united" to the earlier. Then, in terms of the objective point of view alone, all action is logical. The differentiating criterion therefore involves the subjective point of view and can be stated in two ways: (a) Action is logical in so far as the operations are logically united to their end from a subjective as well as an objective point of view. . . . (b) The subjective end must coincide with the objective end. (Parsons 1949: 190–191)

Both Pareto and Parsons hold that an action's objective end must agree with its subjective purpose for the action to be logical. A significant difference of emphasis, however, lies between them. Pareto states that "from the *subjective* point of view nearly all human actions belong to the logical class" while Parsons states that "in terms of the *objective* point of view alone all action is logical."[5] Consider the example offered by Pareto—the practice of Greek mariners offering sacrifices to Poseidon as a means for safe navigation. To Pareto, this is nonlogical because, although the sailors considered the sacrifices to be logical, there is no scientific effect resulting from their *actions*.

In Parsons's interpretation, the sacrifices are nonlogical because there is no scientific validity for the *beliefs* held by the sailors. Thus the emphasis changes from the rationality of the objective action to the rationality of the subjective belief. Although Parsons arrives at the same answer as Pareto—sacrifices to Poseidon are nonlogical—an important element in the latter's thought is lost, particularly Pareto's view that people have a strong tendency to rationalize their behavior with theories or beliefs they consider to be subjectively logical. This view is nicely expressed in the following extract from Pareto's sociological lectures at Lausanne University:

> Il y a proportionnellement plus de vérité dans la proposition: les hommes croient certaines choses parce qu'ils agissent d'une certaine façon, que dans l'autre : les hommes agissent d'une certaine façon parce qu'ils croient certaines choses. Mais comme les hommes aiment à donner un vernis logique à leurs actions, ils s'imaginent que cette dernière proposition représente la vérité. (Pareto 1905: 17–18, cited in Valade 1990: 187)[6]

Parsons's change of Pareto's emphasis becomes significant when he then identifies analytical sociology with nonlogical actions only, since it is easily forgotten that, while the purposes of such actions are objectively nonlogical, the opposite is typically true *subjectively* (in Pareto's theory). Thus a potential point of contact between sociology and subjective rationality highlighted by Pareto is lost in Parsons's interpretation.

IV

Economics and Sociology

IN HIS BIOGRAPHICAL ENTRY ON VILFREDO PARETO for the *Encyclopedia of the Social Sciences*, Parsons (1933) observed that Pareto's whole sociological theory turned on the concepts of logical and nonlogical action. He then put forward the claim that: "The former is formulated with the type of economic action primarily in mind, as action rational with reference to a given subjective end. The main analytical problems of Pareto's sociology, however, concern the other type." (1933: 106) This identification of economics with logical action and sociology with nonlogical action was carried over (although in a less explicit way) to *The Structure of Social Action*:

Action which meets closely the criteria of "logicality" is, to a first approximation, that for which economic theory is most nearly adequate as an explanatory tool. Hence it is a reasonable supposition that the study of cases which involve departure from these criteria will lead to the isolation of some, at least, of the important noneconomic elements. (Parsons 1949: 186)

[Pareto] has first abstracted from the logical elements of action, leaving the nonlogical. Then of nonlogical action he has discarded the overt acts . . . leaving only the linguistic manifestations or theories involved in nonlogical action. The nucleus then of the analytical, as distinct from the synthetic, part of Pareto's treatise is *an inductive study of the theories or linguistic expressions involved in nonlogical action.* (Parsons 1949: 196)

Parsons acknowledged at several points that Pareto himself did not take the step of considering action in systems analytically, but argued that such a step was implied by his approach (see, for example, Parsons 1949: 186, 229, 267, 300). This is the view of Pareto's *Trattato* that has passed into the folklore of economists and sociologists. Pareto's thought, however, is again more subtle than Parsons's sharp distinction allows.

Pareto certainly regarded pure economics or political economy as restricted to logical behavior. In his *Manual,* Pareto (1972: 103) defined political economy as the study of "the many logical, repeated actions which men perform to procure the things which satisfy their tastes." Similarly, in *Trattato,* Pareto (1935: 491) observed that "pure economics has the advantage in fact of being able to draw its inferences from very few experimental principles; and it makes such a strict use of logic as to be able to state its reasonings in mathematical form." This does not mean, however, that what Pareto then termed "applied economics" or "sociology" was restricted to nonlogical behavior. To the contrary, Pareto (1935: 1734) observed that sociology is more complicated than economics precisely because "in addition to logical conduct, which is alone envisaged in economics, one has to deal with non-logical conduct, and then again, in addition to logical thinking, with derivatives" (see also Aspers 2001: 524, who points out how Pareto used the example of money to illustrate this distinction).

More damaging than the exclusion of logical behavior from the discipline of sociology, however, is the way in which Parsons's original approach separated "logical" economics from "nonlogical" sociology. Pareto was very clear that such a separation, which he himself had adopted earlier in his academic career, was an error:

> I succumbed, to some extent at least, to a common preconception among economists that the economic factor can be isolated from other social factors. Not till I had completed the investigation presented in these volumes did I become altogether aware of that error, which kept me from taking the short step that leads from the particular theory of economic crises to the general theory of social phenomena. (Pareto 1935: 1908–1909)

Many modern economic sociologists remain concerned about the common precept held by economists that economic factors can be isolated from other social factors. Contrary to the widespread belief among both economists and sociologists, however, Pareto explicitly rejected such a preconception. It is this point, perhaps more than any other, that makes Pareto an important figure in the history of economic sociology as a discipline.[7]

V

Conclusion

THE INTRODUCTION OF THIS ARTICLE CITED A NUMBER OF EMINENT SCHOLARS who attribute last century's separation of economics and sociology to a division originally proposed by Vilfredo Pareto. Arthur Stinchcombe (1986: 1) refers to this as a "birth myth" created by Talcott Parsons: "In *The Structure of Social Action* Parsons (1937) had presented us with a birth myth in which sociology was born out of the decay of utilitarianism, as Durkheim, Weber, Pareto and even Alfred Marshall realized that the framework of rationality was given by deeply irrational value commitments embedded in religion, or in habitual commitments to the values embedded in work activities, or simply, in Pareto, in the unreasonableness of humankind." This article has argued that this myth reflects more of Parsons's own early thinking on the boundary between economics and sociology in the 1930s than it reflects Pareto's actual text in his *Trattato di Sociologia Generale* written in 1916.

Of course, Parsons himself did not maintain the sharp division between economics and sociology that he thought he had found in the *Trattato*. In his Marshall Lectures, delivered at Cambridge University in November 1953, Parsons described his change of mind in these terms:[8]

> The other horn of the dilemma was what at that time I called the "analytical factor view" and associated above all with the name of Pareto. This was the view that economic theory dealt with a special class of the *variables* involved in social action. It then needed to be supplemented by the theory of *the other variables* which controlled the "social" and "political" aspects. This is what Pareto in his General Sociology set out to provide. I personally followed Pareto's lead in this respect.
>
> I am now of the opinion that this was a false dilemma. The non-economic aspects are not the resultants of the operation of one or more sets of "non-economic" variables whereas the economic aspect is the resultant of a different and independent set of variables, of an independent though abstract "theoretical system." The correct view is rather that there is *one* set of fundamental variables of the social system which are just as fundamental in its economic aspect as in any other, and of course vice versa. (Parsons [1953] 1991: 16)

The Marshall Lectures represented a fundamental reconsideration by Parsons about the boundary between economics and sociology. They led three years later to his important book with Neil Smelser (1956), *Economy and Society: A Study in the Integration of Economic and Social Theory* (see Parsons 1970: 845–846; Smelser 1981, 1991), in which "economic theory is a special case of the general theory of social systems" and "an economy, as the concept is usually formulated by economists, is a special type of social system" (Parsons and Smelser 1956: 306). *Economy and Society* is often cited as a founding pillar of modern research in economic sociology (Swedberg 1990: 319; Granovetter and Swedberg 1992: 5; Holton 1992; Smelser and Swedberg 1994: 15), and so all the more reason to correct the myth that Pareto's writings are contrary to its basic schema. In particular, this article has shown that for Pareto: (1) sociology is a synthetic discipline concerned with the study of human society in general; (2) human behavior is nearly always logical from a subjective point of view; and (3) sociology studies both logical and nonlogical behavior judged from an objective viewpoint.

Thus Aspers, Levine, and Zafirovski are right to draw attention to

Pareto as an important intellectual ancestor for economic sociology. Pareto's work must not be accepted uncritically, of course, but his approach to economics and sociology contains important insights for modern debates about the boundary between the two disciplines. In particular, Pareto would be dismayed by the tendency for many sociologists to downplay the subjectively rational aspect of human action, and for many economists to analyze real-world problems without recognizing the need to incorporate sociological facts and theories. In this context it is appropriate to give Pareto the last word, which is as relevant at the beginning of the 21st century as it was in 1916:

> A number of economists today are aware that the results of their science are more or less at variance with concrete fact, and are alive to the necessity of perfecting it. They go wrong, rather, in their choice of means to that end. They try obstinately to get from their science alone the materials they know are needed for a closer approximation to fact; whereas they should resort to other sciences and go into them thoroughly—not just incidentally—for their bearing on the given economic problem. The economists in question are bent on changing—sometimes on destroying—instead of supplementing. They go round and round like squirrels in their cages, chattering forever about "value," "capital," "interest," and so on, repeating for the hundredth time things known to everybody, and looking for some new "principle" that will give a "better" economics—and for only a few of them, alas, does "better" mean in better accord with the facts; for the majority it means in better accord with certain sentiments they hold. Even with those few their effort, for the present at least, is doomed to disappointment. Until economic science is much further advanced, "economic principles" are less important to the economists than the reciprocal bearings of the results of economics and the results of the other social sciences. (Pareto 1935: 1413)

Notes

1. All citations from *The Structure of Social Action* in this article come from the second edition, which the preface explains was a reprint by a new publisher of the original book without any changes.

2. Samuels (1974: 9) also argued that for Pareto "economics must be part of a larger general sociology, ultimately because of the interdependence of nominally economic and sociological variables," but called the resulting analysis "economic policy" rather than "economic sociology."

3. A referee reports that the same can be said of the way Talcott Parsons

(1931, 1932) interpreted Marshall. A good overview of Marshall's economic sociology is provided by Aspers (1999).

4. The idea that Pareto refused to set up a precise definition of sociology may have come from Parsons's mentor, Lawrence Henderson (1935: 19).

5. Parsons appears to have been nervous about his reworking of this aspect of Pareto's theory, commenting that "such an interpretation of Pareto's scientific 'objectivism' would seem on the face of it so far-fetched as to be ridiculous" (Parsons 1949: 190, fn. 1). Parsons defended his interpretation as an answer to a critique by Murchison (1935) that Pareto's distinction of logical and nonlogical action is meaningless because all action must necessarily to the scientist be logical.

6. "There is proportionately more truth in the proposition that people hold certain beliefs because they act in a certain fashion, than in the converse that people act in a certain fashion because they hold certain beliefs. But since people like to give a logical veneer to their actions, they imagine this latter proposition represents the truth."

7. Two other English-language writers have offered a similar interpretation of Pareto. Pitirim Sorokin (1928: 38), who was the founding Professor of Sociology at Harvard University and Parsons's head of department in 1931, summarized Pareto's approach as follows: "The one science which uses the conclusions of pure economics and of other pure social sciences, making a synthesis of their data is sociology. Thus, as pure economics begins to take more and more into consideration all the important human traits, and proceeds its synthetic way, it begins to turn more and more into sociology, as the synthetic science of a real man and of real social phenomena." Similarly Vincent Tarascio (1968: 71) recognized that "Pareto was emphatic in stating over and over again that a 'synthesis' or integration of the theories of the separate disciplines had to take place in order to arrive at better approximations to human society" and that "to the 'synthesis' of all specialized disciplines dealing with the study of human society, Pareto gave the name sociology" (see also Tarascio 1969, 1976, 1983).

8. These lectures were not published until 1991, after the originals were rediscovered by Richard Swedberg in Harvard University archives. Swedberg (1991) introduces Parsons's lectures with an essay explaining the various stages in his intellectual development on the relationship between economic theory and sociological theory.

References

Aspers, Patrick. (1999). "The Economic Sociology of Alfred Marshall." *American Journal of Economics and Sociology* 58(4): 651–667.
——. (2001). "Crossing the Boundaries of Economics and Sociology." *American Journal of Economics and Sociology* 60(2): 519–545.

Baron, James, and Michael Hannan. (1994). "The Impact of Economics on Contemporary Sociology." *Journal of Economic Literature* 32(3): 1111–1146.

Camic, Charles. (1987). "The Making of Method: A Historical Reinterpretation of the Early Parsons." *American Sociological Review* 52(4): 421–439.

——. (1989). "Structure After 50 Years: The Anatomy of a Charter." *American Journal of Sociology* 95(1): 38–107.

——. (1991). "Introduction." In *Talcott Parsons: The Early Essays*. Ed. C. Camic. Chicago: University of Chicago Press.

Coleman, James, and Thomas Fararo. (1992). "Introduction." In *Rational Choice Theory: Advocacy and Critique*. Eds. J. Coleman and T. Fararo. Newbury Park: Sage Publications.

Davern, Michael, and Stanley Eitzen. (1995). "Economic Sociology: An Examination of the Intellectual Exchange." *American Journal of Economics and Sociology* 54(1): 79–88.

Friedland, Roger, and A. F. Robertson. (1990). "Beyond the Marketplace." In *Beyond the Marketplace: Rethinking Economy and Society*. Eds. R. Friedland and A. F. Robertson. New York: Aldine de Gruyter.

Granovetter, Mark. (1990). "The Old and the New Economic Sociology: A History and an Agenda." In *Beyond the Marketplace: Rethinking Economy and Society*. Eds. R. Friedland and A. F. Robertson. New York: Aldine de Gruyter.

Granovetter, Mark, and Richard Swedberg. (1992). "Introduction." In *The Sociology of Economic Life*. Eds. M. Granovetter and R. Swedberg. Boulder, CO: Westview.

Henderson, Lawrence. (1935). *Pareto's General Sociology: A Physiologist's Interpretation*. Cambridge: Harvard University Press.

Heyl, Barbara. (1968). "The Harvard 'Pareto Circle'." *Journal of the History of the Behavioral Sciences* 4(4): 316–334.

Hodgson, Geoffrey. (2001). *How Economics Forgot History: The Problem of Historical Specificity in Social Science*. London: Routledge.

Holton, Robert. (1992). *Economy and Society*. London: Routledge.

Homans, George. (1984). *Coming to My Senses: The Autobiography of a Sociologist*. New Brunswick, NJ: Transaction Books.

Homans, George, and Charles Curtis. (1934). *An Introduction to Pareto: His Sociology*. New York: Alfred A. Knopf.

Ingham, Geoffrey. (1996). "Some Recent Changes in the Relationship Between Economics and Sociology." *Cambridge Journal of Economics* 20(2): 243–275.

Johnston, Barry. (1986). "Sorokin and Parsons at Harvard: Institutional Conflict and the Origin of a Hegemonic Tradition." *Journal of the History of the Behavioral Sciences* 22(2): 107–127.

Mason, Edward. (1982). "The Harvard Department of Economics from the

Beginning to World War II." *Quarterly Journal of Economics* 97(3): 383–433.

Murchison, Carl. (1935). "Pareto and Experimental Social Psychology." *Journal of Social Philosophy* 1(1): 53–63.

Pareto, Vilfredo. (1905). *Programme et Sommaire du Cours de Sociologie.* Rpt. in *Oeuvres Complètes de Vilfredo Pareto*, vol. XI. Ed. G. Busino. Geneva: Librairie Droz, 1967.

———. (1906). *Manuale di Economia Politica.* Milan: Societa Editrice Libraria.

———. (1916). *Trattato di Sociologia Generale.* Florence: Barbara.

———. (1917). *Traité de Sociologie Générale.* French translation of *Trattato di Sociologia Generale.* Trans. P. Boven. Paris: Payot.

———. (1935). *The Mind and Society.* English translation of *Trattato di Sociologia Generale* (2nd ed., 1923). Trans. A. Bongiorno and A. Livingston. London: Jonathan Cape.

———. (1972). *Manual of Political Economy.* English translation of *Manuale di Economia Politica* (French ed., 1927). Trans. A. S. Schwier. Eds. A. S. Schwier and A. N. Page. London: Macmillan.

Parsons, Talcott. (1928). "Capitalism in Recent German Literature: Sombart and Weber, I." *Journal of Political Economy* 36(6): 641–661.

———. (1929). "Capitalism in Recent German Literature: Sombart and Weber, II." *Journal of Political Economy* 37(1): 31–51.

———. (1931). "Wants and Activities in Marshall." *Quarterly Journal of Economics* 46(1): 101–140.

———. (1932). "Economics and Sociology: Marshall in Relation to the Thought of His Time." *Quarterly Journal of Economics* 46(2): 316–347.

———. (1933). "Vilfredo Pareto." In *Encyclopedia of the Social Sciences*, vol. 11. Ed. E. Seligman. London: Macmillan. Rpt. 105–108 in Camic (1991).

———. (1935a). "Sociological Elements in Economic Thought: The Analytical Factor View." *Quarterly Journal of Economics* 49(4): 646–667.

———. (1935b). "Review of *The Mind and Society* and *Pareto's General Sociology.*" *American Economic Review* 25(4): 502–508.

———. (1936). "Pareto's Central Analytical Scheme." *Journal of Social Philosophy* 1: 244–262. Rpt. 133–150 in Camic (1991).

———. (1937). *The Structure of Social Action.* New York: McGraw-Hill.

———. (1949). *The Structure of Social Action*, 2nd ed. New York: Free Press.

———. [1953] (1991). "The Marshall Lectures—The Integration of Economics and Sociology." *Sociological Inquiry* 61(1): 10–59.

———. (1970). "On Building Social Systems Theory: A Personal History." *Daedalus* 99(4): 826–878.

Parsons, Talcott, and Neil Smelser. (1956). *Economy and Society: A Study in the Integration of Economic and Social Theory.* London: Routledge and Kegan Paul.

Robertson, Roland, and Bryan Turner. (1991). "An Introduction to Talcott

Parsons: Theory, Politics and Humanity." In *Talcott Parsons: Theorist of Modernity*. Eds. R. Robertson and B. Turner. Newbury Park: Sage.

Samuels, Warren. (1974). *Pareto on Policy*. Amsterdam: Elsevier.

Samuelson, Paul. (1947). *Foundations of Economic Analysis*. Cambridge: Harvard University Press.

Smelser, Neil. (1981). "On Collaborating with Talcott Parsons: Some Intellectual and Personal Notes." *Sociological Inquiry* 51(3/4): 143–154.

———. (1991). "The Marshall Lectures and *Economy and Society*." *Sociological Inquiry* 61(1): 60–67.

Smelser, Neil, and Richard Swedberg. (1994). "The Sociological Perspective on the Economy." In *The Handbook of Economic Sociology*. Eds. N. Smelser and R. Swedberg. Princeton: Princeton University Press.

Sorokin, Pitirim. (1928). *Contemporary Sociological Theories*. New York: Harper.

———. (1963). *A Long Journey*. New Haven, CT: College and University Press.

Steiner, Philippe. (1995). "Vilfredo Pareto et le Protectionnisme: L'Economic Politique Appliquée, La Sociologie Générale et Quelques Paradoxes." *Revue Economique* 46(5): 1241–1262.

Stinchcombe, Arthur. (1986). *Stratification and Organization: Selected Papers*. Cambridge: Cambridge University Press.

Subrahmanyam, Sanjay. (1992). "The Decline of Sociological Economics: A Comment." *Indian Economic Review* 27(S): 475–481.

Swedberg, Richard. (1987). "Economic Sociology: Past and Present." *Current Sociology* 35(1): 1–221.

———. (1990). *Economics and Sociology: Redefining Their Boundaries: Conversations with Economists and Sociologists*. Princeton: Princeton University Press.

———. (1991). "Introduction to Talcott Parsons' Marshall Lectures." *Sociological Inquiry* 61(1): 2–9.

———. (1997). "New Economic Sociology: What Has Been Accomplished, What Is Ahead?" *Acta Sociologica* 40(2): 162–182.

Swedberg, Richard, and Mark Granovetter. (1992). "Introduction." In *The Sociology of Economic Life*. Eds. M. Granovetter and R. Swedberg. Boulder, CO and Oxford: Westview.

Tarascio, Vincent. (1968). *Pareto's Methodological Approach to Economics: A Study in the History of Some Scientific Aspects of Economic Thought*. Chapel Hill: University of North Carolina Press.

———. (1969). "Paretian Welfare Theory: Some Neglected Aspects." *Journal of Political Economy* 77(1): 1–20.

———. (1976). "Pareto: A View of the Present Through the Past." *Journal of Political Economy* 84(1): 109–122.

———. (1983). "Pareto's *Trattato*." *Eastern Economic Journal* 9(2): 119–131.

Valade, Bernard. (1990). *Pareto: La Naissance d'une Autre Sociologie.* Paris: Universitaires de France.

Weintraub, Roy. (1991). *Stabilizing Dynamics: Constructing Economic Knowledge.* Cambridge: Cambridge University Press.

Zafirovski, Milan. (1999). "Economic Sociology in Retrospect and Prospect: In Search of its Identity Within Economics and Sociology." *American Journal of Economics and Sociology* 58(4): 583–627.

Zafirovski, Milan, and Barry Levine. (1997). "Economic Sociology Reformulated: The Interface Between Economics and Sociology." *American Journal of Economics and Sociology* 56(3): 265–285.

Economics, Sociology, and the "Professional Complex"

Talcott Parsons and the Critique of Orthodox Economics

By JOHN HOLMWOOD*

ABSTRACT. This article discusses the relationship between economics and sociology in the context of Parsons's analytical theory of action and systems and his criticisms of orthodox and institutional economics. The article also addresses his view of the importance of the professions to an understanding of the nature of advanced capitalism. The professions are discussed as both an illustration of his theoretical argument and a substantive problem that stimulated the development of his theory. The "professional complex" is an emergent phenomenon in capitalism that modifies its operation and points to the complexity of systems of social action that require to be analyzed without being reduced to one of their elements. This reductionism is evident in orthodox economic theory and also in the more sociologically-oriented approach of institutional economics. Parsons argues that each is a form of what, following Whitehead, he calls the "fallacy of misplaced concreteness." Although Parsons offers a significant critique of dominant approaches in economics, major flaws within his own theory create the appearance that he has simply carried over the deficiencies of orthodox theory into his own general statement of theory. These flaws contribute to major misunderstandings of Parsons's project and, therefore, indicate continuing problems in the relation between economics and sociology.

*John Holmwood is Professor of Sociology at the University of Birmingham, UK; e-mail: j.holmwood@bham.ac.uk. He was formerly Professor of Sociology and Dean of the School of Social Sciences and Cultural Studies at the University of Sussex, UK. His main research interests are the relation between social theory and explanation and social stratification and inequality. He would like to thank Gurminder Bhambra, Steve Kemp, Matthias Klaes, Laurence Moss, and an anonymous referee for their helpful comments on this article.

American Journal of Economics and Sociology, Vol. 65, No. 1 (January 2006).

A number of recent commentaries point to a renewed interest in the relationship between economics and sociology (Swedberg 1991; Smelser and Swedberg 1994). What is also evident is that this relationship is uneasy and, seemingly, contradictory. Economists, for example, have shown an interest in applying economic models to phenomena more usually addressed by sociologists, such as the family, crime and deviance, and the like. This has extended to the application of economic analysis to what might be regarded as the quintessential object of sociology, institutions, and the elaboration of a "new" institutional economics on neoclassical foundations (Williamson 1981). At the same time, some sociologists and economists have sought to unify economics and sociology within a single framework of rational choice (Hirshleifer 1985; Coleman 1990). Other sociologists have returned the favor, arguing that the quintessential object of economics—exchange—should be approached from a sociological perspective, emphasizing its character as an institution (Granovetter 1985, 1990). Here sociologists have found an alliance with "heterodox" economists—for example, contemporary advocates of "old" institutional economics, radical economists, and Marxist economists—to challenge the utilitarian assumptions of the neoclassical framework and to argue for a "new" economic sociology (Swedberg and Granovetter 1992; Ingham 1996).

It is evident that economics and sociology are not neatly distinguished, with some sociologists accepting assumptions that are strongly associated with economics and, vice versa, with heterodox economists accepting what are often regarded as sociological assumptions. Nonetheless, there seems to be an underlying division, and it is one that is frequently used to characterize the two disciplines. Baron and Hannan, for example, comment that:

> Economics, at least in its neoclassical micro variants, relies on a highly simplified model of individual action (rational choice) and a simple mechanism (market equilibrium) to aggregate individual actions to derive system-level implications. Most sociology uses complicated models of individual behavior (including effects of values, prior experience, commitments, location in social networks and context), and complicated mechanisms to aggregate interests and actions. (1994: 1114)

Economics, then, utilizes a simple model that claims general relevance, while *sociology* tends to be particularistic and descriptive.

I do not wish to go into all the nuances associated with this distinction, except to say that it also gives rise to confusion over terms. For example, from the perspective of economics, sociology is often argued to be "not theoretical" and to be "empiricist," while sociologists typically vehemently deny that charge and accuse the former of "positivism." These misunderstandings, or ways of talking past each other, have characterized debates across the years, going back to the 19th-century *Methodenstreit* between proponents of the general theory in economics and the German historical school; they have determined the reception of Parsons's critique of orthodox economics; and they continue into the present.[1]

In this article, I will address these issues of the theoretical form of economics and sociology in discussion of the work of Talcott Parsons. I shall suggest that his arguments remain significant, but are also frequently misunderstood. For example, some advocates of the "new" economic sociology have argued that Parsons contributed to the dominance of orthodox economics by his acceptance of its categories and his rejection of "old" institutional economics (Camic 1992; Swedberg and Granovetter 1992; Velthuis 1999; Hodgson 2001). For Swedberg and Granovetter, and for Velthuis, this reinforced disciplinary boundaries between sociology and economics and set back the cause of a proper sociology of economic phenomena (see also Brick 2005). In contrast, Gould (taking issue with Camic 1989) argues for the contemporary relevance of Parsons's early writings precisely because he believes that Parsons provided an effective critique of orthodox economic categories, writing:

> in our current situation, where economists are seeking to apply utilitarian models to everything . . . where utilitarian rational-choice models seem once again to be making inroads into the heart of sociology and where methodological empiricism is stronger than ever, it is well to read Parsons's fifty-year-old demolition of those very same points of view. (1989: 649; see also Alexander 1984)[2]

What is it that can make sense of these contrasting views? I shall argue that Parsons's critique of orthodox and institutional economics is intimately associated with his claims for his *action frame of reference* as a means of overcoming and synthesizing dualisms in the epistemological foundations of social science (Adriaansens 1979), including those indicated by the division between sociology and economics. Indeed, his early characterization of the problem is very similar to that of Baron and Hannan, with several important qualifications. He accepts that when sociological elements are introduced in the application of economic theory to concrete reality, this is frequently done in an empiricist way (Parsons [1935] 1991: 186). Moreover, when this is combined with an emphasis on the "unreality" of economic assumptions, this tends to the radical and dismissive critique of economic orthodoxy that is found in institutional economics (perhaps especially Veblen).[3] However, he also argues that a similar empiricism characterizes orthodox economics itself insofar as it is held that "the principles of economic theory . . . are directly, without essential qualifications for other factors, applicable to concrete 'economic activities,' to 'business'" ([1935] 1991: 186). For Parsons, what is necessary is for the sociological "factors" to be theorized with an equivalent rigor to those of economics. It is only when this is done that an analytical theory that incorporates all relevant factors can be applied to concrete circumstances without an empiricist confusion of analytical factors with corresponding concrete domains, or what he calls "the fallacy of misplaced concreteness." The concrete domain of the "economy" is no less subject to the operation of sociological factors, but the latter need to be stated within an abstract social science comparable to orthodox economics (once it, for its part, is properly understood outside the constraints of a positivist epistemology).

In this way, Parsons sought to retain some of the *substantive* insights of the institutional critique of orthodox economics, while providing a theoretical framework that would transcend the limits both of orthodox economics *and* the institutionalist critique. At the same time, this framework was to secure the professional status of sociology in its relation to economics and other disciplines. Central to this ambition is the problem of a proper understanding of the institutionalization of activities (including economic activities), for which the role of the professions represents a test case.

If I disagree with some part of the interpretation put forward by commentators like Camic and Granovetter, I have considerable sympathy with their conclusion. As I shall show in a subsequent section of the article, Parsons's theory does contain serious flaws, and these flaws allow the impression that he has simply carried over the deficiencies that sociologists typically associate with neoclassical economics into his general theory (for example, by transposing the economist's concern with market equilibrium to the wider social system itself, and in his evident difficulties in providing an empirical reference for his theory).[4] However, this was not his initial intention, and any understanding of the current problems facing "economic sociology" requires a proper appreciation of how Parsons's critique of orthodox economics was integral to his argument for an action frame of reference.[5]

I

The "Professional Complex"

FOR CAMIC AND OTHERS (Camic 1992; Wearne 1989; Granovetter 1990; Velthuis 1999; Brick 2005), Parsons was seen as initially sympathetic to institutional economics but later rejecting it. Part of their explanation of why Parsons turned away from institutional economics is to do with his appointment at Harvard in 1927 and the lower status accorded to sociology when compared with economics.[6] This had both a particular expression, in the dominance of orthodox economics within Harvard itself (compared with Parsons's alma mater Amherst, where he had imbibed institutional economics), as well as a general expression. Institutional economics was on the wane (Yonay 1998), and sociology itself was experiencing greater problems of public acceptance than economics (evidenced by much later acceptance into university teaching and research arrangements). To some degree, being seen to be closer to the accepted form of science was to have greater status, and the emulation of economics was a potential route to the successful institutionalization of sociology, as well as serving Parsons in terms of his personal career.

However, there is no reason to believe that Parsons's reasons were simply self-serving, as Hodgson (2001) suggests. As we shall see, as befits someone who was concerned with the integration of self-interest and altruism (and their explanation in terms of "social structure"), rather than their expression as opposites, Parsons had clearly articulated reasons for this shift. If Parsons turned away from institutional economics in particular (Camic 1992; Velthuis 1999), and economics in general (Brick 2005), at least in his own mind, it was because he had transcended the limits of orthodox economics in his general frame of reference, the further elaboration of which was the primary focus of his attention after the writing of *The Structure of Social Action*. Moreover, he regarded its sociological aspect not to be in direct opposition to institutional economics, but to be its more adequate successor (in the sense of providing a better theoretical account of the very processes of the institutionalization of activities, including those deemed to be "economic").

Parsons's concern with the professions (including the profession of sociology) coincides with his engagement with the problem of the relation between economics and sociology.[7] Two general themes emerge: first, concerning how capitalism is to be characterized and the importance of an understanding of the professions in reframing the standard characterization; second, concerning changes in the complexity of the institutional evolution of capitalism as the context for the emergence of sociology as a discipline.

In his earliest article on the professions, Parsons argues that capitalism is frequently associated with the rise of "free enterprise" and associated motives of acquisitiveness and self-interest. "By contrast with business in this interpretation," Parsons writes, "the professions are marked by 'disinterestedness'" ([1939] 1954: 35). Although the business economy received greater empirical emphasis, Parsons believes that the professions are equally significant. Thus, Parsons writes that "it seems evident that many of the most important features of our society are to a considerable extent dependent on the smooth functioning of the professions. Both the pursuit and the application of liberal learning are predominantly carried out in a professional context" ([1939] 1954: 34).

Nonetheless, the general dominance attributed to pecuniary motives within the modern capitalist economy creates an apparent tension where any social structures organized in terms of professional disinterestedness are either thought to be *really* determined by the operation of self-interest, or where those distinctive structures are held to be becoming increasingly commercialized so that they are likely to disappear (Parsons [1939] 1954).[8] In contrast, Parsons writes that "the fact that the professions have reached a uniquely high level of development in *the same society* which is also characterized by a business economy suggests that the contrast which has been mainly stated in terms of the problem of self-interest, is not the whole story" ([1939] 1954: 36).

According to Parsons, the professions exhibit a particular kind of authority, one based not on social status, but on a functionally specific technical competence. The advice offered by a professional has the form of a "command" in the sense that the professional person's expertise entails knowing the best interests of the client. This technical competence is based upon general university learning and is associated with universalistic values. Despite a profession's monopoly of expertise, Parsons suggests that the corporate form of professional organization provided an ethical self-regulation of relations with clients such that any apparent monopoly operates in the general public interest, rather than in the private interest of professionals themselves.

Although Parsons's argument was directed at one strand in the institutionalist critique of capitalism, which emphasized the dominance of pecuniary motives over other motives, including those of the professions (see, for example, Veblen 1904), his purpose was to uphold another institutionalist point. This is that the seemingly radical difference (when considered empirically) between business motives and professional motives is to do with different social structures; that is, it is "situational" rather than "motivational." Parsons writes: "the difference is not so great as our predominantly economic and utilitarian orientation of thought would lead us to believe. Perhaps even it is not mainly a difference of typical motive at all, but one of different situations in which much the same commonly human motives operate. Perhaps the acquisitiveness of modern business is institutional rather than motivational" ([1939] 1954: 36).[9]

In this way, Parsons is just as concerned to criticize any simple association of the professions with "altruistic" motives. The *individual* medical practitioner may be no less self-interested than someone engaged in business. In this situation, a practitioner may have an "interest" in offering unnecessary services, but he or she must accommodate the existence of professional ethics that rule against it. This is not to say that the individual practitioner does not act on the basis of his or her "interest," but that interest now has to include the calculation of the consequences of any ethical breaches. Insofar as professional ethics are institutionalized, they are significant factors in the definition of the situation of acting.[10] Moreover, Parsons suggests that it is not simply that professional ethics serve to protect against the operation of the "profit motive." The nature of the "profit motive" itself is a product of social structure, and social structure has to be understood in sociological as well as economic terms. At least part of the reason why professional ethics can serve practitioner-client relations is because there is not the strong tension between professional practice and the business activities that otherwise predominate in the economy.

Parsons's point is one concerning the *social structural* governance of activities, and he makes the further claim that the "universalism" predominant in professional activities comes to extend to other spheres: "the role of universalism is by no means confined to the professions. It is equally important to the patterns governing contractual relationships, for instance in the standards of common honesty, and to administrative office" ([1939] 1954: 42). In other words, "business enterprise"—what is often regarded as the concrete object to which the principles of economic theory can be directly applied—also requires to be understood in terms of the operation of sociological factors. The functional specificity of the professional role and its special "authority" also applies to administrative office and the authority of commands within any hierarchy, including that of the modern corporation. As Parsons puts it, "the concentration of much of our social theory on the problem of self-interest has served to obscure the importance of functional specificity, an institutional feature common to the professional and commercial spheres" ([1939] 1954: 40).

This point is reinforced by the recognition that the sharp "empirical" differentiation between business motives and professional motives recedes with the increasing complexity of the modern economic system and its occupational order. The "firm" no longer corresponds to that which was analyzed by Marx, for example, or by other classical political economists (and by extension, orthodox economists as well, though there are suggestions in Marshall that go beyond the standard approach).[11] It is increasingly complex and, while that complexity might seem to indicate a greater concentration of economic power, that assumption reflects a form of sociological empiricism (Parsons [1935] 1991). The growth of the large-scale corporation, for Parsons, is predicated upon a differentiation of functions of ownership and managerial control, where managers increasingly take on a professional ethos and direct companies toward longer term and more socially diffuse goals (Parsons [1949] 1954; see also Parsons and Smelser 1956).[12]

It seems clear, then, that from his early essays onward Parsons is concerned with understanding the "economy" as more than the aggregate of self-interested exchanges among individual actors (and, as I have emphasized, he is concerned with seeing "self-interest," itself, as socially complex). The latter conception he regarded as typical of expression of utilitarian thinking, which he understood to be empiricist in character; that is, it confused the economic factor as a dimension of activities with concrete "economic" actions as such. At the same time, he also understood the dominance of utilitarian accounts in sociological terms, that is, in terms of the evolution of the institutional structures of capitalism. Disciplines such as economics and psychology had come to the fore during the period of early and developing capitalism when the elision between principles of economic theory and their concrete application was easier to make (and, consequently, a direct association could be sought between economic motivations and their psychological grounding, for example, in a "hedonistic" principle).

Parsons's account in *The Structure of Social Action* of the "1890–1920 generation" as a transitional generation presaging a synthesis that would be the basis of future scientific endeavors, then, was also underpinned by a sociological analysis of the changing social context for sociology itself. It was a transitional generation in part because it was located in a transition in the institutional development of capitalism. The particular authors were selected because they bore upon the relation between sociology and economics that was crucial to the emerging discipline and what Parsons saw as its necessary formation. This was how Parsons sought to define his own role, unifying sociology and economics within the categories of a general theory in order to provide a secure basis for the discipline in its coming of age.

It was not so much concern to be associated with the higher status of orthodox economics that drove Parsons forward as his concern to establish the scientific foundations of sociology.[13] In the course of doing so, however, from his own perspective, he must settle the relationships between economics and sociology and between analytical categories and their empirical referents, which in turn led him to revise the methodological and epistemological assumptions of the orthodox framework. It should be clear, then, that Parsons did not so much "turn away" from economics as produce an analysis that explains why an institutional analysis—based, as we shall see, on what Parsons ([1935] 1991) calls an "analytical factor" view—must replace the standard, utilitarian account. This institutional analysis is wide in scope and would be illustrated in a range of phenomena (other than the professions) to which Parsons also turned his attention, phenomena such as social stratification, gender and generation, the nature of fascism, the family, and the relation between psychoanalysis and sociology. Nonetheless, this analysis is held by Parsons to be equally applicable to "economic phenomena" and, in its crucial character, derives from his engagement with the problem of understanding economic phenomena.

Parsons's critique of the empiricist interpretation of orthodox economic analysis is no less radical than that of the institutionalists. However, sociology does not displace orthodox economics, as is implied by Veblen (Parsons [1935] 1991: 198). Rather, it is to be understood on a par with economics, when each is properly understood as providing the elucidation of a "factor" (or set of factors) within an integrated *analytical* factor view of the organization of disciplines. If Parsons's critique of orthodox economics is also combined with a less radical social critique than is found among the more radical institutionalists, it is partly because Parsons believed that they had failed to follow through the implications of a thoroughgoing analytical account of action (and, paradoxically, had overestimated the dominance of the commercial interests that they decried).[14]

II

The "Analytic Factor View": A General Framework for Economics and Sociology?

THE MAIN WORK in which Parsons addressed the requirement of a general framework of analytical categories as the necessary foundation of social scientific inquiries is *The Structure of Social Action* (1937) (*TSofSA*). An early indication of that scheme and its direct application to the problem of economics, however, is also to be found in his earlier article on "Sociological Elements in Economic Thought" (Parsons [1935] 1991). Although the scheme of categories goes through several later modifications, it is my contention that its general features remain fundamentally unchanged in these elaborations (see Holmwood 1996).

Parsons begins *TSofSA* with a characterization of systems of scientific (including social scientific) theory and their associated criteria of validity. Crucial to his analysis is the identification of indicators of the breakdown of a theoretical system. He identifies two kinds of category relevant to the dynamic processes of theory development. These are the *positive* categories of a theoretical system and its *negative*, or *residual*, categories, writing that "a theoretical system must always involve the positive definition of certain empirically identifiable variables or other general categories" (1937: 17). By *positive* definition, he means that they have a consistent definition within a system.

However, Parsons believed that there will also emerge categories that are *negatively* defined, for example, "facts known to exist, which are even more or less adequately described, but are defined theoretically by their *failure* to fit into the positively defined categories of the system" (1937: 17). Such residual categories are of fundamental importance, and their role "may be deduced from the inherent necessity of a system to become logically closed," insofar as "the obviously unattainable, but asymptotically approached goal of the development of scientific theory . . . is the elimination of all residual categories from science in favor of positively defined empirically verifiable concepts" (1937: 19). According to Parsons, this process of "elimination" is not a matter of simple addition: "theoretical systems change. There is not merely a quantitative accumulation of 'knowledge of fact,' but a qualitative change in the structure of theoretical systems" (1937: 19). It is not simply the residual categories that are transformed by redefinition, but also the positively defined categories of previous statements as explanations are extended and new relationships postulated: "the process of the carving out of positive categories from residual categories is also a process by which the reconstruction of theoretical systems is accomplished as a result of which they may eventually be altered beyond all recognition" (1937: 19).

According to Parsons, recognition of the proper nature of theoretical systems is itself the product of a long period of scientific development, in which "the earlier phases are almost always concerned directly with the understanding of pressing concrete, though not necessarily practical, problems which are attacked in whatever way at the time promises results, without bothering very much about the exact logical nature of the procedures involved or the relation of the various approaches to each other" ([1935] 1991: 182). It is clear that Parsons believed that the social sciences were now at the point when clarity about these procedures and the relations between approaches was both possible and imperative.

Fundamental to his conception of a theoretical scheme is that it is both *selective*, in that it cannot deal with all possible problems, and that it proceeds by *abstraction*. The issue of the relation between economics and sociology will be resolved by identifying the appropriate level of abstraction and form of empirical reference. Residual categories frequently arise in relation to concrete facts, but the conversion of residual categories into positively defined categories entails their statement within an *analytical* scheme as an issue that is logically prior to any question of their empirical application. As Parsons's treatment of the professions reveals, however, the tendency hitherto has been to regard the analytical element of economic theory as having a direct empirical reference, reducing the "self-interested" element to concrete motivation, rather than an element of a complex of interaction that includes other elements. As we have seen, Parsons refers to this as the "fallacy of misplaced concreteness" and, as such, he argues that it derives from an inappropriate empiricist methodology. For him, it is a characteristic of the positivistic approach to action that dominates in orthodox economics.

Parsons agrees that any scheme of analytical categories for the social sciences must take as its point of reference human *action*. As a first step in clarifying his difference from the orthodox approach, Parsons identifies what he calls the "unit act" and its component elements. Parsons is clear that the "unit act" should not be understood as referring to something that exists *concretely*.[15] It does not have any immediate reference to the concrete individual acts of any specific person. Parsons's aim is to identify by a process of logical abstraction the most basic elements of a wider scheme. Any issues of the concrete manifestation of action can only be addressed once that wider scheme has been fully elaborated. Its categories do not refer directly, but, ultimately, the scheme will be used to generate mechanisms with direct empirical implications; at least, that is what Parsons argues.

According to Parsons, action is a process oriented to the realization of an end. It occurs in conditional circumstances that must be calculated upon and utilized by actors in the pursuit of their ends. However, "ends" and "conditions" (including "means") are analytically distinct categories. This claim is important because it means that action cannot be understood as an emanation of cultural values, as is the case with some forms of idealism: action is not free from determination by circumstances. Consequently, action involves "effort" to conform to norms (which govern ends and the selection of their means of realization) since it must transform circumstances and, therefore, accommodate and calculate upon conditions if it is to be successful. In addition, action, to be rational, must be adequate in terms of the knowledge necessary to the realization of ends. Thus, Parsons refers to the "intrinsic rationality of the means-end relation" in terms of the necessary role of "valid knowledge as a guide to action" (1937: 600). However, action cannot be reduced to its conditions, since an understanding of the agency of the actor and, consequently, of the subjective meaning of an action is necessary in any adequate account. With conditions and means classified as technical in substance and, as such, external to any given actor, the "subjective," voluntary aspect of action is associated with the actor's capacity to form ends.

Parsons saw the problems of positivism as consisting in the problematic role of the category of "ends" within their schemes. Parsons addressed his criticism to the utilitarian conception of action in orthodox economics, where ends are "given" in the sense that how actors arrive at their preferences is not addressed, only the processes by which they are to be realized through rational choice. Parsons's view was that to take ends as "given" is to assign them a necessary status within a scheme but to fail to account adequately for them. The implication, he suggests, is that ends vary "at random relative to the means-end relationship and its central component, the actor's knowledge of his situation" (1937: 63). Within "positivism," an assumption of the "randomness" of ends would also be regarded as unsatisfactory (because of its implicit indeterminacy), but the tendency is for theorists to move in the other direction to that suggested by Parsons. Thus, radical positivists attempt to deny the analytical independence of "ends," reducing them to the "situation" of action; that is, they attempt to see action as entirely the product of determining stimuli located in the external environment. There is, then, what Parsons called a "utilitarian dilemma" within positivism where:

> either the active agency of the actor in the choice of ends is an independent factor in action, and the end element must be random; or the objectionable implication of the randomness of ends is denied, but then their independence disappears and they are assimilated to the conditions of the situation, that is to elements analyzable in terms of nonsubjective categories, principally heredity and environment, in the analytical sense of biological theory. (1937: 64)[16]

It is easy to misunderstand Parsons's arguments around the nature of the "unit act" to imply that what he is trying to do is to provide a legitimate domain of concern for economics, namely, the relation between means and ends, while sociology should be concerned with the category of ends. For example, Swedberg and Granovetter comment that "[Parsons] came to see sociology as focusing exclusively on the values, or 'ends,' in 'means-end' chains, with economists assigned to the task of analyzing the most efficient ways to achieve ends taken as given" (1992: 5). This is incorrect. The discussion of "unit acts" provides only the basic elements of an analytical frame of reference and, according to Parsons, such a discussion "serves only to arrange the data in a certain order, not to subject them to the analysis necessary for their explanation" (1937: 48).

Failure to recognize this is a form of the "fallacy of misplaced concreteness," where the unit act is regarded as having a concrete reference in terms of individual actions, rather than being conceived correctly as the means of identifying analytical elements and relations.[17] As such, the "unit act" has a "fictional" status because empirical reference is only achieved when analysis has gone beyond the "unit act." Swedberg and Granovetter's misunderstanding is also significant because Parsons's discussion of the unit act is the heart of his critique of institutional economics for the fallacy of misplaced concreteness where orthodox economics is criticized for the lack of realism of its assumptions (see Parsons [1935] 1991: 198ff).[18]

According to Parsons, "explanation"—that is, *analytical realism* rather than *empiricist realism*—requires a further step in the analysis, from "unit acts" to their location within "systems" of action. This step, Parsons argues, "consists in generalising the conceptual scheme so as *to bring out the functional relations* in the facts already descriptively arranged" (1937: 49) This further generalization of the scheme will identify emergent properties of *systems* of action, that is, properties that appear in relation to any consideration of the coordination of actions and that are not reducible to analysis in terms of "unit acts" alone. Thus, Parsons writes that "action systems have properties that are emergent only on a certain level of complexity in the relations of unit acts to each other. These properties cannot be identified in any single unit act considered apart from its relation to others in the same system. *They cannot be derived by a process of direct generalization of the properties of the unit act*" (1937: 739). The concept of emergent properties, then, serves to identify the "elements of structure of a generalised system of action" (1937: 718), and these elements of *structure* are to be further analyzed in terms of their *functional* relations, that is, in terms of the logical relations established within the theoretical system.

This is what underlies Parsons's use of an "organic" analogy, in which "the very definition of an organic whole is one within which *the relations determine the properties of its parts.* The properties of the whole are not simply a resultant of the latter" (1937: 32). The idea of emergent properties of systems of social action is at the heart of how Parsons approached his "problem of order."[19] Action occurs in systems, and these systems have an orderly character. There are two issues of "order," or integration, identified by Parsons. These are what we can term *personal* order and *interpersonal* order. *Personal order* involves the recognition that any given act is, for the actor, one among a plurality of other chosen and possible actions with a variety of different ends in view with different requirements for their realization. *Interpersonal order* involves the recognition that actions occur in contexts that include, as Parsons put it, "a plurality of actors" (1937: 51).

The emergent properties of personal order, according to Parsons, have received more attention in social theory (in particular, in economics) than those of interpersonal order. From the point of view of the analysis of the "unit act," any relation of conditions (including means) to the realization of a given end is a purely "technical" issue of the competent realization of the end in question. However, every action occurs in contexts produced by each individual's past actions, which, in turn, affects the possibilities of his or her future action. Along with the requirement of a "technical" efficacy of means, there is a requirement of consistency in the relation among purposes. Actions occur in what Parsons termed "means-ends chains." For any actor, there is a mutual dependency of acts as means and conditions of other acts. Where means are scarce relative to ends, actors will maximize outcomes by the most efficient selection of means and by placing their ends in a personal hierarchy of preferences. Actors' ends are determined by their preferences and values, but their "cognitive" address to the means of the realization of their ends is also governed by what Parsons termed a "normative standard," the "norm of efficiency." Thus, one of the emergent properties of personal order is "economic rationality."[20] As Parsons put it: "economic rationality is thus an emergent property of action which can be observed only when a plurality of unit acts is treated together as constituting an integrated system" (1937: 40).

However, even where Parsons is closest to the form of orthodox economics within his own analysis of the unit act, he is already moving beyond it. For Parsons, more fundamental issues of social theory arise when systems of social action involving a *plurality* of actors are the focus of attention. These are the issues of *interpersonal* order. He offers his analysis of emergent properties in terms of the increasing complexity of systems of action. Interpersonal systems are more complex than personal systems because, analytically, they presuppose the latter. Thus, what Parsons was concerned with identifying were additional emergent properties of interpersonal order beyond but incorporating those of personal order. Such systems are *interpersonal systems of personal systems of action.* Interpersonal order concerns the coordination of systems of action where these systems include the activities of a number of actors. According to this conception, the actions of any given actor form the conditions and means of other actors in the system. Just as there is a mutual dependence of acts within the means-end chains of an actor's system of personal order, so there is a mutual dependence of acts and means-end chains among the interactions of a plurality of actors.

This analysis applies equally to the domain of activities addressed by orthodox economics, and Parsons should not be implied as arguing that the move from personal systems to interpersonal systems is equivalent to a move from economics to sociology. An example will suffice to make this point. It is not just professionals who potentially face consumers with less knowledge than they have. It is also the case for many other services. For example, when taking a car to a mechanic for servicing, the consumer is frequently dependent on the mechanic's judgment of what parts require replacement. However, insofar as the mechanic has an interest in customers returning for further services, or believes that the maintenance of a customer base is reputational, then the mechanic has an "interest" in acting in the interests of the customer. The "noncontractual" element in a contract includes longer-term relations of contracting as aspects of any specific contract thought of as an individual event. "Economic" actions are systems of "social" action.

As Parsons elaborated this general analytical theory of systems of social action, he stressed the role of a common culture, both as the source of the standards governing interaction and internalized within personality as the basis of dispositions to act. However, he was far from arguing that the stability of systems of action depends only on the functioning of common value elements, as many of his critics suggest. Parsons's conception of normative order is more subtle than is usually allowed, and he intended it to include a treatment of issues of power. Thus, in his hierarchical presentation of "emergent properties," Parsons offered coercion as "above" economic rationality, but below "common values." He wrote: "where others are concerned coercion is a potential means to the desired control, which is not included in the economic concept as such. It also has a similar double aspect—the exercise of coercive power as a means and its acquisition as an immediate end" (1937: 239–240). However, according to Parsons, "coercive power" does not *define* the system, in the sense that the system is founded upon it. Coercive power is a relation *within* the system. Thus, Parsons wrote: "it cannot be a property of the *total* action system involving a plurality of individuals; it can only apply to some individuals or groups within a system *relative* to others. Coercion is an exercise of power over others" (1937: 740). Camic (1989), then, is wrong to imply that Parsons is overly concerned with normative constraints on action to the neglect of power. It may occupy fewer pages of his first book, but it has a very clear place within the analytical scheme.[21] In particular, it is identified as the domain of "theoretical political science" as an abstract social science.

The final emergent property of the total action system is the requirement that "in order that there may be a stable system of action involving a plurality of individuals there must be normative regulation of the power aspect of individuals within the system; in this sense, there must be a distributive order" (1937: 740). In other words, the distribution of resources within the system and, therefore, the actions within which those resources are produced and reproduced must be governed by some legitimating principles or norms.

Sociology as a specific systematic theoretical discipline, then, is associated with the common ultimate value element, but it should be recalled that this does not mean that the object of sociology as an empirical discipline is a domain of value-rational actions. Once again, it is the analytical scheme as a combination of factors that provides the basis of empirical reference and not any single factor taken on its own. This is crucial to understanding the frequent observations in Parsons's early essays and in *The Structure of Social Action* that the analytical factor view must not be confused with specific domains of activity and with concrete forms of action. Thus, he writes:

> human life is essentially one and no concretely possible degree of functional differentiation can destroy its unity. But although its concrete reality is a unity, it can, like all other complex phenomena, be broken down for purposes of analysis into different factors. However predominant any one of these factors may be in a particular set of concrete activities, it is never present to the complete exclusion of the others. The only way of maintaining a positive role for economic theory as a systematic generalizing science is to make it the science of *one* of those factors in concrete human action, to be sure more conspicuous in those concrete activities we call "business" than elsewhere, but neither confined to them, nor excluding others there. ([1935] 1991: 224)

His discussion of the professions was designed precisely to show the operation of the "sociological factor" conjointly with the "economic factor" (and other analytic factors) in order to provide a complex understanding of the concrete activities associated with "business."[22]

As Parsons developed his theory—in *The Social System* and after— he offered a distinction between different *levels* of analysis, namely, personality, social system, and culture (adding a fourth level of "organism," once the four-fold scheme of functional imperatives is fully elaborated).[23] Although this involves a marginal modification of the relationships among the different social sciences (which are now specified in terms of levels as well as within the level of the social system), the "analytical factor" view that underpins the earlier analysis remains unchanged. The levels correspond to the analytical distinctions made in the earlier statement of the action frame of reference (see, especially, 1951: 549–550). Thus, the level of personality corresponds to the individual actor viewed as a system. The level of culture refers to the symbols and meanings that are drawn upon by actors in the pursuit of their personal projects and their negotiation of social constraints and facilities. As Parsons argues, the three key features of the cultural system are "that culture is *transmitted*, it constitutes a heritage or a social tradition; secondly, that it is *learned*, it is not a manifestation, in particular content, of man's genetic constitution; and third, that it is *shared.* Culture, that is, is on the one hand the product of, on the other hand a determinant of, systems of human social interaction" (1951: 15). Finally, the "social system" corresponds to that level of interaction among a "plurality of actors," which was a primary focus of the earlier work. The "social system" constitutes an institutional order of interaction; it is a structure of positions and roles organized by normed expectations and maintained by sanctions (including coercion). It is the social system that is the domain of the analytical sciences of action, namely, economics, sociology, and political science.

Parsons proposes that each of the "levels" forms a system in its own right, where the characteristics of a system are relations of logical coherence among its parts. At the same time, each system functions in relation to the other systems and interpenetrates with them. In other words, their interpenetration, or interdependence, also constitutes a "system." This is what Parsons had previously referred to as the "total action system." However, his main focus of attention remains that of the social system. Parsons (1960; Parsons and Smelser 1956) proposes four functional prerequisites, or imperatives, that are necessary to its constitution and operation. Two of the imperatives—pattern maintenance and integration—are concerned with normative issues and two—adaptation and goal attainment—are concerned with the nonnormative. Similarly, two are concerned with cultural principles—integration and goal attainment—and two with issues of integrity in a potentially hostile lower-level environment—pattern maintenance and adaptation. Together they supply the axes of the two-by-two tables that proliferate throughout Parsons's later writings. They are the coordinates of the account of "social structures" and institutionalized action that he promised in his earlier work.

It is not necessary to follow Parsons through every further specification of his scheme, where everything is divided by four and four again. The social system, for example, is further divided into subsystems defined by the priority accorded to one or other of the functional prerequisites in its organization (for example, the "economy" subsystem defined by the "adaptation" prerequisite; the "polity" subsystem defined by the "goal-attainment" prerequisite; the "societal community" subsystem defined by the "integration" prerequisite; the "socialization" subsystem defined by the "pattern-maintenance" pre-requisite), but where each is also specified by the subordinate but mutual operation of the other prerequisites.

It is clear that Parsons's account transforms the categories of ortho-dox economics—at least in principle—by virtue of their location within a "holist" scheme. If this is readily apparent in the later work, it is no less the case for his earlier position. From the outset, the determining relations that analytical theory was to establish were understood by Parsons to be invariant, and the "economic factor" was subsumed within those relations. Thus, in *The Structure of Social Action*, Parsons writes that "analytical elements, once clearly defined, will be found to have certain uniform modes of relation to each other which hold independently of any one particular set of their values" (1937: 36). These "uniform modes of relation" have the status of "ana-lytical laws" where "an analytical law . . . states a uniform mode of relationship between the values of two or more analytical elements" (1937: 622). In contrast, the analytical categories of the scheme itself are not empirical. Parsons writes that "the action frame of reference may be said to have . . . 'phenomenological' status. It involves no con-crete data that can be 'thought away,' that are subject to change. It is not a phenomenon in the empirical sense. It is the indispensable logical framework in which we describe and think about the phe-nomenon of action" (1937: 733).

Concrete differences are to be accounted for by differences in the "values" (in the technical meaning of the content and levels of vari-ables) of the elements that have been identified analytically. It is pre-cisely the understanding of uniform modes of relationship between elements, which the analytical theory of action provides, that enables the prediction of changes in the "values" of the variables of empiri-cal systems consequent upon changes in the "value" of some other variable in the system. The point is further elaborated in his later work in the context of a discussion between economics and sociology, when Parsons, in collaboration with Smelser, writes:

> The specifically economic aspect of the theory of social systems, there-fore, is a *special case* of the general theory of the social system. If this is true, we must clarify the position in which this special case stands rela-tive to other possible special cases, in order to "locate" economic theory

in relation to other branches of theory. But the *basic* variables operative in all the special cases are the variables of a more general theory. The peculiarity of economic theory, therefore, is *not* the separate class of variables it employs but the *parameters* which distinguish the special case or classes of cases we call economic in the use of the general variables of social theory from the other important types of special case. (1956: 6)

This is glossed further in a footnote with the comment—a recurrent theme from his analysis of the professions—that "empirically most so-called 'economic' processes must be regarded as resultants of economic and non-economic factors" (1956: 6). It is the very argument that the "concrete" is made up of "systems," rather than "individual acts," that underlies the later claim of Parsons and Smelser that "if we view the goal of the economy as defined strictly by socially structured goals, it becomes inappropriate even to refer to utility at this level in terms of individual preference lists or indifference curves. . . . Therefore, it is correct to speak, with only apparent paradox, of the 'maximization of utility' in a social context without at the same time making *any* statements about the interpersonal measurability of utility" (1956: 22).

It is evident that Parsons's transformation of orthodox economics is more fundamental than his critics from within the "new" economic sociology allow. However, it is Parsons's very concern to set out a general framework of analytical categories (or factors) that elicits the charge that he capitulated to what subsequently came to be seen as neoclassical orthodoxy. The problems seem to be twofold. One is the emphasis on the integration of the "total action system." Parsons frequently argues that this is an *analytical* assumption, rather than a *concrete* description, but while this is a qualification of fundamental importance, it does not eliminate the issue of empirical reference. The analytical theory is intended to refer to concrete circumstances, and its reference is in terms of the mechanisms identified through the idea of functional imperatives. These identify tendencies toward integration as a property of concrete systems of action, *insofar as they can be analyzed as systems.* This is directly analogous to the status of equilibrating tendencies within orthodox economics.

The second issue is that of how the empirical reference of the scheme bears upon its adequacy. Any lack of integration in concrete systems of action is precisely that, *concrete*, lacking any *equivalent* theorization to that of integration in terms of the scheme and its analytical categories. A specific example is that of the ownership and control debate mentioned above, where Parsons takes issue with those who interpret the rise of large-scale corporations in terms of a concentration of economic power. It is central to Parsons's understanding of the role of the professions in modern society that the separation of ownership and control allows for managers to take on a "political" role oriented to more diffuse social interests. There is no doubt that Parsons's argument is "counterintuitive" and, therefore, potentially deeply interesting. However, he does not suggest that it is something to be resolved by research.[24] It would be possible to read his early articles on the professions, for example, as constituting a research program where he provides detailed theoretical arguments for considering that the professions are not reducible to self-interest and that an economic order in which the professions are a significant part is, itself, significantly different from one in which they are absent. Given the existence of competing accounts of the rise of the modern corporation, this might be regarded as something for comparative research. At least initially, Parsons seemed to suggest that this was a possibility; analytical theory would serve empirical research. However, his primary purpose in the discussion of the professions is to identify the necessity of the distinction between the *analytical* and the *concrete*, while it is the very elaboration of the analytical theory that gives rise to the attenuation of empirical research as having a bearing on the further development of his scheme.

The detail of Parsons's treatment of empirical phenomena comes to be derived from the categories of a scheme that is itself held to be nonempirical. In this way, it proves all too easy for Parsons to assimilate all arguments to his general theory, that is, to a general argument about the progressive differentiation of social structures around specialized functions. Differentiation and functional specialization are argued to be integral to complex systems and their integration. At the same time, as each interchange in the complex contributes to the interdependence of the system, so there is a possibility of "strain" at each nodal point. "Conflict" and "oppositional" (in its specific Parsonian sense of oppositional to collective goals) uses of power are "admitted" as possibilities, without questioning the underlying statement that denies them a more fundamental status.[25] This is a problem that he had initially associated with the emergence of residual categories that would reveal the limitations of a scheme and the need for its reconstruction.

Were the categories of his scheme to be merely the categories of a descriptive approach to societies (including the economy), then it might be argued that they could serve a heuristic purpose in which the extent of their realization in practice would be an "empirical" issue. Parsons sometimes appears to argue that this is so, writing that "the concept 'integration' is a fundamental one in the theory of action. It is a mode of relation of the units of a system by virtue of which, on the one hand, they act so as collectively to avoid disrupting the system and making it impossible to maintain its stability, and, on the other hand, to 'co-operate' to promote its functioning as a unity" ([1953] 1954: 71). He was at pains to point out that this is a conceptual, not an empirical, claim: "A generalised social system is a conceptual scheme, not an empirical phenomenon. It is a logically integrated system of generalised concepts of empirical reference in terms of which an *indefinite number of concretely differing empirical systems* can be described and analyzed" ([1953] 1954: 71; emphasis added).

However, the *variance* of empirical systems in terms of the specific "values" of their elements, as we have seen, occurs alongside *invariant relations* between their elements, and so the idea that there can be an "indefinite number of concretely differing empirical systems" is somewhat compromised. Certainly, when Parsons set out a classification of types of society, they are limited by the logic of the categories, whether this is the generation of a typology out of the scheme of pattern variables found in the earlier work (Parsons 1951), or the generation of a typology and developmental account of the emergence of modern societies in terms of stages logically derived from the application of the four-function paradigm (Parsons 1966, 1971). The typologies are all generated by the logic of the a priori categorical scheme; the "indefinite number of concrete empirical systems" is not itself the basis for a reconsideration of types or the categories from which they are derived. The categories were not empirically derived and their "applications" have no consequence for the theory.

This is, perhaps, not surprising, given that Parsons describes the analytical scheme very precisely as "phenomenological" and not empirical. Although the analytical factor approach is presented as emergent—that is, as a phase in the development of scientific thought in which there was an engagement with concrete problems—its definition and development of the approach is in terms of a purely "logical" analysis of the relations among factors. As Burger puts it, Parsons was so concerned with avoiding the problems of empiricism and the "fallacy of misplaced concreteness" that he rendered his scheme unfalsifiable: "the only thing that could be tested is the synthetic explanation of concrete phenomena by the combined totality of all the specialized sciences. Yet how can these sciences be developed to begin with if they are not testable?" (1977: 328).

III

Conclusion

It might be responded that "sociology" could provide the "particular" answer to concrete instances of deviation from the "rational," equilibrating models of social systems by accounting for those deviations in terms of power or nonrational influences on behavior. This is implied by Baron and Hannan's construction of the relation between sociology and economics with which I began this article. However, it must be recalled that Parsons provided a form of (political science and) sociology in which power and values, themselves, serve equilibrium, leaving a "residual" status to those behaviors that are "deviations" from his model and yet logically required by it (for example, there can be no integrative tendencies, except that there are particular concrete circumstances of less-than-perfect integration). The space of accounting for the "residuals" can no longer be filled by sociology, as it can in the case of orthodox economics, precisely because sociology itself is integral to the wider analytical theory.

Although Parsons sought to provide a general theory that would *both* unite economics and sociology *and* unite sociologists, its internal problems created a division *within* sociology that reproduces the division between "economics" *and* "sociology." Given the status difference between economics and sociology that many commentators have identified, it is not surprising that Parsons found it difficult to persuade economists to accept his transformation of their domain. Since he could not persuade sociologists that the residual categories that his scheme generated were insignificant, it is hardly likely that he would have any influence outside his field. After all, it was Parsons (and Smelser) who claimed that the theory of the economic system was a special case of the theory of the social system, and sociologists, by and large, came to reject the latter.

What does this mean for the relation between economics and sociology? In contrast to what is argued by his critics from within the "new" economic sociology, Parsons does offer a view of the relation between economics and sociology that involves a significant modification of the standard assumptions of orthodox economics, not least its assumptions of methodological individualism, rational choice, and equilibrium as an aggregate of individual decisions. He also provides the example of the "professions" as an instance of an emergent phenomenon within capitalist economics that transforms the environment such that other concrete relationships are modified. In this respect, Parsons could be argued to have "discovered" a concept of "social structure" as a sui generis reality, similar to what is proposed by the "new" economic sociology. However, Parsons also committed himself to a form of analytical theorizing in which the mechanisms associated with the functioning of social structures are rendered non-empirical, thereby undermining economic sociology as an empirical research program.

Throughout this article, I have been associating economics with neoclassical economics, but it is also a discipline characterized by debate over its concepts and methods (albeit not so severe as sociology). Neoclassical economics is simply a dominant approach to social phenomena. As such, it has a set of core concepts and mechanisms that it applies to social analysis, frequently giving rise to the problems that constituted Parsons's starting point. It is on this basis that writers such as Gould (1989) or Alexander (1982) suggest that Parsons was ahead of his time, but my analysis suggests that he was *of his time.* Rather than address the relationship between sociology and economics as a question of disciplines and the logical relations among them, we might better think in terms of a series of competing explanations to be resolved in research. *Contra* Parsons, consensus on a theory of action need not be regarded as a starting point. *Contra* Hirshleifer (1985), a "master pattern" is neither desirable nor likely. In the present postpositivist phase of social scientific development, new insights into economic activities are likely to be the product of competing approaches by persons and research groups calling themselves "economists" and "sociologists," but without strong disciplinary identities.

Notes

1. For example, "old institutionalists" were charged with being atheoretical and descriptive by their "orthodox" colleagues, while the current advocates of institutionalism vehemently rebut this charge in the name of an anti-positivist philosophy of science (see Hodgson 2001). It should be evident that this distinction also maps onto that between formalists and substantivists in economic anthropology (for the former, see Cook 1966, Schneider 1974; for the latter, see Polanyi et al. 1957). In that sense, sociology and anthropology can be seen as equivalent disciplines, while psychology tends to be aligned with economics.

2. For Gould (1991), the problem of the false division between sociology and economics is a "failure of will" on the part of Parsons to fully carry through in his later writings the critique of neoclassical economics that was contained in his early voluntaristic theory of action. Nonetheless, for Gould, "Parsons' work provides the most sophisticated economic sociology available. He enunciated a conceptual framework within which it is possible to both reconceptualize microeconomic theory and to draw on macroeconomic theory in the formulation of a viable macrosociology" (1991: 91).

3. Parsons's criticisms of institutionalism were often rather general and, when directed at specific writers, the main target was Veblen, whose writings were not particularly current. See Parsons ([1935] 1991). This is probably explained by his unwillingness to antagonize his teachers at Amherst, where his undergraduate studies had been within an institutionalist milieu.

4. These are similar to charges laid against orthodox economics when Parsons was writing. See, for example, Hutchison ([1938] 1960).

5. A note on terminology: in his early essays, Parsons referred to "classical political economy" associated with Smith, Ricardo, and Malthus (with Marx as a critical variant) and to the "marginalist" position that supplanted it

as forms of orthodox economics. His intention was to identify marginalism with the emergence of an analytical factor view of economics, but for this to be properly emergent and its implications to be fully developed requires the recognition of other analytical factors alongside the "economic" factors (see Parsons [1934] 1991, [1935] 1991). In the absence of this recognition of other analytical factors, economic orthodoxy is drawn back to various forms of positivist and empiricist understandings, of which utilitarianism is the most dominant, linking classical political economy with its marginalist successor. In this way, the "analytical factor view" is Parsons's own contribution to the understanding of economics as one of the analytical sciences of action.

6. In reflecting on the nature of Parsons's contribution in light of these developments, there seem to be several distinct positions. Those who seek to emphasize his continuing relevance suggest that Parsons was ahead of his time in articulating an essentially postpositivist philosophy of science, where the relative autonomy of theory from fact is emphasized and where the reduction of science to social context is avoided (Alexander 1982; Gould 1989). Others, such as Camic (1992), have contested this anachronistic interpretation and have offered an interpretation more along the lines of recent social studies of science, emphasizing the particular social context of Parsons's early writings. According to Alexander and Sciortino (1996), this is an unsatisfactory, reductionist approach. I shall suggest that there is no need to regard an explanation in terms of social context to be incompatible with a claim for the intellectual substance of Parsons's contribution. However, it is difficult to see that Parsons's own conception of the philosophy of science is directly equivalent to postpositivism, not least because the latter is anti-foundational and Parsons is clearly setting out a foundational statement (see Holmwood 1996).

7. Essentially, Parsons's most important writings on the professions span the period between the writing of *The Structure of Social Action* (1937) and *Economy and Society* (co-authored with N. Smelser, 1956), with *The Social System* (1951) in between. His writings on the professions include general treatments of the topic (Parsons [1939] 1954) and their specific applications to law (Parsons [1952] 1954) and medicine (Parsons 1951) and to sociology itself (Parsons 1959). In this article, I shall pay particular attention to Parsons's early writings around *The Structure of Social Action*, since these are most at issue in the debate over his critique of institutional and orthodox economics.

8. Similar arguments emerged again in the 1970s in criticism of Parsons's emphasis on the professions, with writers arguing for the dominance of self-interested motivations (Collins 1977), or for the "proletarianization" of the professions (Larson 1977). The expansion of the professions, which Parsons took to be of prime sociological significance as a distinctive social structure, is associated by these writers with their assimilation to the social structure of

capitalism, in which the professions are seen to have no particular sociological significance.

9. Parsons ([1940] 1954) elsewhere suggests that the dominance of acquisitive motives may not have an institutional explanation but may be related to anomie. "Ours is a society," he writes, "which in a number of respects is far from being perfectly integrated. A very large proportion of the population is in this sense insecure to an important degree. It is hence suggested that another component of this acquisitiveness, especially of the kind which is most offensive to our moral sentiments, is essentially an expression of this widespread insecurity" ([1940] 1954: 67).

10. As Parsons says in the context of a more general discussion of power and legitimacy in *The Structure of Social Action*, it is necessary to distinguish "between the fact of orientation to a legitimate order and the motives for acting in relation to it. The two elements of interest and legitimacy are interwoven in a complex way. The fact that an order is legitimate in the eyes of a large proportion of the community makes it ipso facto an element in the *Interessenlage* of any one individual, whether he holds it to be legitimate or not. Suppose he does not, his action, to be rational, must be nonetheless oriented to this order" (1937: 652).

11. Parsons allows that Marx introduces a "sociological element"—that of power—into classical political economy by making the firm his central unit of analysis. See Parsons ([1935] 1991).

12. This understanding of the market economy as "embedded" is given more formal articulation in Parsons's later writings, where the economy is understood to operate in terms of institutionalized values of the wider social system of which it is part. For example, Parsons and Smelser write that "the goal of the economy is not simply the production of income for the utility of an aggregate of individuals. *It is the maximization of production relative to the whole complex of institutionalized value-systems and functions of the society and its sub-systems*" (1956: 22; emphasis added).

13. Of course, it is the perceived closer relation of economics to science that is the origin of the status claims made on behalf of economics, so the two are not neatly separated.

14. Recent arguments by Brick (1993) and Nielsen (1991) have transformed the lazy critique of Parsons as being conservative in his orientations, suggesting that he had a socially liberal and progressivist outlook.

15. However, most interpretations of Parsons typically have regarded the unit act as referring to concrete individual acts. See, for example, Schutz ([1940] 1978), Martindale (1971), and Menzies (1976). A similar view is found in the "new" economic sociology, as we shall see.

16. In these respects, Parsons identifies a tendency within utilitarianism to seek the direct integration of economics, psychology, and biology, a tendency that is evident in the recent statement of Hirschleifer, who writes "there

is only one social science" (1985: 53) and "in pursuing their respective impe-
rialist destinies, economics and sociobiology have arrived in different ways
at what is ultimately the same master plan of social theory—one into which
the phenomena studied by the various social sciences to some extent already
have been, and ultimately will all be, fitted" (1985: 66). In these terms, it is
significant to Parsons that institutional economists had resort to biological
evolution in their approach to economic development (see Parsons [1935]
1991: 202).

17. Thus, Parsons writes that "the sense in which the unit act is here
spoken of as an existent entity is not that of *concrete* spatiality or otherwise
separate existence, but of *conceivability* as a unit *in terms of a frame of reference*" (1937: 43–44; emphasis added).

18. In this context, the structure of Parsons's ([1935] 1991) earlier two-part
essay on the sociological elements in economic thought is significant. The
first part, which includes a discussion of institutional economics, is "concerned with theories on the empiricist basis," while the second part rehearses
the argument to come in *The Structure of Social Action* and takes up "the
alternative of an *abstract* economic theory in relation to other abstract social
sciences" ([1935] 1991: 187).

19. Contrary to much of the secondary literature, then, from his earliest
statement of the action frame of reference onward, Parsons was concerned
with the identification of "unit acts" in order to locate their elements within
wider systems. The discovery of a "systems" approach was not a later development in which Parsons gave up an earlier attachment to "action," as is
commonly argued (Scott 1963; Menzies 1976).

20. See, especially, Parsons's discussion of Pareto (1937: 228ff).

21. Ironically, given Camic's general hostility to "presentist" interpretations
of texts, his heavy emphasis on normative action in *The Structure of Social
Action* derives from the later observation in the secondary literature that
Parsons's weakness lies in the domain of power and conflict. While this may
be true, it is clear that Parsons does not foresee this problem and he intends
his scheme to be adequate to problems of power and conflict. Moreover, the
later specification of the social system and its subsystems clearly identifies a
political subsystem, albeit with power functionally defined as serving collective goals and operating *over* actors to the extent that it serves to secure
compliance with those goals. Nor is it correct to suggest, as does Whitford
(2002), following Camic (1989), that all Parsons does is "tweak" the "missing
link" of ultimate values, leaving neoclassical economic theory otherwise
untouched, "implying that it successfully models those aspects of the social
world to which it is applied, and so cedes paradigmatic privilege to rational
choice" (2002: 332).

22. Parsons is quite clear that assigning sociology and economics to different analytical elements (or factors) within a single scheme is not the same

as saying that each discipline has its own domain of empirical problems. Thus, in a footnote to the statement that economics "must reconcile itself to be limited to the analytical abstraction of one of the fundamental factors in human action and its study for the purposes of the systematic formulation of theory in 'artificial' isolation from the rest" [1935] (1991: 213), Parsons comments that "artificial isolation" does not refer to the concrete division of labor of scientists and that "it seems to me that all important concrete research problems cut across several of the divisions between theoretical sciences" ([1935] 1991: 213). Ironically, Swedberg and Granovetter (1992) reproduce the very division that Parsons held to be problematic, in charging him with reinforcing disciplinary boundaries. They write that "American sociologists basically came to see themselves as dealing only with 'social' problems, which by definition were different from 'economic' problems. This development was due in part to the sharp division of labor recommended by Talcott Parsons in the 1930s" (1992: 5). They fail to acknowledge Parsons's critique of the fallacy of misplaced concreteness as well as the substance of what he says about the professional complex and its implications for understanding what were typically regarded as "economic" problems.

23. As with some other commentators (see, for example, Adriaansens 1979; Alexander 1984), I regard Parsons's scheme as complete once he establishes the functional imperative scheme as the means of distinguishing *levels* of systems and *dimensions* of the social system (see Holmwood 1996 for a discussion). Significantly, this development is associated with his return to consider the relations between economics and sociology (Parsons and Smelser 1956; Parsons 1960).

24. See, for example, Parsons's (1975) exchange with Gintis (1975) around the issue of ownership and control within the capitalist enterprise, which Parsons conducts entirely as a matter of correct specification in terms of the theory of the social system, with no consideration that there may also be issues of empirical adequacy in their competing accounts.

25. This is described by Alexander in the following way: "functionalism is concerned with integration as a possibility and with deviance and processes of social control as facts. Equilibrium is taken as a reference point for functionalist systems analysis, though not for participants in actual social systems as such" (1985: 9).

References

Adriaansens, H. P. (1979). "The Conceptual Dilemma: Towards a Better Understanding of the Development in Parsonian Action Theory." *British Journal of Sociology* 30: 5–24.

Alexander, J. C. (1982). *Theoretical Logic in Sociology, Volume I: Positivism,*

Presuppositions and Current Controversies. London: Routledge and Kegan Paul.

———. (1984). *Theoretical Logic in Sociology, Volume IV: The Modern Reconstruction of Classical Thought: Talcott Parsons*. London: Routledge and Kegan Paul.

———. (1985). "Introduction." In *Neofunctionalism*. Ed. J. C. Alexander. Beverley Hills, CA: Sage.

Alexander, J. C., and G. Sciortino. (1996). "On Choosing One's Intellectual Predecessors: The Reductionism of Camic's Treatment of Parsons and the Institutionalists." *Sociological Theory* 14: 154–171.

Baron, J. T., and M. T. Hannan. (1994). "The Impact of Economics on Contemporary Sociology." *Journal of Economic Literature* 32: 1111–1146.

Brick, H. (1993). "The Reformist Dimension of Talcott Parsons's Early Social Theory." In *The Culture of the Market: Historical Essays*. Eds. T. H. Haskell and R. F. Teichgraber III. Cambridge: Cambridge University Press.

———. (2005). "Talcott Parsons' 'Shift Away from Economics,' 1937–1946." *Journal of American History* 87: 490–514.

Burger, T. (1977). "Talcott Parsons, the Problem of Order in Society and the Program of an Analytical Sociology." *American Journal of Sociology* 83: 320–334.

Camic, C. (1989). "*Structure* After 50 Years: Anatomy of a Charter." *American Journal of Sociology* 95: 38–107.

———. (1992). "Reputation and Predecessor Selection: Parsons and the Institutionalists." *American Sociological Review* 57: 421–445.

Coleman, J. S. (1990). *Foundations of Social Theory*. Cambridge, MA: Belknap Press.

Collins, R. (1977). *The Credential Society*. New York: Academic Press.

Cook, S. (1966). "The Obsolete 'Anti-Market' Mentality: A Critique of the Substantive Approach to Economic Anthropology." *American Anthropologist* 68: 323–345.

Gintis, H. (1975). "Welfare Economics and Individual Development: A Reply to Talcott Parsons." *Quarterly Journal of Economics* 89: 291–302.

Gould, M. (1989). "Voluntarism Versus Utilitarianism: A Critique of Camic's History of Ideas." *Theory, Culture and Society* 6: 637–654.

———. (1991). "Parsons' Economic Sociology: A Failure of Will." *Sociological Inquiry* 61: 89–101.

Granovetter, M. (1985). "Economic Action and Social Structure: The Problem of Embeddedness." *American Journal of Sociology* 91: 481–510.

———. (1990). "The Old and the New Economic Sociology: A History and an Agenda." In *Beyond the Marketplace: Rethinking Economy and Society*. Eds. R. Friedland and A. F. Robertson. New York: Aldine De Gruyter.

Granovetter, M., and R. Swedberg (Eds.). (1992). *The Sociology of Economic Life*. Boulder, CO: Westview Press.

Hirshleifer, J. (1985). "The Expanding Domain of Economics." *American Economic Review* 75: 53–68.

Hodgson, G. M. (2001). *How Economics Forgot History: The Problem of Historical Specificity in the Social Sciences.* London: Routledge.

Holmwood, J. (1996). *Founding Sociology? Talcott Parsons and the Idea of General Theory.* London: Longman.

Hutchinson, T. W. ([1938] 1960). *The Significance and Basic Postulates of Economics.* New York: Augustus M. Kelley.

Ingham, G. (1996). "Some Recent Changes in the Relationship Between Economics and Sociology." *Cambridge Journal of Economics* 20: 243–275.

Larson, M. S. (1977). *The Rise of Professionalism: A Sociological Analysis.* Berkeley: University of California Press.

Martindale, D. C. (1971). "Talcott Parsons' Theoretical Metamorphosis from Social Behaviourism to Macro-Functionalism." In *Institutions and Exchange: The Sociologies of Talcott Parsons and George Caspar Homans.* Eds. H. Turk and R. L. Simpson. New York: Bobbs-Merrill.

Menzies, K. (1976). *Talcott Parsons and the Social Image of Man.* London: Routledge and Kegan Paul.

Nielsen, J. K. (1991). "The Political Orientation of Talcott Parsons: The Second World War and Its Aftermath." In *Talcott Parsons: Theorist of Modernity.* Eds. R. Robertson and B. S. Turner. London: Sage

Parsons, T. ([1935] 1991). "Sociological Elements in Economic Thought." In *Talcott Parsons: The Early Essays.* Ed. C. Camic. Chicago: University of Chicago Press.

———. (1937). *The Structure of Social Action.* New York: Free Press.

———. (1951). *The Social System.* London: Routledge and Kegan Paul.

———. ([1939] 1954). "The Professions and Social Structure." In *Essays in Sociological Theory.* New York: Free Press.

———. ([1940] 1954). "The Motivation of Economic Activities." In *Essays in Sociological Theory.* New York: Free Press.

———. ([1952] 1954). "A Sociologist Looks at the Legal Profession." In *Essays in Sociological Theory.* New York: Free Press.

———. ([1953] 1954). "A Revised Analytical Approach to the Social Stratification." In *Essays in Sociological Theory.* New York: Free Press.

———. (1959). "Some Problems Confronting Sociology as a Profession." *American Sociological Review* 24: 547–558.

———. (1960). "Pattern Variables Revisited: A Response to Professor Dubin's Stimulus." *American Sociological Review* 25: 467–483.

———. (1966). *Societies: Evolutionary and Comparative Perspectives.* Englewood Cliffs, NJ: Prentice-Hall.

———. (1971). *The System of Modern Societies.* Englewood Cliffs, NJ: Prentice-Hall.

———. (1975). "Commentary on Herbert Gintis, 'A Radical Analysis of Welfare Economics and Individual Development.'" *Quarterly Journal of Economics* 89: 280–290.

Parsons, T., and N. J. Smelser. (1956). *Economy and Society: A Study in the Integration of Economic and Social Theory.* London: Routledge and Kegan Paul.

Polanyi, K., C. M. Arensberg, and H. W. Pearson. (Eds.). (1957). *Trade and Market in Early Empires: Economies in History and Theory.* New York: Free Press.

Scott, J. F. (1963). "The Changing Foundations of the Parsonian Action Scheme." *American Sociological Review* 28: 716–735.

Schneider, H. K. (1974). *Economic Man.* New York: Free Press.

Schutz, A. ([1940] 1978). "Parsons' Theory of Social Action." In *The Theory of Social Action: The Correspondence of Alfred Schutz and Talcott Parsons.* Ed. R. Grathoff. Bloomington, IN: Indiana University Press.

Smelser, N. J., and R. Swedberg. (Eds.). (1994). *The Handbook of Economic Sociology.* Princeton: Princeton University Press.

Swedberg, R. (1991). "Major Traditions of Economic Sociology." *Annual Review of Sociology* 17: 251–276.

Veblen, T. (1904). *The Theory of the Business Enterprise.* New York: Scribner.

Velthuis, O. (1999). "The Changing Relationship Between Economic Sociology and Institutional Economics: From Talcott Parsons to Mark Granovetter." *American Journal of Economics and Sociology* 58: 629–649.

Wearne, B. (1989). *The Theory and Scholarship of Talcott Parsons to 1951: A Critical Commentary.* Cambridge: Cambridge University Press.

Whitford, J. (2002). "Pragmatism and the Untenable Dualism of Means and Ends: Why Rational Choice Theory Does Not Deserve Paradigmatic Privilege." *Theory and Society* 31: 325–363.

Williamson, O. E. (1981). "The Economics of Organization: The Transaction Cost Approach." *American Journal of Sociology* 87: 548–577.

Yonay, Y. P. (1998). *The Struggle Over the Soul of Economics: Institutionalist and Neoclassical Economists in America Between the Wars.* Princeton: Princeton University Press.

Interpenetration Versus Embeddedness

The Premature Dismissal of Talcott Parsons in the New Economic Sociology

By Jens Beckert,* translated by Lissa Janoski

ABSTRACT. The economy and economics are important fields in Talcott Parsons's work. Parsons's contributions on this subject were, however, mostly critically received in the new economic sociology. In this article, main points of criticism of Parsons's economic sociology will be discussed and the question asked whether the importance of Parsons's works in economic sociology was adequately treated. It will be demonstrated that the critical assessments was based for the most part on theoretical conceptions Parsons developed during his structural-functionalist period. Hence the assessments neglected to discuss the theory of expressive-symbolic communication of affect that Parsons developed in his later systems-functionalist period. However, precisely these later theoretical developments correlate

*Jens Beckert is Professor of Sociology and Director of the Max Planck Institute for the Study of Societies in Cologne. Previously, he was Professor of Sociology at the Georg August University Göttingen and Associate Professor of Sociology at the International University Bremen. He studied sociology and business administration at the Freie Universität Berlin and the New School for Social Research in New York. He received his Ph.D. in sociology from the Freie Universität in 1996 and his Habilitation in 2003. Beckert was a visting fellow at the sociology department of Princeton University in 1994–1995 and at the Center for European Studies of Harvard University in 2001–2002. His book *Beyond the Market: The Social Foundations of Economic Efficiency* was published by Princeton University Press in 2002. His second monograph, "Unverdientes Vermögen. Soziologie des Erbrechts" (Campus Verlag 2004), will also be published in English by Princeton University Press. Other publications include: "Economic Sociology and Embeddedness: How Shall We Conceptualize Economic Action?" *Journal of Economic Issues* 37: 769–787, 2003; "Agency, Entrepreneurs and Institutional Change: The Role of Strategic Choice and Institutionalized Practices in Organizations," *Organization Studies* 20: 777–799, 1999; "What Is Sociological about Economic Sociology? Uncertainty and the Embeddedness of Economic Action," *Theory and Society* 25: 803–840, 1996. This is the revised version of an article that was originally published in German in the *Berliner Journal für Soziologie* in 2002. The author thanks Harald Wenzel for his excellent suggestions.

American Journal of Economics and Sociology, Vol. 65, No. 1 (January 2006).
© 2006 AJES, Inc.

directly with the concept of social embeddedness as a key concept in the new economic sociology. A stronger linking with this development in Parsons's theory could bring economic sociology closer to finding a foundation in action theory, which has been missing up to the present.

I

Introduction

TALCOTT PARSONS WAS ALSO AN ECONOMIC SOCIOLOGIST. In fact, his works in this field represent an already impressive sociological oeuvre. Even before *The Structure of Social Action* ([1937] 1949a) was published, Parsons (1991) had produced a series of theoretical essays in leading economics journals in which he dealt critically with economic action theory and with the role of "noneconomic factors" on the economy. In the 1940s, more essays followed, regarding economic action theory (1949b, 1954a) and regarding the professions (1951, 1954b). In the 1950s, Parsons gave the Marshall Lectures ([1953] 1986) in Cambridge, which became the basis for *Economy and Society* (1956). Both texts describe the workings of the economic system and its integration in the social system of society using the AGIL pattern. Finally, the article on the sociology of money (1963), which was written in the context of his media theory, is also part of Parsons's work in economic sociology.

This is a remarkable legacy for economic sociology! However, at the time of their publication, neither the works from the 1930s nor *Economy and Society* were great successes for Parsons (Parsons 1977; Smelser 1981). And, later, when the importance of *The Structure of Social Action* was recognized in sociology, it was not the economic sociology entailed in it that was considered interesting. Rather, his convergence thesis, the canonization of sociological classics that were suggested in the work, and the rejection of utilitarianism as a theory of social order became influential in sociological discourse. Parsons's works were hardly considered important contributions to economic sociology at the time of their publication.

A probable reason for this is the fact that economic sociology, although it had an excellent debut with classic sociologists such as

Emile Durkheim, Karl Marx, Georg Simmel, and Max Weber, received little attention for many decades from the late 1930s onward. How could someone then become seriously interested in Parsons's significance as an economic sociologist? Only during the last 25 years did the situation in economic sociology change dramatically. It developed from a marginalized area of sociological research to an innovative and prominent field. This is especially true for the United States, where today "the new economic sociology" is an important field of sociological scholarship (Guillén et al. 2003; Smelser and Swedberg 1994; Zukin and DiMaggio 1990). In this scenario, it would have been expected that as a part of the increasing interest in economic sociology the works of Talcott Parsons in this area of scholarship would have received late credit.

Parsons's works on the economy were indeed debated in the 1980s and 1990s (Deutschmann 1999; DiMaggio and Powell 1991; Ganssmann 1989, 1996; Granovetter 1985, 1990; Holton 1986, 1992; Saurwein 1988; Swedberg 1987; Zelizer 1994). However, all in all, these receptions were mostly critical. Important proponents of the new economic sociology distanced themselves from Parsons, even defining today's economic sociology against his theoretical concepts.[1]

In this article, I will use these critics as a starting point and analyze to what degree they do justice to Parsons's works in economic sociology. I will follow three main lines of critical debate: (1) the discussion over Parsons's action theory, (2) the debate on the relationship between economy and society, and (3) the criticism of his theory of money. I will argue that the criticisms from the new economic sociology often point to problematic aspects in Parsons's economic sociology. But they do so in an abbreviated and incomplete sense. As a result, they obscure important theoretical contributions that are contained in Parsons's economic sociology, which might be fruitful for the further development of the new economic sociology. Particularly Parsons's detachment from a primarily value-oriented understanding of integration of economic functions in his systems-functionalist period is practically ignored. In consequence, even important similarities between Parsons's ideas in economic sociology and the term *embeddedness* as a key concept in the new economic sociology—which can be discerned from Parsons's writings in this period—were not recognized. In conclusion, I will argue, building on my own work (Beckert 2003, 2005) and Harald Wenzel's (2001), that there are basic elements for a theory of market integration in Parsons's later works that can be linked to the concept of embeddedness and that also allow this concept to receive a foundation in social theory.

II

On the Criticism of Action Theory

THE MOST INFLUENTIAL CRITICISM on Parsons in the new economic sociology was brought forth by Mark Granovetter (1985).[2] In the prominent essay "Economic Action and Social Structure: The Problem of Embeddedness," Granovetter introduced the term *social embeddedness*, which has since become a key concept in economic sociology. The term is explicitly defined in opposition to Parsons. According to Granovetter, economic sociology must keep its distance from two action-theoretical positions. On the one hand, it must distance itself from an "undersocialized" understanding of economic action. Contrary to the assumption of individual utility maximization of economic theory, actors do not act as isolated *monads*, but are embedded in social network structures that are themselves relevant for the explanation of economic results.

In addition to the action concept of economic theory, Granovetter rebuts a second position in action theory, which is this time connected to Parsons. As he argues, economic sociology could be attached to an "oversocialized" concept of action (Wrong 1961) that views action as culturally determined and therefore does not give credit to freedom of action. The actors thus appear to be "cultural dopes" (Garfinkel 1967), marionettes being led by the strings of their functionally integrated culture.

Granovetter's concerns readily find consensus. Every concept of economic sociology that is worthy of its name distances itself from the atomistic assumptions of the rational actor model. At the same time, the assumption that decisions are not *determined* by the actors' integration in social and cultural relations can be regarded as a widely accepted result of the debate on the relationship between structure and agency that has continued up to the present. However, it can be questioned (1) to what extent the formulated criticism on Parsons is actually justified and (2) to what extent Granovetter is successful in developing a theoretical alternative.

1. An answer to the first part of this question depends particularly on which parts of Parsons's works are examined. In fact, it is arguable that Parsons in his structural-functionalist period from the 1940s onward focused on the internalization of values in the socialization process, while the actors' freedom of action played little systematic role in *this* theoretical conception.[3] This was not the case in his earlier works. The voluntaristic theory of action that Parsons developed in his early works ([1937] 1949a) had its starting point specifically in the rejection of deterministic theories from behaviorism and utilitarism, which are criticized for being inappropriate as theories of social order (Alexander 1983; Beckert 2002; Münch 1988). In his voluntaristic theory of action, Parsons was committed specifically to the anchoring of freedom of action in decision making. In the theoretical model, Parsons introduced norms and values as elements of the "unit act" while at the same time considering the category of "effort," pointing to the voluntaristic element of action. This theory therefore cannot be labeled as culturally deterministic.

Of course, one does not have to recognize a normative action theory as the sought alternative to rational actor theory from economics (Joas and Beckert 2001; Beckert 2003). Still, Granovetter's critique of Parsons's action theory relies too heavily on simplified formulations of Parsons's critics and therefore does not do justice to the richness of the conceptions of action in his work.[4]

Immanent criticism might claim that in the voluntaristic theory of action the category of "effort" was introduced as a residual category without being adequately determined theoretically (Wenzel 2001: 300). Parsons took on this task only much later, when he developed a theory of symbolic communications media of the generalized system of action. In this work he developed a theory of expressive-symbolic action (*ibid.*: 288ff.) that detaches itself from the greatly value-oriented explanation of social order. I will specifically treat this below. For now, it should only be kept in mind that the criticism on normative overdetermination is neither fair to Parsons's early works nor to his conception in his later period of systems functionalism.

2. In order to completely reject Parsons's action theory as outdated for economic sociology, Granovetter should have suggested an alternative action theory. Granovetter's (1985) key concept consists in taking social embeddedness as a starting point for economic sociology. *Social embeddedness* in this case means the integration of actors in networks of social relations. According to this view, the network structures themselves are the most important explanatory variable for economic outcomes.

Network analysis has become the most important approach in the new economic sociology (Burt 1992; Uzzi 1997; White 2002). To what degree, however, does network analysis provide a way out of Granovetter's outlined dilemma between an oversocialized and an undersocialized concept of action? Doubts are appropriate here. Network analysis is a structuralist theory whose explanations are not based upon action theory. With that, Granovetter's concept of "social embeddedness"—formulated as a starting point of economic sociology—should not be regarded as a "solution" to the problems associated with Parsons's value-based conception. Rather, both concepts are established on categorically different levels (Beckert 2003), and the question regarding the appropriate basis in action theory remains unanswered. To the extent that network analysts search for explicit connections to action theory, they find them foremost in the model of rational action—in other words, in the undersocialized concept of action. Few works try to combine network research with more interpretative concepts in action theory.[5] This limited interest in action theory is problematic, since the connection between network analysis and action theory could raise some of the most interesting research questions for economic sociology: How are existing network structures interpreted in differing cultural and political contexts? What influence on this do attributes such as gender, class, race, or ethnicity have? What influence do values have? How do social bonds develop between actors in networks, and how are they strengthened? How can employers use network structures contingently for their interests?

Regardless of the answers to these questions, the problem of what a nonnormativistic and nonrationalistic theory of economic action might look like has been opened. Could a closer look at Parsons contribute to resolving it?

III

Evaluative Versus Cognitive Integration of Economic Action

BEFORE EXPLORING THE POTENTIAL OF PARSONS'S THEORY on these questions, I will discuss a further line of criticism. A second influential opinion on Parsons's action theory from the new economic sociology was brought forth by Paul DiMaggio and Walter Powell (1991), who examined Parsons's basic concepts on action theory more thoroughly than Granovetter. Their main point of criticism consists of the fact that Parsons's conceptualization of the influence of culture on the decisions of actors in economic contexts overestimates the evaluative dimension of culture (see also Warner 1978).

According to DiMaggio and Powell (1991: 16ff), a strong orientation toward Freud during the structural-functionalist period erroneously led Parsons to understand social order as depending on the precondition of internalization of culture in the socialization process. Institutional integration would be understood by Parsons as an agreement between a society's general value patterns and the structure of individual needs located in the personality system. Problematic for DiMaggio and Powell is not first and foremost the steering of action through culture but rather Parsons's limited understanding of culture.

Their criticism is based on ethnomethodological and phenomenological approaches. In their view, Parsons followed a limited strategy by reducing his own concept of culture—initially comprised of cognitive orientations and a cathectic dimension, in addition to the value dimension—to the dimension of values. With this reduced understanding of culture, Parsons's theory would not do justice to the diverse ways in which culture influences decisions. The often strategic usage of culture through actors was not considered.[6] In addition, according to DiMaggio and Powell, the level of purely cognitive-based integration in routine action would not become clear, which is effectively independent of the evaluative dimension of culture. Ignoring routines leads to an ultimately incomplete break with utilitarianism because, for Parsons, action is oriented quasi-intentionally toward gratification, which can be achieved by actors by means of value-conforming action.

DiMaggio and Powell also focused their criticism on Parsons's structural-functionalist period. Unlike Granovetter's critique of Parsons's "oversocialized" concept of action, criticism on the underrepresentation of the cognitive dimension of action cannot be diffused through reference to Parsons's early works. This holds true despite the fact that Parsons in his early essays (1991) put forward an entire palette of noneconomic factors that were relevant for the integration of economic exchange processes. Among these were routine and habit. Yet these elements are not categorically anchored in the "unit act." DiMaggio and Powell, however, do not take into account Parsons's later theory development. In the development of his media theory, as Harald Wenzel (2001: 300f.) points out, Parsons emphasized the importance of expressive-symbolic action and no longer saw generalized meaning as rising foremost from internalized value attitudes but rather from the process of concrete interaction between ego and alter. With this, the cathectic dimension and prereflective phenomena such as routines and habits come into view.

That this theoretical development is not taken into account is especially unfortunate, as DiMaggio and Powell's suggestions for a foundation of economic sociology in action theory might have been connected to *this* development of Parsons's theory. Instead, DiMaggio and Powell refer to the attempts at a "new synthesis" in sociological theory that have been developing since the 1970s. Among the promising approaches the authors argue should be integrated in the new economic sociology are the phenomenological approaches from Harold Garfinkel, Peter Berger, Thomas Luckmann, and Mary Douglas, as well as the advances from Randall Collins, Anthony Giddens, and Pierre Bourdieu. A more exact elaboration of the action-theoretical foundations of a phenomenologically-based economic sociology is not, however, provided by the two authors.[7]

IV

Economy and Society

ALONG WITH THE REJECTION of a primarily norm-based action theory, criticism from the new economic sociology was directed at Parsons's way of viewing economic structures, which Mark Granovetter and Richard Swedberg designated the "economy-and-society perspective" (Granovetter 1990: 90ff.; Swedberg 1987: 62). This criticism is aimed at the compartmentalization of the fields of sociology and economics, not only in the early works but also in *Economy and Society* (1956).

What exactly is meant by that? Parsons's theoretical essays from the 1930s should be seen in the context of the controversy in American economics between institutionalists on the one hand and neoclassical economists on the other. In this debate, Parsons is on the side of the institutionalists insofar as he, like them, particularly emphasizes the role of economic institutions for economic exchange. For Parsons, institutions are a noneconomic factor that is not based in the economic system itself but rather in the value attitudes of society. They are a "set of normative rules, obligatory on the participants" (1991: 170). Neoclassical economics keeps these factors out of its theoretical models and treats them as restrictions that enter into the data set of economic decision making. Institutionalists, however, claim that institutions must be recognized in economic theory as constituting economic action. This is exactly what Parsons disputed. On the basis of methodological arguments, which can mainly be traced back to Alfred North Whitehead (Wenzel 1990), Parsons criticized institutionalist economics, saying that with their method they could not achieve anything more than a photographic rendition of reality. The task of science, however, should be abstraction.

Parsons therefore advocated the existence of multiple disciplines in the social sciences that would be *analytically* separated and that would find their subject in the study of *one aspect* of the general scheme of action. Economics should deal with means-end relationships. The analytically limited area of study in sociology, on the other hand, would be made up of the study of the system's ultimate ends, the "value factors" (Parsons 1991: 163). As a result of this, Parsons recognized orthodox economics as a legitimate approach. However, at the same time, a place for sociology is found within the realm of scientific disciplines, which makes sociology appear "equal" to other social sciences, especially to economics. One can suspect that this construction was inspired by motives to legitimize sociology as an academic subject and that controversies with the field of economics were preferably avoided (Camic 1987, 1991).

Economic sociology, however, is left pretty helpless in this theoretical framework. Orthodox economics is recognized, and sociology's task consists of investigating which values actors orient themselves toward when acting rationally. Because of that, sociological findings cannot in principle lead to *revisions* of economic theory.

Parsons himself must also have had his doubts about this compartmentalization of sociology and economics. For one, his essays on economic sociology from the 1940s (1949, 1954) do not adhere to this separation but rather can be characterized as institutional. Additionally, Parsons abandoned his focus on the theoretical conceptualization of the relationship between sociology and economics at the end of the 1930s (Brick 2000; Parsons 1977).

It is therefore even more surprising that Parsons took up this theme again in the 1950s, first in the Marshall Lectures ([1953] 1986) and then in *Economy and Society* (1956), written jointly with Neil Smelser. At first glance it would appear as if Parsons had given up on the compartmentalization of sociology and economics. His point of reference in the 1950s was no longer microeconomics but Keynesian theory. However, closer inspection reveals an astonishing continuity. In the Marshall Lectures, Parsons wanted to show again that economic theory—this time in the form of Keynesianism—fits into a metatheoretical scheme and can be located there. The higher ranking point of reference for economics and sociology became the AGIL scheme. Once again, his concern was not with sociological criticism on economic theory but with its location within a given theoretical frame.

V

The Interpenetration of Economy and Society

This economy-and-society approach followed in *Economy and Society* contributed to the widespread rejection of the book in the new economic sociology (Granovetter 1990: 92). Nevertheless, the dismissal of Parsons's economic sociology from the 1950s based on the critique of the economy-and-society perspective could be premature for two reasons. First, because it does not do justice to the achievements of the book in the analysis of the systematic interconnectedness of the economy with cultural, socially integrative, and political realms of the social system and with the personality system. With their analysis of interdependent relationships between economic and other social functions, Parsons and Smelser contributed to the core of economic sociology. Second, in *Economy and Society*—under the influence of Keynes's theory—a new orientation for the understanding of market integration is indicated, which is of importance for the theoretical advancement of economic sociology.

Hence, for the judgment of *Economy and Society*, the close investigation of Parsons and Smelser's analysis of the boundary exchanges between the economic system and the other societal subsystems *as well as* the evaluation of the suggested conception of integration of economic action are crucial. Both aspects, however, were hardly acknowledged by Parsons's critics from the new economic sociology. I will illustrate what fruitful results could have been reaped from this on the basis of two examples.

A. Consumer Markets

The first example is the analysis of consumer markets. Parsons and Smelser did not see consumption primarily in its function of satisfying biological needs for reproduction but rather as reflecting role expectations of a culturally defined lifestyle standard. Through spending on consumption, the social system "household" fulfils institutionalized demands to live according to a certain lifestyle. Expenditure levels are determined by a culturally defined basket of goods that determines the "cultural survival" (Parsons and Smelser 1956: 221) of the household. Beyond that, expenditures for entertainment, leisure, and vacations are given a function for intra-family conflict management and, with that, status symbols assume an integrative function by positioning the household in relation to other households and thus symbolizing membership in a group.

Interest is thus directed toward institutional structures that add to the explanation of the integration of diverging interests of market parties. With that, the principal problem is formulated as follows: "For there to be stability in the retail consumers' market there must be an integration between the values and norms on the one hand of the economy, on the other of the family" (Parsons 1986: 28). Parsons regarded two institutions that make this integration possible. On the one hand, there are universally valid prices, whereby the opportunity to determine prices by negotiation between sellers and interested buying parties is rendered impossible. On the other hand, there are quality signals of the producers in the form of image building for brands and through warranties.

Through fixed prices, the consumer is left with only two options: whether to buy the product, and how much of it to purchase. The product seller is at the same time prevented from reacting to differing social backgrounds of the customers with price changes. Through this, the economy's differentiation from other social systems and a tendency toward universalized structures is expressed.

The situative fixing of prices, depending on the social situation (particularly of the individual buyer) expresses on the other hand a " 'particularistic' nexus of relationships'" (1986: 59) that contains duties that go beyond economic transactions. If consumers are socially bound to buy goods from a specific company and the seller sets prices based on the social status of the individual buyer (relative/stranger, poor/wealthy, etc.), the competition between suppliers is effectively stopped. Through price fixing, the economic transaction is freed from particularistic restrictions, and the consumer's competitive behavior is directed toward alternative suppliers. Compared to the regulation of prices through situative bargaining, the institution of price fixing reveals itself to be more efficient, if market control of prices remains. This consensus with economic theory does not, however, mean that the institution of price fixing can be *explained* by economic interests. Instead, Parsons and Smelser pointed out that the differentiation process of economies and the interest in increasing economic productivity in society must be culturally legitimized in itself.

The second institution of consumer markets, which serves to guarantee continuing consumer demand and also ensures high economic performance, consists of quality signals in the form of image creation and warranties that are provided by the producer. The function of these signals lies in the reduction of consumer risks in purchasing decisions, which stem from the asymmetrical distribution of information. In particular, the quality of technologically complex, durable consumer goods cannot really be judged by consumers. Trust is necessary, which the consumer "invests" in the producer through his or her purchases. Here, Parsons and Smelser anticipated debates on incomplete contracts and on trust that became important fields of research in the new economic sociology.

B. Financial Markets

A theoretically significant part of *Economy and Society* is the analysis of financial markets. Here, the move away from the concept of mainly normative integration of economic action clearly can be recognized. Parsons and Smelser see financial markets as internal economic markets. The investor is not bound by the norms and interests of society but rather can act indepently from social considerations, solely oriented toward maximization criteria. Paradoxically, the necessity of the institutionalization of decisions arises precisely from this nonstructuredness in financial markets. Here, Parsons ties into the problem of action in conditions of uncertainty (Beckert 1996). In financial markets there is a maximum of alternative possibilities for decisions and a minimum of normative predispositions for decisions, from which risky and uncertain situations result (Parsons and Smelser 1956: 234). However, how can the ability for action be maintained under these circumstances of double contingency? Parsons and Smelser refer to Keynes, who in his *General Theory* ([1936] 1949) had explained the orientation toward conventions and the significance of mimetic behavior on financial markets with the problem of uncertainty. The authors went even beyond Keynes by supporting anthropological findings on action in situations with uncertainty: the origin of magic and superstition is located in such situations. Comparable mechanisms are apparent in financial markets: investors orient themselves not on facts but rather on the *opinions* of those believed to have insider knowledge, or they make decisions by using rules of thumb (Parsons and Smelser 1956: 238). For financial markets, the point is that the actors have to create confidence for investment decisions *independently from any value order* that could otherwise guide their decisions in order to keep these markets functioning.

Of course, Parsons and Smelser could have written much more on the link between uncertainty and institutionalization in market contexts. The remarks on this topic were kept very short in *Economy and Society*. By pointing to the nonnormative social mechanisms that stabilize actors' expectations on financial markets, they show in principle, however, that noneconomic elements flow into this market and that sociology can contribute to the understanding of the functioning of financial markets by analyzing these mechanisms. At the same time, these mechanisms do not rest on a preceeding value order but must be created by the actors in the action process. Especially in this, an important perspective can be recognized for the action-theoretical foundations of economic sociology that was not adequately valued in the reception of *Economy and Society*.

The investigation of the institutional bases of consumer markets and the study of financial markets thus are examples for the analysis of the interconnectedness of economic action and society. This is the primary concern in economic sociology. The concrete empirical insights achieved by Parsons and Smelser nevertheless received little appreciation from the new economic sociology criticism on Parsons.[8] Rather, this criticism concentrated on Parsons's meta-theoretical recognition of economic theory and concluded that such "self-restriction" hindered the study of the economy from a sociological perspective.

This does not imply that one must agree with the findings of Parsons's economic sociology in every detail. Particularly the studies on consumer markets reveal the problematic assumption of the orientation of action on internalized values. However, instead of primarily ignoring Parsons's findings, it would have been more appropriate to ask, for example, what a different understanding of culture—with a stronger emphasis on the cognitive dimensions— would mean for the conceptualization of consumer markets. Or whether the important insights on the functioning of financial markets may be informative to the investigation of other market contexts. In this sense, however, Parsons's economic sociology was not taken up, and the potential of his works was not exhausted in the new economic sociology. For Parsons's *empirical discoveries*, this can hardly be made up for today because the new economic sociology has progressed much further in the understanding of cultural, political, and cognitive embeddedness of economic processes than Parsons had half a century ago.

This is different from the *theoretical insights* in *Economy and Society*, which Parsons and Smelser derived from Keynes and that were central to their discussion of financial markets and the workings of credit in the economy. Here, a conceptualization of economic action is indicated that is no longer based on normative action, but rather on the generalization of meanings of action in the process of action itself (Wenzel 2001: 237ff.).[9] Due to the lack of normative integration and the uncertainty developing from this, decisions on financial markets can come into existence only when actors succeed in establishing confidence in the future outcomes of their investment decisions. This cannot be achieved through values but instead refers to an integration that can merely be achieved by communication in the action process. This aspect is closely connected to the theory of money.

VI

Money as a Symbolically Generalized Medium

THE THEORY OF MONEY REPRESENTS the third area of critical discussion on Parsons's economic sociology, along with the criticism on his theory of action and his conception of the relationship between sociology and economics. German economic sociologists, in particular, thoroughly discussed Parsons's theory of money (Deutschmann 1999; Ganssmann 1989, 1996; Habermas 1984; Luhmann 1988; Paul 2004).[10] The reason for this is probably the great resonance of Parsons in the work of the two most influential German post–World War II social theorists, Jürgen Habermas and Niklas Luhmann. In their media theories, Luhmann (1988, 1995) and Habermas (1984) directly connected with Parsons, thereby directing attention to Parsons's original contributions.

Building on Max Weber, Parsons sees the precondition for the functional differentiation of the economy in the development of a money economy. In an economy that is characterized by highly specialized production processes, the direct exchange between labor and consumer goods would not be practicable and, besides, would not take the diverging interests of families and companies into account. While a company's production decisions are oriented toward expected profits, consumer choices are made—as we have seen—on the basis of lifestyles that are culturally anchored. The differentiation between production and the consumption of goods requires the relative detachment of employment and consumer purchasing decisions. It is only through abstraction from concrete goods and value storage by means of the medium of money that production plans can be developed independently of the concrete needs of the workers and be adjusted to the profit motive. Through the medium of money, consumers can attain independence from the products they produce, which makes it possible to adequately speak of the development of lifestyles on the basis of consumer choices. The different needs of the economy and the family can be reconciled as consumer demand and labor demand become separated by the exchange medium of money from concrete producers and at the same time remain connected to each other on a generalized level. By adding the mechanism of money, the qualitative dimension of connecting the economy and the household disappears, and the potential conflict of interests between household and company is reduced to a conflict over wages.

Despite this central role of money in explaining functional differentiation, the discussion of money plays only a subordinate role in *Economy and Society*. Parsons developed his theory of money as a symbolically generalized medium of exchange only in the 1960s (particularly Parsons 1963). The analysis of money as a medium of interaction through which the economy regulates its boundary processes with other subsystems became Parsons's model for his entire media theory.[11] Appealing to economic theories of money, Parsons described money as a medium of exchange whose function consists in measuring value (Parsons 1963: 236). Money is thereby symbolic, "in that though measuring and thus 'standing for' economic value or utility, it does not itself possess utility in the primary consumption sense— it has no 'value in use' but only 'in exchange', i.e. for possession of things having utility" (Parsons 1963: 236). The offers to buy or sell goods or services are communicated through the medium of money. Parsons traced the development of money to its roots in precious metals, which have intrinsic value. This connection is fully lost in differentiated money economies, to the extent that money becomes worthless in regard to its use value. The theoretical problem arising from the worthlessness of money (why should ego be willing to exchange a good for worthless money in the exchange process?) is deciphered by Parsons pointing to the four degrees of freedom that actors achieve through the medium of money: the buyer can spend money on any goods; he or she can buy from any producer; the buyer can freely decide on the time of purchase; and he or she is free to accept or reject the terms of purchase. The disadvantage of the worthlessness of money is compensated by the gain in options and motivates acceptance of the medium in exchange.

However, the risk remains that money will not be accepted by third parties or that it will become worthless due to inflation. This risk remains because money is not tied to a product that has a use value. However, the disconnection of money from its historical origins in precious metals is, according to Parsons, a precondition for its functional efficiency as a medium of exchange, which is why this risk is part of the structure of differentiated economies. Only the actors' *trust* in the stability and acceptance of the symbolic medium can be supported through its institutionalization. "There must be an element of bindingness in the institutionalization of the medium itself—e.g. the fact that the money of a society is a 'legal tender' which must be accepted in the settlement of debts which have the status of contractual obligations under the law" (1963: 240). At the same time, the institutionalization of money allows a separation of economic exchange processes from their anchoring in culturally sanctioned expectations of reciprocity. Only under these conditions do the degrees of freedom, which have been attained through acquisition of money, become relevant, which could otherwise not be exercised due to institutionalized obligations. What, from whom, when, and for what price something is purchased is no longer culturally decided. The resulting uncertainty of economic decisions can no longer be normatively reduced. This points again toward the detachment of Parsons's economic sociology from the concept of normative integration of exchange processes.

The criticism from economic sociology of Parsons's theory of money is sparked by several arguments. One aspect of this was the assumption of trust in the enduring value of money. Heiner Ganssmann (1989: 293) argues that Parsons's theory of money has always assumed that an institutional trust in money exists, without, however, explaining where this trust comes from. According to Ganssmann, the theory therefore describes a functioning economy but cannot explain its origins. The main point of criticism for Parsons's theory of money was based on his obvious underestimation of money's societal relevance. By considering money merely as a symbol—which was already problematic (1963: 290ff.)—Marx's and Weber's insight that the monetary economy enables an orientation toward profits as its own end was ignored. Money is the central instrument for the orientation toward the profit motive and makes possible the principally unlimited dynamics of capitalist economies, detached from concrete needs (1963: 292). Parsons's theory of money, however, completely in the tradition of the neoclassical theory of money, plays down the possible social implications of money by understanding it only as a neutral means to simplify exchange. Christoph Deutschmann's (1999: 44) criticism follows these same lines. He accuses Parsons's theory of money of not recognizing "wealth characteristics of money" and with this its potential to reach beyond the economic system and to attain social power.[12] This suggests that money is not only a neutral means of exchange; it contains the "additional usefulness" of freedom of choice. Compared to the owner of a good, the owner of money can transfer his or her wealth easily from one use to the next and achieve social power by strategically exploiting this possibility. On the other hand, according to Deutschmann, Parsons ignores the imaginary dimension of action, which is embodied in money and consists of the possibility to attain not only existing wealth but even imaginable future wealth. Only monetary wealth initiates "the production of today unknown products by not yet known producers" (1963: 54).

All in all, this criticism of Parsons's theory of money from economic sociology practically amounts to the point that he underestimates the social-structural importance of money (compare also to Zelizer 1994). The reason for this is suspected to lie in Parsons's premise to acknowledge the neoclassical theory of money.[13] A completely new perspective on Parsons's theory of money was opened, however, by Harald Wenzel (2001: 246ff.). He referred to the connection between Parsons's theory of money and Keynes's. In his Marshall Lectures and in *Economy and Society*, Parsons had indeed relied heavily on Keynesian economic theory. And for Keynes, it holds true that "money matters"! Even though money is discussed only marginally in the Marshall Lectures and in *Economy and Society*, Keynes's theory of money enters into it indirectly in an important way.

According to Keynes, a stable underemployment equilibrium can arise precisely because economic actors can reserve parts of their investment funds in liquidity. This hoarding of money for speculative reasons can lead to depriving the economy of sufficient investment funds. Keynes thus establishes a connection between money and the real economy, a connection that is largely refuted in neoclassical theory. The actual amount of money that is kept in liquid form decisively depends on a noneconomic entity according to Keynes, namely, the *expectations* of the investors concerning the further development of the interest rate and the long-term revenues from capital investments. Here, Keynes refers to the "state of confidence," in other words, the trust in market development, as relevant for the rate of investment (Keynes 1949: 149). The actual expectations actors hold with regard to future states of the economy do not, however, reflect a rational estimate. This is impossible due to uncertainty. Instead, the expectations and the level of confidence are an expression of "mass psychology" and "animal spirits," making "economic prosperity . . . excessively dependent on a political and social atmosphere" (1949: 162).[14] This implies that the integration of economic processes depends to a high degree on the creation of confidence (or trust) in processes of social interaction.

Parsons's media theory follows this central characteristic of modern money economies by no longer primarily referring to mechanisms of normative integration for explaining the interpersonal generalization of meaning, but instead turning to the expressive-symbolic communication of affect. What matters is convincing alter in situations that are principally characterized by uncertainy, that is, to produce a "state of confidence." The result of Parsons and Smelser's analysis of financial markets was specifically that no general value orientations guide action, but rather that the contingent achievement to convince actors of the positive prospects of their investments is what really counts. The state of confidence can be created only through communication—the possibility of which is established by the very same differentiation processes, induced through the medium of money, that represent the expansion of the freedom of choice for the actor. With that, economic sociology is guided toward an interactionist theory of the communication of affect. None of the critiques from economic sociology on Parsons recognized this theoretical aspect that paves a way to a pragmatist understanding of action in economic contexts (Beckert 2003). An important theoretical basis for the sociological understanding of the integration of market processes could lie in this because it offers an alternative to the less plausible assumption of primarily normative integration of modern economies.

VII

Conclusions

WHAT SIGNIFICANCE DOES the economic sociology of Talcott Parsons have in view of the manifold criticisms from the new economic sociology? Parsons's action theory from his structural-functionalist period was rightly criticized for its strong orientation toward values and the use of a limited concept of culture. This leads to a restricted understanding of the integration of economic processes. Yet at the same time, it must be kept in mind that this justified criticism was rarely made into a starting point in the development of alternative concepts of action in the new economic sociology until now.

That Parsons's works in economic sociology were used too little as stimuli for further development holds true also in one other respect. The boundary processes between the economy and other societal subsystems and intra-economic exchange processes, which were analyzed by Parsons and Smelser in the 1950s, point to areas of analysis that were only taken up again 30 years later in economic sociology. For example, the study of financial markets, which has become an important topic today (Abolafia 1996; Baker 1984; Knorr Cetina and Preda 2004), could have used Parsons's suggestions to its advantage. In this case, the reception of the book by the new economic sociology—which first gave the work little attention and later ignored the details by focusing on the problematic conceptionalization of the relationship between the economy and society—wasted its potential.

In the criticism on Parsons's theory of money, it was rightly pointed out that Parsons neither analyzes money in view of its social-structural effects nor adequately addresses the effects of the developed money economy on the dynamic of capitalist economies. An attempt to develop economic sociology further as part of social theory is most evident in these criticisms on the theory of money. However, these criticisms are not successful in recognizing the importance of theoretical developments expressed in Parsons's media theory, of which the theory of money is one important part. Parsons himself—not just his critics from the 1960s and 1970s—developed an action theory that conceives social integration much less as originating from an established consensus of values than in his structural-functionalist writings. In reference to Keynes, Parsons brings the problem of uncertainty (or double contingency) to the fore as a core problem of sociological theories of order and social action. The question of how actors make decisions in economic contexts in which they cannot calculate the consequences of their decisions rationally and their actions are not culturally determined can in fact be recognized as the central starting point for economic sociology (Beckert 1996). Parsons's conceptionalization of the expressive-symbolic communication of affect points toward a theoretically important change in the basic assumptions of mutual coordination of action in the economy. Normative patterns that precede action play a much more limited role. Instead, the rather short-term and contingent creation of willingness to cooperate through expressive or performative action sits center stage. The creation of voluntary willingness to cooperate in situations with uncertainty—that is, out of trust—is one crucial basis of a market's ability to function (Beckert 2005).

This "created trust" cannot exist without any institutional and normative "backing." Values and norms continue to play a role. However, the main focus of Parsons's explanation for action no longer lies in existing cultural states but rather in the creation of willingness to cooperate in the process of action itself (Beckert 2002: 259ff., 2003; Wenzel 2001: 317). With that, economic sociology's core concept of embeddedness can find a foundation in an action theory that is distinct from the rational actor model. This removes the concept of embeddedness from a purely structuralist reading, which reduces the understanding of coordination of markets quasi mechanically to the structure of networks. Instead, the role of "skillful actors" (Fligstein 2001) or "institutional entrepreneurs" (Beckert 1999) that produce "stable worlds," that is, confidence, can take center stage in the explanation of how markets function. This does not deny the crucial insight that goal-oriented action is always "embedded in concrete, ongoing systems of social relations" (Granovetter 1985: 487) that provide opportunities for entrepreneurial action.

Mark Granovetter's (2003: 46) reference to structural differentiation, which separates social spheres of action, is obviously closely related to the puzzle providing the starting point of Parsons's theory of differentiation. That is, how can these differentiated spheres be reintegrated in a way that allows for social order? Following Granovetter, social differentiation can be understood as constituting social structures that contain structural holes. Entrepreneurial activity signifies mobilization of social resources through the bridging of such holes. This occurs through trust building and through social power (Granovetter 2003: 49ff). For Granovetter, the connection between structual preconditions and mobilization strategies makes an understanding of concentration of economic power and the expansion of markets possible. This starting point, however, is in direct agreement with Parsons's (building on Keynes) analysis of bringing about a "state of confidence," in which investments can be mobilized on the basis of forming contingent behavioral expectation into joint action, which cannot be explained by norms and values. With this, Parsons and the new economic sociology are not opponents but complement each other in an important way. Both see trust building as developing in the contexts of social interaction. The strand of the new economic sociology that is based on network theory teaches us that trust-building opportunities and economic power depend on the structure of the actors' social relationships. Parsons's conceptualization of the expressive-symbolic communication of affect contributes a nonnormative foundation in action theory for the understanding of this process of expectation building that allows for cooperation. Such a foundation has not yet been provided by the new economic sociology, and it was also not recognized in the reception of Parsons. This makes the reexamination of Parsons 50 years after the publication of *Economy and Society* worthwhile for the theoretical development of the new economic sociology.

Notes

1. The rejection of Parsons, particularly from American sociology, is not limited to his works in economic sociology but rather expresses general objections to the "grand theory." The critical assessment was directed specifically against Parsons and is not to be viewed as an anti-historical iconoclasm. Other works from classic sociologists, especially Weber (Hamilton and Biggart 1992; Swedberg 1998) and Durkheim (Steiner 1992), were readily built upon.

2. Granovetter, however, draws heavily on Ronald Burt's *Toward a Structural Theory of Action* (1982).

3. Many of the boundary processes between economic and other societal subsystems conceptualized in *Economy and Society* (1956) were problematic due to their orientation toward the principle of value integration. Two examples serve to illustrate this.

First is the normative theory of innovation that was developed in *Economy and Society* (1956: 265ff). According to this theory, the motivation for innovation originates from a conflict between the integrative part of the economic system and the personality systems of the actors. The inefficient use of production resources supposedly leads to dissatisfaction on the part of economic actors because it contradicts the internalized value of efficient resource use. Innovations, or changes in combinations of factors, aim at increased productivity and thus resolve intra-personal tensions. The motivation behind economic innovation cannot be explained through aspiration toward utility maximization but is rather the result of the interpenetration of personality systems and the economic system.

Second, Parsons and Smelser explain the pacification of the conflict between capital and labor by means of socialization processes that workers go through as they learn professional roles, leading to an internalization of the value of stable productivity. The dimension of social power is left out of this normative conception of the relationship between capital and labor. Using this argument against Parsons and Smelser, Alexander (1983: 234) stressed that normative orientations did not decide the course of action in the labor market but rather "economic class-position and material resources." Though labor market relations are also normatively integrated—which was already established by Durkheim—Parsons's theory is problematic due to its exclusion of the importance of social power.

4. Perhaps one should consider Granovetter's criticism less as a critical discussion of Parsons's works and more as a theoretical delimitation that could also have been formulated independently of Parsons. The reference to Parsons could merely serve to underline a position set apart from the concept of normative integration of economic action.

5. For criticism on this, see Emirbayer and Goodwin (1994). An exception to this are some of the later works by Harrison White, especially his *Identity and Control* (1992).

6. This point of criticism relates to Swidler's (1986) concept of culture as a "tool kit."

7. In the new economic sociology, the demand for an alternative action theory that is neither normativistic nor rationalistic in an economic sense has hardly become a focus (compare, however, Beckert 2002, 2003; Friedberg 1995; Storper and Salais 1997). This could be due to an avoidance of often unproductive debates with proponents of rational choice theory; the dominating self-conception of the new economic sociology as a "middle-range" approach; and the inherent difficulty in operationalizing more interpretative conceptions of action for quantitative empirical research. That the new economic sociology appears to be treading water theoretically despite a number of highly interesting studies could be due to a lack of a sophisticated microfoundation as well as a lack of a social theory. As warranted as the criticism on Parsons's action theory from the 1950s may be, Parsons does teach us the importance of a sociotheoretical foundation in economic sociology. Only on such a foundation can individual empirical studies lead to a general sociological perspective on the economy. Parts of Parsons's work could be helpful today for this task.

8. Compare, however, e.g., Holton (1986, 1992) and Münch (1994).

9. The emphasis on trust for the functioning of consumer markets points in this direction.

10. See also, however, Dodd (1994) and Zelizer (1994).

11. Habermas (1984). See also Wenzel (2001).

12. Indeed, Parsons (1963: 242) does mention the consequences of unequal distribution of money. According to Parsons, the owner of greater wealth has an advantage in that the marginal value of the price of a specific product is smaller for him or her than for a less wealthy person.

13. If money can be recognized as a socially consequential aspect at all, then only in its egalitarian effect: "All dollars are 'created free and equal'" (Parsons 1963: 242). This is because, in monetarily regulated exchange

processes, the buyer's or seller's social status is neglected. Only the amount of money offered is deciding.

14. See also the very interesting article by DiMaggio (2003) on the usefulness of these Keynesian ideas for economic sociology.

References

Abolafia, M. (1996). *Making Markets: Opportunism and Restraint on Wall Street.* Cambridge: Harvard University Press.

Alexander, J. (1983). *The Modern Reconstruction of Classical Thought: Talcott Pasons.* Berkeley: University of California Press.

Baker, W. (1984). "The Social Structure of a National Securities Market." *American Journal of Sociology* 89: 775–811.

Beckert, J. (1996). "What is Sociological about Economic Sociology? Uncertainty and the Embeddedness of Economic Action." *Theory and Society* 25: 803–840.

——. (1999). "Agency, Entrepreneurs, and Institutional Change. The Role of Strategic Choice and Institutionalized Practices in Organizations." *Organization Studies* 20(5): 777–799.

——. (2002). *Beyond the Market: The Social Foundations of Economic Efficiency.* Princeton. Princeton University Press.

——. (2003). "Economic Sociology and Embeddedness: The Problem of the Structure of Action." *Journal of Economic Issues* 37: 769–787.

——. (2005). *Trust and the Performative Construction of Markets* MPIfG Discussion Paper 05/8. Cologne: MPIfG.

Brick, H. (2000). "Talcott Parsons's 'Shift Away from Economics' 1937–1946." *Journal of American History* 87: 490–514.

Burt, R. (1982). *Toward a Structural Theory of Action.* New York· Academic Press.

——. (1992). *Structural Holes.* Cambridge, MA: Harvard University Press.

Camic, C. (1987). "The Making of a Method: A Historical Reinterpretation of the Early Parsons." *American Sociological Review* 52: 421–439.

——. (1991). "Introduction." In *Talcott Parsons: The Early Essays.* Ed. Charles Camic. Chicago: University of Chicago Press.

Deutschmann, C. (1999). *Die Verheissung des absoluten Reichtums. Zur religiösen Natur des Kapitalismus.* Frankfurt: Campus Verlag.

DiMaggio, P. (2003). "Endogenizing 'Animal Spirits': Toward a Sociology of Collective Response to Uncertainty and Risk." In *The New Economic Sociology: Developments of an Emerging Field.* Eds. Mauro F. Guillén, Randall Collins, Paula England, and Marshall Meyer. New York: Russell Sage Foundation.

DiMaggio, P., and W. Powell. (1991). "Introduction." In *The New Institutionalism in Organizational Analysis*. Ed. P. DiMaggio and W. Powell. Chicago: University of Chicago Press.

Dodd, N. (1994). *The Sociology of Money: Economics, Reason and Contemporary Society*. Cambridge, UK: Polity Press.

Emirbayer, M., and J. Goodwin. (1994). "Network Analysis, Culture and the Problem of Agency." *American Journal of Sociology* 99: 1411–1453.

Fligstein, N. (2001). *The Architecture of Markets*. Princeton: Princeton University Press.

Friedberg, E. (1995). *Ordnung und Macht. Dynamiken organisierten Handelns*. Frankfurt: Campus.

Ganssmann, H. (1989). "Money—A Symbolically Generalized Media of Communication? On the Concept of Money in Recent Sociology." *Economy and Society* 17: 285–316.

——. (1996). *Geld und Arbeit*. Frankfurt: Campus.

Garfinkel, H. (1967). *Studies in Ethnomethodology*. Englewood Cliffs, NJ: Prentice-Hall.

Granovetter, M. (1985). "Economic Action and Social Structure: The Problem of Embeddedness." *American Journal of Sociology* 91: 481–510.

——. (1990). "The Old and the New Economic Sociology: A History and an Agenda." In *Beyond the Market*. Eds. Roger Friedland and A.F. Robertson. New York: de Gruyter.

——. (2003). "A Theoretical Agenda for Economic Sociology." In *The New Economic Sociology: Developments of an Emerging Field*. Eds. Mauro F. Guillén, Randall Collins, Paula England, and Marshall Meyer. New York: Russell Sage Foundation.

Guillén, M. F., R. Collins, P. England, and M. Meyer (Eds.) (2003). *The New Economic Sociology: Developments of an Emerging Field*. New York: Russell Sage Foundation.

Habermas, J. (1984). *Theory of Communicative Action*. Vol. 2. Boston: Beacon Press.

Hamilton, G. G., and N. W. Biggart. (1992). "Market, Culture, and Authority: A Comparative Analysis of Management and Organization in the Far East." In *The Sociology of Economic Life*. Eds. Mark Granovetter and Richard Swedberg. Boulder, CO: Westview Press.

Holton, R. J. (1986). "Talcott Parsons and the Theory of Economy and Society." In *Talcott Parsons on Economy and Society*. Eds. Robert J. Holton and Bryan S. Turner. New York: Routledge Kegan.

——. (1992). *Economy and Society*. London: Routledge.

Joas, H., and J. Beckert. (2001). "Action Theory." In *Handbook of Sociological Theory*. Ed. Jonathan H. Turner. New York: Kluwer.

Keynes, J. M. ([1936] 1949). *The General Theory of Employment, Interest, and Money*. London: Macmillan.

Knorr Cetina, K., and A. Preda. (2004). *The Sociology of Financial Markets.* Oxford: Oxford University Press.

Luhmann, N. (1988). *Die Wirtschaft der Gesellschaft*, Frankfurt: Suhrkamp.

———. (1995). *Social Systems.* Stanford, CA: Stanford University Press.

Münch, R. (1988). *Theorie des Handelns. Zur Rekonstruktion der Beiträge von Talcott Parsons, Emile Durkheim und Max Weber.* Frankfurt: Suhrkamp.

———. (1994). "Zahlung und Achtung. Die Interpenetration von Ökonomie und Moral." *Zeitschrift für Soziologie* 23: 388–411.

Parsons, T. ([1937] 1949a). *The Structure of Social Action.* Glencoe, IL: Free Press.

———. ([1939] 1954a). "The Professions and Social Structure." In *Essays in Sociological Theory.* Glencoe, IL: Free Press.

———. ([1940] 1954b). "The Motivation of Economic Activities." In *Essays in Sociological Theory.* Glencoe, IL: Free Press.

———. (1949b). "The Rise and Fall of Economic Man." *Journal for General Education* 4: 46–53.

———. (1951). *The Social System.* Glencoe, IL: Free Press.

———. ([1953] 1986). "The Marshall Lectures." In *Research Reports from the Department of Sociology.* Vol. 4. Uppsala: Uppsala University.

———. (1963). "On the Concept of Political Power." *Proceedings of the American Philosophical Society* 107: 232–262.

———. (1977). "On Building Social System Theory: A Personal History." In *Social Systems and the Evolution of Action Theory.* Ed. Talcott Parsons. New York: Free Press.

———. (1991). *The Early Essays.* Ed. Charles Camic. Chicago: University of Chicago Press.

Parsons, T., and N. Smelser. (1956). *Economy and Society.* Glencoe, IL: Free Press.

Paul, A. (2004). *Die Gesellschaft des Geldes. Entwurf einer monetären Theorie der Moderne.* Wiesbaden: VS Verlag.

Saurwein, K.-H. (1988). *Ökonomie und soziologische Theoriekonstruktion. Zur Bedeutung ökonomischer Theorieelemente in der Sozialtheorie Talcott Parsons'.* Opladen: Westdeutscher Verlag.

Smelser, N. J. (1981). "On Collaborating with Talcott Parsons: Some Intellectual and Personal Notes." *Sociological Inquiry* 51: 143–154.

Smelser, N., and R. Swedberg (1994). *The Handbook of Economic Sociology.* Princeton, NJ: Russell Sage Foundation.

Steiner, P. (1992). "Le fait social économique chez Durkheim." *Revue française de sociologie* 33: 641–661.

Storper, M., and R. Salais. (1997). *Worlds of Production: The Action Framework of the Economy.* Cambridge: Harvard University Press.

Swedberg, R. (1987). "Economic Sociology: Past and Present." *Current Sociology* 35: 1–221.

———. (1998). *Max Weber and the Idea of Economic Sociology.* Princeton: Princeton University Press.

Swidler, A. (1986). "Culture in Action: Symbols and Strategies." *American Sociological Review* 51: 273–286.

Uzzi, B. (1997). "Social Structure and Competition in Interfirm Networks: The Paradox of Embeddedness." *Administrative Science Quarterly* 42: 35–67.

Warner, S. (1978). "Toward a Redefinition of Action Theory: Paying the Cognitive Element its Due." *American Journal of Sociology* 83: 1317–1349.

Wenzel, H. (1990). *Die Ordnung des Handelns.* Frankfurt: Suhrkamp.

———. (2001). *Die Abenteuer der Kommunikation.* Weilerwist: Verlbrück Verlag.

White, H. (1992). *Identity and Control: A Structural Theory of a Social Action.* Princeton: Princeton University Press.

———. (2002). *Markets from Networks: Socioeconomic Models of Production.* Princeton: Princeton University Press.

Wrong, D. (1961). "The Oversocialized Conception of Man in Modern Sociology." *American Sociological Review* 26: 183–193.

Zelizer, V. (1994). *The Social Meaning of Money.* New York: Basic Books.

Zukin, S., and P. DiMaggio. (1990). "Introduction." In *Structures of Capital: The Social Organization of the Economy.* Eds. Sharon Zukin and Paul DiMaggio. Cambridge: Cambridge University Press.

The Global System of Finance

Scanning Talcott Parsons and Niklas Luhmann for Theoretical Keystones

By Alexandra Hessling and Hanno Pahl*

ABSTRACT. In the last decades, revolutionary changes in financial markets, instruments, and institutions have stimulated empirical and theoretical investigations into the interaction of the financial and the "real" side of economic systems. While a considerable body of empirical investigations seems to provide evidence of positive correlations between stock market development and economic growth, there is no consensus in other social sciences as to whether there are two-way linkages, and if so, how to conceive a possible mechanism of interaction. Particularly, the hypergrowth and ubiquity of financial markets has triggered controversial debates on how to understand today's economic landscape. With the objective of clarifying the relationship between finance and economy, this article restructures the present debate through the lenses of Talcott Parsons's and Niklas Luhmann's theories of social systems. Basic system-theoretical ideas on social aspects of finance and economy as well as on uncertainty and risk hint at new insights into the global system of finance that might go far beyond explanatory models of causality.

I

Introduction

How can we explain a seemingly limitless growth of financial transactions that "is close to 1500 trillion dollars a day, which is more than seventy times the daily volume of international trade of goods"

*Alexandra Hessling is a graduate student with a Diploma in Sociology from the University of Bielefeld. She may be contacted at the Institute for World Society Studies, Faculty for Sociology, University of Bielefeld, PO Box 100131, 33501 Bielefeld, Germany; e-mail: hessling@uni-bielefeld.de. Hanno Pahl is a graduate student with a Diploma in Political Sciences from the University of Bremen and may be contacted at the Institute for World Society Studies at the address given above.

American Journal of Economics and Sociology, Vol. 65, No. 1 (January 2006).

(Goldfinger 2000: 72)? Does the rapid growth of stock markets mirror economic reality (Lowenstein 1988)? What do we observe: One single defining trend? The shift from tangible to intangible, where the economic landscape is no longer shaped by physical flows of material goods and products but by streams of data, images, and symbols (Goldfinger 2002)? And do those streams of data, images, and symbols exist for and refer to the "real" economy of tangibles? If so, the question is how they interact with the real economy.

The academic bazaar of explanations and interpretations of the evolution of the financial system and its impact on the economy is dazzling and multicolored. Some enthusiastic scholars pronounce that the financial system fosters efficient resource allocation. They grasp the financial economy as a vehicle of creative destruction that promotes innovation and eliminates obstacles to development and growth. Other critical thinkers agree on the destructive nature of money but paint a far more pessimistic picture: they proclaim the *financialization* of the economy, where financial assets replace and destroy physical assets (Froud et al. 2000; Fligstein and Shin 2004; Stockhammer 2004). Most economists clearly reject this view and instead dedicate their research to verifying and explaining positive correlations between financial market development and economic growth. And indeed, most empirical investigations suggest strong two-way linkages. But classical concepts of asymmetric information, financial liberalization, and market efficiency—notwithstanding their explanatory potential—have answered only too few questions. And many other issues need to be addressed on other theoretical grounds than economics.

What does sociology contribute to understanding the relationship of society, economy, and finance? As early as about half a century ago, Parsons and Smelser (1956) declared that sociology has tools that can help explain noneconomic phenomena in economic settings. And programmatically they noticed that "much study is needed to probe to deeper levels of understanding, but it is a very promising field" (1956: 239). Since then, sociologists have contributed various theoretical approaches to understanding social phenomena and mechanisms in the economic and financial settings of our society. Despite their different epistemological backgrounds, they basically share the idea of modern finance as a social reality sui generis. Anthony

Giddens (1990: 21ff.), for instance, perceives financial markets as a central aspect of what he calls the *disembedding of social systems*, a lifting out of social relations from local and national contexts. In the same way, Manuel Castells (1989, 1996) talks about *spaces of flows* to conceive the development of strong ties between social actors who are spatially divided, and first of all, he makes reference to financial markets. These spaces of flows bear similarities to Saskia Sassen's (1999) *spatio-temporal configurations* of dematerialized/digital activities of finance on the one hand and materialized activities on the other. But while Sassen claims interacting and overlapping spatial and temporal orders, advocates of postmodern approaches disagree with interactions, and instead declare the *uncoupling of financial markets from the "real" economy* (Heine 2001). Along these lines and to put it into metaphorical words, financial markets don't mirror economic reality. They are halls of mirrors, "where reflections of reflections, images of images constitute the only reality that matters" (McGoun 1997: 111). Drawing on Jean Baudrillard's (1983) philosophical works, the *hyperreality of finance* (McGoun 1997) is proclaimed. Finance has become a "hyperreal" game, an emergent social reality that is not a reflection of the "real" economy any more.

Without going into further details of the underlying theoretical positions, many of the social studies on finance turn more or less explicitly round the relationship between finance and economy. Either they seem to assume complex interdependencies, or they suggest the autonomy of finance operations from economic production. But do we have to perceive interdependency and autonomy as mutually exclusive concepts? If we keep an eye on recent changes in financial markets, instruments, and institutions, we might witness both: finance operations have unfolded their own systemic qualities in terms of autonomy and globality, and yet, the financial system somehow bears upon the economy. However, certainly one of the most promising approaches that is complex enough to transcend dichotomous perceptions is Talcott Parsons's *theory of social systems* and its further development by Niklas Luhmann. The theory of social systems—and this is the explanatory strength and common feature of both adaptations—radically disclaims any model of causality. That is to say, neither do financial activities reflect "real" economic activities, nor do they simply destroy or foster them in a linear measure. Instead, and this absolutely is one of the most striking highlights of Parsons's theory, we can understand the hypergrowth of finance as a social phenomenon that derives from processes of internal differentiation in economy and society. Along with the idea of differentiation and interlocking subsystems, the financial system has developed from evolutionary peculiarities of the economic system. This is why their relationship ought to be explained in terms of co-evolutionary and functional (not causal!) interdependency, while the financial system itself builds on its own, autonomous, mode of operation.

With the intention of clarifying this somehow paradoxical relationship of finance and economy, the article restructures the debate on global finance through the lenses of Talcott Parsons's and Niklas Luhmann's theory of social systems. Both contributions will be scanned for theoretical keystones to put the relations between global finance, economy, and society on more theoretical grounds. For these purposes, we will start by introducing some basic conceptual ideas. The second section is thus dedicated to searching out finance in the context of the economy and society along the lines of Parsons's analytical boundaries of the AGIL scheme. From this analytical perspective, special attention is given to patterns of differentiation in society and economy and to credit mechanisms and financial markets at the boundaries between society's and economy's subunits. At this juncture, we will focus on Parsons's *Economy and Society*, where he certainly worked out his most sophisticated ideas on financial markets and the economic system. These ideas were taken up by Niklas Luhmann, a German sociologist, who further developed Parsons's theory of social systems. To draw a distinction between both approaches, Luhmann's adaptation will be presented separately, in the third section. This section begins with a brief description of the differentia specifica of both approaches to functional differentiation and follows up with discussing the question of whether global finance is to be conceptualized as an autonomous social system. The fourth section enters empirical grounds and takes up topical changes in financial markets, instruments, and institutions. We will refer to various academic contributions to our understanding of global finance in order to supplement empirical investigations to our theoretical presumptions about the autonomy of global finance. The concluding section summarizes the arguments and critically reflects Parsons's and Luhmann's contributions to fathoming the relations between finance and economy.

II

Talcott Parsons on Society, Economy, and Finance

MYRIADS OF SCHOLARS across the disciplines of economics, finance, geography, and sociology have contributed deep insights into the dynamics of global finance. And the academic literature on the globalization of finance has mushroomed, akin to the dramatic increase of financial flows in recent years. So, in view of the huge amount of literature at hand, is there a need for other theoretical approaches to conceptualizing global finance than the already available? And why should we search Talcott Parsons's work for theoretical keystones? Talcott Parsons's *Economy and Society*—conceived and written together with Neil J. Smelser in the 1950s—serves us as a starting point because his general social theory might help in conceiving global finance from an evolutionary perspective. We argue that three of Parsons's conceptual ideas sharpen the view for evolutionary peculiarities of finance: first, his concept of differentiation and interlocking subsystems; second, his notions on credit mechanisms at the boundary between economy and polity; and third, his idea of financial markets at the boundary between capitalization and production.

A. Patterns of Differentiation in Society and Economy

The first theoretical keystone that allows us to put the relations between finance, economy, and society on theoretical grounds is Parsons's AGIL scheme. With his general model of social systems, Parsons introduced an analytical framework to look at society as a social system that must serve basic functions in order to maintain existence. In the AGIL scheme, Parsons identifies four functional imperatives each society—whether modern or premodern, capitalistic or noncapitalistic—has to deal with: adaptation (A), goal attainment (G), integration (I), and latent-pattern maintenance (L). Parsons and

Smelser argue that, in line with these analytical boundaries, society as a whole tends to differentiate into four primary subsystems: the economic subsystem that is specialized in relation to the adaptive function of society, and three other primary subsystems that likewise meet the goal-attainment function, the integration function, and the latent-pattern-maintenance function of society (see Figure 1).

As the authors argue, this mechanism of functional differentiation also recurs on the level of society's primary subsystems. With regard to the economic subsystem, for instance, we can distinguish between four analytical subsystems: the capitalization and investment subsystem (A_A), the production subsystem (A_G), the organizational subsystem (A_I), and the economic commitments subsystem (A_L) (see Figure 2). The same procedure of decomposition into subsystems can be carried out over and over again to conceptualize progressive levels of differentiation into interlocking subsystems. Along these lines, we can think of society as a highly differentiated social system; we can consider the economy as a subsystem of society that is internally differentiated; and we can look at finance as serving specific functions within and at the boundaries of the economic subsystem.

Before we continue to conceptualize finance through the analytical lenses of the AGIL scheme, some general notions on concepts of

Figure 1

The Social System

A		**G**
adaptive		**goal-attainment**
subsystem		**subsystem**
(economy)		**(polity)**
integrative		**latent-pattern-**
subsystem		**maintenance**
		subsystem
I		**L**

Figure 2

The Economic System

A_A		A_G
capitalization and investment subsystem		production subsystem
organizational subsystem		economic commitments subsystem
A_I		A_L

differentiation must be made. Parsons and Smelser introduced a concept of *functional differentiation* that does not necessarily correspond to concrete patterns of structural differentiation. The differentiation of concrete structures according to the analytical boundaries of the AGIL scheme may vary over time and from society to society. So while premodern societies do not necessarily dispose of a monetary differentiated economic system, although they have to meet society's adaptive function, capitalistic societies are more likely to develop concrete structures and roles along the line of functional imperatives. Regardless of these structural differences, Parsons and Smelser presume a "tendency of social systems to develop progressively higher levels of structural differentiation under the pressure of adaptive exigencies" (Parsons and Smelser 1956: 47).

But do we really witness concrete shifts toward a highly differentiated economic system? And are current changes in financial markets, instruments, and institutions brought about by processes of internal differentiation? Several investigations suppose so. They draw a picture of today's economic landscape by pointing to social structures that seem to follow *spatial and temporal patterns of differentiation*. There is, for instance, a growing body of research that goes under the banner of "economic geography" or the "geography of money." This research program mainly focuses on ways in which socio-spatial relations of actors are intertwined with processes of economic changes at various geographical levels—global, local, or glocal. Along these lines, one may possibly identify finance at the global level—most obviously in the metropolitan centers of Tokyo, London, and New York—and relations of production on the local or glocal level. However, while perceptions of space provide the intellectual framework for economic geographers, sociological thinkers have proposed other concepts of time and space to reach for the global: Anthony Giddens recognizes new opportunities opened up by what he calls time-space distantiation, Manuel Castells campaigns for a network society of global reach in which the space of flows (information, technology, and finance) replaces the space of places, and Saskia Sassen promotes interacting and overlapping spatial and temporal configurations of the economy. All of these approaches, as well as Parsons's concept of interlocking subsystems, suggest that one shouldn't understand finance as a "leveling force" of society and economy but instead should conceptualize the economy as a highly differentiated part of society. Based on Parsons's functionalist investigation of society, one may look at the global architecture of finance as a phenomenon that has developed from functional differentiation as the basic principle of social change. And just as the aforementioned approaches illustrate, this very basic principle seems to go along with temporal and spatial patterns of differentiation within the economic system.

B. Credit Mechanisms at the Boundary Between Economy and Polity

Based on the assumption that the evolutionary peculiarities of social systems actually differentiate into specialized subsystems, the next challenge is to pinpoint global finance in the context of society's interlocking subsystems. This is a much more complex endeavor than fathoming the relations between economy and society, since according to the AGIL scheme we cannot simply think of global finance as a subsystem of the economic system. Instead, we can discover finance as a specific function within the economic system and at the same time as an *intermediary mechanism* at the boundaries between society's and economy's subsystems. One therefore has to look at the boundary exchanges between the adaptation subsystem (economy) and the goal-attainment subsystem (polity) on the one hand, and between the economy's subsystems of capitalization/investment and production on the other.

The *boundary relationship between the economy and the polity* is of particular importance to tracing Parsons's ideas on the financial sphere because at this point he and Smelser expound their position on the *problem of credit* that relates both subsystems. Here, the authors argue that "the flow from the polity into the economy is the creation of capital funds through credit; [and that] the reverse flow is the control of the productivity of the economy" (Parsons and Smelser 1956: 59). When seen from this angle, there are no casual linkages between the economy and polity in terms of direct input-output exchanges; both subsystems instead stand in a reciprocally adaptive relationship to each other. This reciprocity is rendered possible by intermediary mechanisms such as the creation of credit at economy's and polity's boundaries. So the problem of credit can be exclusively assigned neither to the economy nor to the polity. Instead, it is decomposed into the creation of capital funds on the part of the economy and into the control of productive capacities on the part of the polity. Along these lines, it is the differentiatedness of social structures that causes the need for integrative mechanisms to regulate interchange processes between society's subsystems. But to think of credit as a mechanism that integrates economic and political spheres definitely overvalues the influence and capacities of political control over economic developments. The picture Parsons and Smelser drew of the economic and political landscape seems absolutely questionable from today's point of view. When they presented *Economy and Society* in the mid-1950s, they focused on the challenges of social integration during the postwar period and thus reflect the historical settings of that time.

Nonetheless, this can serve as a starting point to trace structural changes within economy's and polity's interplay during the last decades. There seems to be, for instance, a broad shift from the intermediated creation of credit toward a *new world of disintermediated global finance*. As the term suggests, disintermediation involves a qualitative change in the predominant forms of credit instruments and in the role of banks as intermediaries. While the creation of credit was once directly intermediated in the form of bank loans, it has now been transferred into a more indirectly intermediated issuing of capital and equity market instruments. And in the meantime, the sheer volume of disintermediated credit instruments dwarfs bank loans (Langley 2002). For that reason, we can assume that credit decision-making processes have for the most part moved from the boundaries to the interior of the economic subsystem. So the problem of credit should therefore, contrary to Parsons's concept of intermediary mechanism, be conceptualized as an inner-economic phenomenon. Besides this global trend toward disintermediation of financial services and institutions, we can instance other developments that challenge Parsons's perception of economy's and polity's interactions. While Parsons basically assumed high degrees of political control over economic activities, *new forms of regulation* have emerged in the course of financial globalization. These regulatory changes are currently debated under the catchphrase of "global governance" and include in particular the following central elements: blurring boundary lines between public and private, fragmentation of power and control, self-regulation and self-organization, and complexity of interactions and interdependencies. Taken together, they suggest a "decentered understanding" of regulation (Black 2002), which measures up to changing interactions between economy and polity. Again, there seems to be a shift of regulatory functions from the subsystem's boundaries into the economic subsystem itself.

C. Financial Markets at the Boundary Between Capitalization and Production

On more microscopic levels of the economic system, Parsons and Smelser paid special attention to the *investment function*, which is placed at a central point in the whole economic process—namely, at the *internal boundary of the investment-capitalization subsystem and the production subsystem*. As Parsons and Smelser stated, the investment function is relevant to the "intra-economic allocation of already-earmarked monetary facilities to already-demanded production"

(1956: 212). Here, one can as well generally speak of investment markets or, rather, financial markets. In these markets, the argument goes, investment funds are balanced against investment returns, and supply-demand relations govern the input and output balance between the two elements of interchange. Above all, these markets are seen as prototypes of unstructured situations and spheres of uncertainty and risk. While structured situations are thought to minimize possible courses of action, financial markets can be taken as the antipode. The investment market, Parsons and Smelser state, "fails to adhere to any of these characteristics of a structured situation: the range of adaptive responses (i.e., speculation) is not limited in a formal sense; there is a great deal of room to manoeuvre, as the daily quotations on the stock market show; and the loose definition of the appropriate adaptations (i.e., moves all made on the basis of 'hunches,' 'tips,' 'shrewdness', etc.) produces a great deal of psychological confusion and strain" (1956: 236). And since uncertainty and risk are considered to be unique characteristics of unstructured situations, Parsons and Smelser add:

> Situations of uncertainty and risk are the classical foci of magic and superstition. . . . Where there can be no reliable prediction of some future state, there arise extremely important attempts to interpret the significance of plausible and tangible "sign" of what is going to happen. In the case of speculation this often takes the form of basing decisions not on the available facts of market developments, but on the indications of the *opinion* of these developments on the part of the "one who knows," the alleged insider, or the fellow with a reputation for shrewdness; or the speculator may rely on traditionalized "rules of thumb," which may or may not be "objective." (1956: 237)

Parsons and Smelser's description of exchange on financial markets certainly lines up with research on behavioral finance. Advocates of this research program generally turn down the efficient market hypothesis, which says that the prices in mature capital markets reflect all the information available and respond only to unexpected news. Instead, behaviorists try to augment or replace traditional ideas of economic rationality (*homo economicus*) with decision-making models borrowed from psychology. That is to say, for instance, that investors respond not just to new information but also to irrational fads, fashions, and fears. Along these lines of behavioral economics, Parsons and Smelser argue that situations of uncertainty and risk may cause two types of effects: "psychologically irrational mass phenomena, and deviance of several types" (1956: 237).

From today's point of view, the boom and bust of the new economy is a classic illustration of Parsons and Smelser's main argument: that unstructured situations may cause catastrophic crashes or, rather, psychologically irrational mass phenomena. Next to this behavioral conception, we could at this point add several approaches of understanding financial markets as cultural and social phenomena (Sjöberg 2004; Clark 2004; Langley 2002; Hannigan 2002; Abolafia 1998). For the most part, these approaches focus once more on temporal and spatial patterns of capital flows, cultural aspects of financial markets, and social spaces of global finance. They first and foremost take the globality of finance as a starting point for further investigations, while implicitly drawing a distinction between the global financial sphere and the "real" economy. This dichotomy between the financial and the "real" economy, however, seems to move through large parts of the recent literature. Nevertheless, there is one crucial difference between recent approaches and the Parsonian perspective on finance. In both cases, the line of argumentation follows a completely different logic. While recent studies pinpoint differences in social structures and perceived experiences of social time and space, Parsons and Smelser focus on processes of differentiation and integration along the analytical boundaries of the AGIL model. The benefits of the latter approach are obvious: the general model of social systems allows us to move between and combine different levels of abstraction and analytically locate the financial sphere within society's and economy's interlocking subsystems. But the cost of this strategy is just as obvious: the analytical sharpness of the AGIL scheme goes to the debit of empirical investigations of concrete social structures.

D. Critical Comments on Parsons's Decomposition of Economy and Finance

With *Economy and Society*, Parsons and Smelser contributed a huge general research program for economic sociology. A comprehensive investigation of finance would have required many more levels of abstraction. But for our purposes here, conceptualizing the relations between finance, economy, and society, we give weight to some theoretical keystones that turn around differentiation and integration. In so doing, at least three different references to conceptualize the financial sphere may be identified: first, the problem of credit at the boundary between economy and polity; second, the level of the economy's subunits capitalization/investment and production; and third, the problem of investment at the boundary between economy's subunits. While this approach certainly sharpens the view for evolutionary processes of functional differentiation, the financial sphere is in consequence functionally decomposed into a multiplicity of system-references. The "paradigm of decomposition" as such is not questioned here. But with a view to the revolutionary changes in financial markets, instruments, and institutions, we may find sound arguments for conceptualizing finance as an autonomous subsystem of the economy. One broad empirical trend that must be taken into account concerns shifts of credit decision-making processes and regulatory functions from the boundary toward the interior of the economic system.

III

Niklas Luhmann on Society, Economy, and Finance

NIKLAS LUHMANN HAS REPEATEDLY MENTIONED that Parsons's theory of functional differentiation is still unique in its capability to make possible comparisons of heterodox social phenomena (e.g., Luhmann 1988: 232). Nevertheless, he decided to build his own version of a theory of functional differentiation on a quite alternative grounding. First, this alternative grounding, as well as some distinctive features of Luhmann's concept of differentiation, will be briefly outlined. In order to understand the consequences of this theoretical approach, the question of whether global finance is to be conceptualized as an autonomous system will then be discussed.

A. Patterns of Differentiation in Society and Generalized Media

In all of his work, Luhmann paid special attention to critiques of how Parsons's analytical boundaries of the AGIL scheme might correspond to concrete social structures in the evolutionary process of society. By critically assessing this intricate question, Luhmann introduced a theory of generalized media of interchange that is quite different from Parsons's intermediary mechanisms at the boundaries of society's subsystems. While Parsons developed his concept of interchange media in a deductive way, that is to say, as a consequence of functional differentiation, Luhmann's line of argument follows the reverse logic. He took interchange media as a starting point to theoretically reconstruct the functional differentiation of society.

In the Parsonian framework, interchange mechanisms are seen as social phenomena that derive from processes of functional differentiation and at the same time solve problems of social integration. "The need for generalized media of interchange is a function of the differentiatedness of social structures: in this sense they are all partly integrative mechanisms" (Parsons 1968: 471). For this reason—here, we use Luhmann's interpretation—"the differentiation of media follows the differentiation of systems and not vice versa" (Luhmann 1976: 507). However, one of the problems of this approach, as various critics have already mentioned, is that the epistemological and ontological status of the media remains somewhat unclear: Are they the results of real interchange in concrete interaction, or are they just an outcome of the analytical theory of functional differentiation (e.g., Alexander 1984: 110ff.; Habermas 1979: 69ff.; Künzler 1989: 120; Willke 1993: 233)?

In contrast to Parsons's deductively developed concept of interchange media, Luhmann turned the whole argument around: generalized media (like power, money, or truth) solve the problem of double contingency at the level of concrete interaction through the transmission of reduced complexity. They are regarded as meaningful constellations of combined selectivity that "employ their selection pattern as a motive to accept the reduction, so that people join with others in a narrow world of common understandings, complementary expectations, and determinable issues" (Luhmann 1976: 512). Following this conception, we can understand media of interchange as "catalytic principle(s) of subsystem-building within the internal environment of the society" (Luhmann 1977: 39). If this is a suitable assumption, a theory of functional differentiation of the society must no longer refer to any given functions. But it can instead try to reconstruct subsystem-building inductively by analyzing "how inside a society forms of connectivity of communications develop expectations in which further connections are more probable" (Nassehi 2004: 4).

We can clarify these distinctions between Parsons and Luhmann by taking a cursory look at the Luhmannian version of the differentiation of the primary societal subsystems. Just like Parsons, Luhmann regards the functional differentiation of society as an emerging concrete and empirical process (Luhmann 1977, 1997: 601). While premodern societies were mainly structured through segmental or stratified types of differentiation (archaic societies and the early advanced cultures, respectively), Luhmann assumes that modern society comes along with a shift toward functional differentiation. This pattern of functional differentiation is not seen from the perspective of the Durkheimian tradition as a more or less harmonic division of labor. It was instead inspired by what Max Weber called the "polytheism" of increasingly independent "value-spheres" in modern society. Weber

> portrayed the birth and composition of modern society as the emergence of a number of autonomous "value-spheres." One after the other, science, law, art, politics, economics, sexuality, and others freed themselves from their former domination by religious ideas. These "value-spheres" became societal domains of their own which cultivate their particular central value without concern for the value-orientations of other domains. (Schimank 2002: 3364)

While premodern societies were characterized by a hierarchical and in some degree total form of integration with, for example, political or religious leaders claiming to represent and integrate the whole society, the modern society gets "decomposed in perspectives of function systems which cannot become organized as a whole" (Nassehi 2004: 4–5). Each function system is thought to constitute its own claims and to evolve its own imperatives of systems continuation.

To theorize this gigantic structural transformation, Luhmann mainly focused on the way in which the primary societal subsystems of the modern society—economy, science, the arts, law, religion, and polity—have emerged. As mentioned above, Luhmann does not suppose that the number and character of society's subsystems can be predicted or deduced from functional exigencies. Instead, he assumes that functional differentiation "selects communication processes around special functions to be fulfilled at the level of the society itself" (Luhmann 1977: 35). As a tool for the description of the constitution and reproduction of society's subsystems, Luhmann introduced the concept of autopoiesis, which traces back to the Chilean biologist Humberto Maturana, into social theory (Maturana and Varela 1980). Although it was originally developed to describe living systems such as cells, Luhmann generalized this concept to emphasize the autonomy of social systems. At this point, Luhmann assumed that social systems gain autonomy through what he called operational closure.

Based on the idea of operational closure, Luhmann drew various consequences and perspectives for societal evolution. At this point, we only want to point out two central aspects that are of vital significance to theoretically framing the relations between economy and finance.

- The relations between the systems, including mutual dependencies and correlations, are expected not as causal linkages. No system can affect the internal structure of another system directly on the level of its operations. For example, political decisions such as appointments of taxes deteriorate the economy, but inside the economic system, these effects are only visible in the language of the prices. "Inputs" from the environment must pass the filters of the system itself. Luhmann uses the concept of *structural coupling* to describe these noncausal connections between operationally closed systems (Luhmann 1997: 100). As stable forms of structural couplings between the economic system and the legal system, for example, Luhmann mentioned the institutions of constitution, contract, and ownership (Luhmann 2000a). These institutions are of great importance to both systems; nonetheless, they do not affect the systems causally on the level of their basic operations. As regards the "theory-architectural status" of this concept, some affinities to the integrative aspects of the Parsonian media conceptualization can be assumed.

- Neither society's spatial nor temporal subsystems are well-defined or determined by territorial frontiers or political borders. Instead, the systems are thought of as prospective world systems. Luhmann argues that all of society's systems come about as *global communication complexes*, which somehow undermine the autonomy of the world's regional cultures and national societies (Stichweh 2003: 3). In other words, for instance, neither the economic reproduction of payments nor scientific claims of truth stop at national or cultural boundaries; instead, they tend to spread globally. The same is assumed for their temporal orders: time is regarded as a system-internal construction generated by functionally specific distinctions between past and future expectations. There are no system-spreading superstructures that synchronize and integrate these time horizons (Luhmann 1997: 768). One example of this is the problem of legal authorities in coping with the dynamics of financial innovations.

B. One Step Beyond: Finance as an Autopoietic System?

Although Luhmann did not explicitly conceptualize finance as an autopoietic system, he discussed aspects of finance in his book on the economic system (Luhmann 1988), as well as in several other writings. Particularly during the last decade, advocates of systems theory have taken up Luhmann's basic assumptions on finance and begun to set up a more detailed theoretical framework on various aspects of this subject (e.g., Baecker 1988; Schmidt 1998; Strulik 2000; Willke 2001a, 2001b; Piel 2003). In this context, one of the most important questions is whether we could speak of today's finance as an autopoietic system in its own right (Schmidt 1998: 183). Empirical findings on the spatial and temporal logic of capital flows as well as observable changes in financial markets, instruments, and institutions would suggest so. But in order to avoid hasty conclusions from perceived experiences of social time and space, namely, the rapidity, volatility, and speed of finance, our aim is first of all to fathom the relations between finance, economy, and society on theoretical *and* empirical grounds.

At this point, a brief excursus on Luhmann's perception of the economic system (1988) may be allowed. In general, and in contrast to Parsons's theory of differentiation, Luhmann does not assume that the society's primary subsystems tend to differentiate into subunits along the lines of functional exigencies. So, in line with Luhmann, we don't think of one and the same pattern of differentiation that recurs over and over again on various levels of abstraction. Instead, we try to make out the specific mode of differentiation by looking at concrete social structures, temporal orders, and spatial configurations of finance within the economic system.

From a conceptual point of view, the modern economic system itself has gradually emerged along recursive chains of monetary operations, and its basic internal structure can be characterized as heterarchic. This means that all of the systems' operations are connected with other operations by myriads of network structures. For example, firms, households, and markets are linked only by decentral operations, without a central control unit or hierarchical constellation. This heterarchic autopoiesis of payments nevertheless must be anchored by a regulation of the medium itself. In early stages of differentiation, the natural properties of gold have served as such an anchor. The operational closure and internal differentiation was limited by an external—and in this case even extrasocial—point of reference. If we now look at the historical evolution of the modern economic system, we can understand the system of Bretton-Woods as a first step in loosening this external point of reference. Parsons and Smelser's assumptions about the central role of the policy to create credit, mentioned in the last section, marked this shift. As a functional equivalent to the natural properties of gold, political decisions such as the coordination of money via monetary policy still anchor the economic system's operational closure, but no longer with reference to extrasocial points of reference such as gold quantities. One may possibly ask to which degree monetary policy is determined politically or economically. We propose to assume that this relationship is not generally fixed but that it can vary over time and that the recent rise of financial markets might mark a further shift toward the autonomy of the economic system from society. One could therefore assume that external points of reference—be they political or extrasocial—are increasingly offset by system-internal structures.

Based on this theoretical foundation, we argue here that the central role of today's financial markets results from their role as functional equivalents to functions once fulfilled system-externally. The external anchors of the economic system's monetary autopoiesis are partly substituted by a system-internal form of a center/periphery differentiation. Financial markets do not govern or control the economic system hierarchically, but nevertheless they play a central role in the system's autopoiesis because of their central position within the heterarchic system. Luhmann (Luhmann 1988: 118) noted that these markets represent the unity of the whole economic system because they are closely linked to all other markets, firms, and households.

But how can one investigate today's economic and financial landscape through the proposed theoretical lenses? One must take the Luhmannian assumptions one step further and ask whether one could conceive finance as an autopoietic system in its own right. According to the system-theoretical approach, this decision is not regarded as a purely heuristic one that lies at the choice of the theoretician. Nor does it imply the use of the term *system of finance* as only a classificatory or an analytical term. Instead, one would have to look inductively for specific communicative operations (decisions, observations) that share unique features and act as points of reference for other communications of the same kind. One would furthermore have to look for the stabilization of recursive chains of communications and observation, analogous to binary codes. In the case of finance, the question is whether it is possible to identify specific couplings of chains of elements within the generalized medium of money.

A promising starting point for this approach has been developed by Dirk Baecker (1988), who has analyzed different forms of operations on various markets (product markets, labor markets, financial markets, future markets). One central element of operations on financial markets are payments that anticipate the reproduction of payments through payments (Baecker 1988: 281). On this basis, it seems legitimate to assume that a financial system might have emerged through a recursive reference of operations of such a kind. In cybernetics, one would probably use the concept of a positive feedback loop to refer to the consequences of this phenomenon of self-

referentiality: while payments that anticipate the reproduction of payments through payments might belong to any monetary economy, it
makes a difference if and when operations increasingly serve as starting points for specific chains of operations. While, following
Luhmann, internal differentiation in general "performs the reproduction of the system in itself" by "splitting it into internal systems and
environments," it is "not simply decomposition into smaller chunks
but, in fact, a process of growth by internal disjunction" (Luhmann
1977: 31). The logic of recursive operations and observations on financial markets establishes a highly selective searchlight for the economic
world, illuminating certain areas and leaving all the rest in the dark.
So what has been addressed as the hyperreality and uncoupling of
finance might be rendered more precisely as a process of system differentiation within the economic system itself. As some empirical
examples in the next section should demonstrate, it surely makes
some analytical sense to not just decompose finance analytically in
the sense that Parsons and Smelser sketched within *Economy and
Society.* While such an approach is essential for outlining finance as
a part of the modern society that maintains many forms of interchanges with other parts of society, the systematic qualities of modern
finance itself would remain underexposed. In order to expose the
least, it could be reasonable and instructive to apply Luhmann's
theoretical approach to recent empirical phenomena.

IV

The Global System of Finance Through the Lenses of Systems Theory

As we have argued in the introductory paragraph, the explanatory
strength of both adaptations of the theory of social systems is that
any models of mono-causality are radically disclaimed. That is to say,
neither do financial activities reflect "real" economic activities, nor do
they simply destroy or foster them in a linear measure. Following
Parsons's general idea of differentiation and interlocking subsystems,
we asked whether finance can be considered as a result of ongoing
processes of internal differentiation within the economic system.
Parsons and Smelser supposed a "tendency of social systems to
develop progressively higher levels of structural differentiation under

the pressure of adaptive exigencies" (Parsons and Smelser 1956: 47). In a further step, we have substantiated this assumption by roughly sketching some aspects of Luhmann's social theory. Based on our theoretical review, we can now enter empirical grounds to discuss whether *today's financial sphere* can be conceived as an *autopoietic system in its own right.* Three examples will serve to demonstrate how the financial sphere gains autonomy and unfolds its own systemic qualities. The autonomy of finance notwithstanding, specific interdependencies between the financial and the economic spheres can be expected. So we then will direct our attention to Luhmann's idea of *structural coupling.* This concept functions as a kind of antonym to the concept of operational closure in order to describe interactions in a nonlinear measure. To empirically illustrate these interactions, we will concentrate on the broad field of corporate disclosure and financial accounting.

A. Systemic Qualities and Operational Closure of Global Finance

Our first example concerns Karin Knorr Cetina and Urs Bruegger's ethnographic research on *microsocial structures of global financial markets.* Their article "Global Microstructures: The Interaction Practices of Financial Markets" (2002) sheds light on the role of face-to-screen situations between traders for the constitution of globally operating financial markets. The authors conceptualize global financial markets as:

> fields in which participants, although geographically distant, are oriented, above all, toward one another and, at the same time, disengaged from local settings [and] are spanned and bound together by global microstructures—that is, patterns of relatedness and coordination that are global in scope but microsocial in character and that assemble and link global domains. (2002: 907)

Knorr Cetina and Bruegger observed everyday activities of traders in foreign exchange markets on the electronic trading floor of a global investment bank in Zurich, Switzerland. Their investigation mainly focuses on computer protocols of "interactions" between traders, which document offers and agreements to deal. These "interactions" are not face-to-face but face-to-screen:

On each of these screens, the same market has a vigorous presence; traders worldwide who deal in the same financial instrument watch the same screen content, which is delivered to them by globally operating firms, such as Reuters, Bloomberg, and Telerate, and by the banks themselves. (2002: 923)

From this perspective, we can look at the screen as a mechanism that simultaneously reduces and increases social complexity. Through the highly selective assortment of content onscreen on the one hand and the observing eyes of traders glued to the screen on the other, social complexity is reduced to the point of single financial numbers. Since these numbers are points of reference for subsequent transactions, the complexity of finance increases along recursive chains of communication. These communication structures are not only equivalents of face-to-face interactions, they are also systemic features that constitute global financial markets.

The recursivity of structures leads over to our second example: the method of *technical or chart analysis*, which aims to anticipate the motion of stock quotations (Piel 2003). In contrast to the traditional method of *fundamental analysis*, which is used to determine the value of a stock by analyzing the financial data that is "fundamental" to a company, technical analysis looks for patterns and indicators on stock charts that will determine a stock's future performance. Fundamental analysis includes external factors such as general economic conditions like inflation and deflation, business data, political decisions, and environmental events; these factors are regarded to enable decisions about whether current market prices are over- or undervalued. Chart analysis does not search for external reasons for price movements but studies the effect of the price movement itself. The goal is to identify periodically stable pattern structures of share price movements (charts). Fundamental analysis has a certain degree of cognitive authority and is regarded as the "astronomy" of financial economics, in contrast to chart analysis, which is sometimes classified as a kind of "astrology." In today's financial sphere, technical analysis can certainly be considered the predominant method of analysis, particularly in portfolio management of big institutional investors (MacKenzie 2003). As Donald MacKenzie has argued, mathematically-based models of financial analysis strongly influence the structure and dynamics of financial markets.

This brings us to our third example, a phenomenon that has recently been discussed under the label *performativity of economics* (MacKenzie 2004). This discussion has played a prominent role in Luhmann's theory of the economic system. The question is whether or how economic theories themselves affect the object they refer to. Luhmann (Luhmann 1988: 81) scrutinized this issue with respect to the practical influence of the Keynesian theory toward economic policy in the second half of the 20th century. Today, we might find even better examples within the financial sphere. While the traditional point at issue between orthodox, neoclassical finance theory and behavioral finance concerns the question of whether the assumptions and axioms of the former (like the efficient market hypothesis or the *homo economicus* conception) are true or false, the following question might be more instructive: Does the *practical use* of models that are based on neoclassical finance theory change patterns of prices toward greater compliance with these models? Along these lines, Donald MacKenzie has explored the impact of the Black-Scholes-Merton option pricing theory on the U.S. option market. The effect of the option pricing model "was to shift both market conditions and patterns of prices towards those posited by theory" (MacKenzie 2004: 310ff.). Besides cases of performativity, MacKenzie also identified contrary phenomena of "counterperformativity," where the adoption of a model undermines the preconditions of its own empirical validity. Once again, he quotes the Black-Scholes-Merton model as an example: while this model became a standard procedure in the 1980s, its large-scale adoption is today widely regarded as having exacerbated the stock market crash in 1987.

From our point of view, these examples of performativity and counterperformativity again stress the supremacy of self-referential operations within global finance. The practical application of models of financial economics must be regarded as an attempt to automate decisions about whether to pay or not pay on financial markets. But, again, these continuous conditionings of the code payment/nonpayment affect the structure of the object they are referring to. The next step that can be expected in this field might entail the development and practical application of models that even take into account the consequences of their own large-scale adoption.

B. Accounting Regulation and Structural Coupling of Finance and Economy

In order to describe the interactions between financial markets and economic organizations in more detail and on empirical grounds, attention is now directed to the broad field of accounting regulation. Accounting regulation is due to the neutrality and objectivity widely ascribed to the use of monetary numbers (Porter 1995), commonly thought to provide for a high degree of transparency and comparability within global finance. As a set of technical procedures for creating calculability and visibility (Burchell et al. 1980), accounting is thought to provide for standardized and unambiguous financial communication. Along these lines, accounting rules can be considered as norms for "organizational talk" (Brunsson 1989) that structure and restrict the way organizations communicate in terms of financial statements; and the accounting procedure can be considered as a linkage between what one might call the *public sphere of financial markets* and the *internal structures of economic organizations.*

Concerning the financial sphere, we first of all witness a broad shift toward a global accounting regulation. Two prevalent bodies of rules have emerged that are commonly thought of as generally accepted: the International Financial Reporting Standard (IFRS) and the U.S. Generally Accepted Accounting Principles (US GAAP). Leaving aside the fact that these two accounting systems claim different origins and compete against each other in some respects, both are capable of superseding national accounting systems, and both aim to provide financial information that is useful to a wide range of users in making economic decisions. The nearly exclusive use of financial information is, inter alia, based on accounting's capacity to achieve high degrees of "epistemic values" (Suzuki 2003) such as generality, comparability, balance, coherence, and simplicity. And it appears that these are exactly the values that structure financial communication, which relies on opportunities to observe, evaluate, and compare financial values across organizations, branches of trade, and even whole economies.

While accounting seems to catalyze specific forms of observation and communication within global finance, the questions are how these are linked to the internal structure of economic organizations, and how calculative practices are involved in ways of managing and governing organizational life. A considerable body of research suggests that business enterprises might have been captured by finance. There is, for instance, Chandler's (1977) historical narrative, which claims that the evolution of business enterprises toward modern multiunit corporations was accompanied by an evolution of management accounting techniques that helped to manage increasingly complex businesses by using numbers. Later, Fligstein (1990) identified a broad shift toward the *finance conception of governance*. What he observed was an increasing dominance of finance personnel in the control of large business corporations, and he stated that "the finance view of efficiency dominates the corporate world today" (Fligstein 1990: 298). More recently, Zorn and Dobbin (2003) have continued this line of argument. They examined the effect of the growing importance of global financial markets on the strategy and structure of over 400 large U.S. firms for the period 1963 to 2000. They documented the rise of a new finance model of corporate governance that contributed to the increasing attentiveness of firms to financial markets and argued that:

> as investors systematically increased their scrutiny of individual firms and evaluated the prospects of firms in terms of how financial markets would value them in the future, firms became acutely aware of the norms for corporate governance that financial markets were developing. As a result, firms became increasingly sensitive to how key actors in financial markets viewed and valued them. (2003: 20)

Based on these empirical findings, one may observe the emergence of a *volonté générale* as a compression of the financial public sphere, which is now speaking more and more with one voice. In this regard, the concrete arrangement of accounting rules is not merely a technical or formal act but rather a result of social balances of power. Generally accepted accounting standards surely do both to a certain degree; they bring about *and* represent the egotism of a global system of finance and its community. This influence is directly enabled through the cognitive authority that is ascribed to global accounting standards as seemingly neutral calculative apparatuses. And this is what empirical studies on the capture of business by finance actually refer to.

But should we think of this capture in a linear measure, that is to say, that the leveling force of finance results in similarity and homogeneity among standard-following organizations? Following Luhmann's general assumptions, the interactions between systems are not to be conceived as causal linkages. "Inputs" from the financial environment have to pass the filters of the economic organizations and vice versa. By crossing the borders, causality gets fractured. Both systems, finance and organization, operate in a self-referential mode and, as a consequence, there is no direct exchange with the environment. The environmental world is explicitly not understood as taken for granted, but in lieu of that, each system enacts its own environment. Both systems create their own view of the world. Instead of talking about the "external environment," the phrase *enacted environment* (Weick 1969) is more adequate, since it draws attention to the process of creating the environment to which the system then adapts. Along these lines, organizations do not react to a given environment—they enact it. So, within the mirror of financial markets, they observe how they are being observed, evaluated, and compared by financial analysts, bankers and brokers, specialized journalists, and institutional and private investors (White 1981).

V

Concluding Comments

In this article, our intention has been to search Talcott Parsons's and Niklas Luhmann's work for theoretical keystones to fathom the relations between economy and finance, and at the same time to reconstruct the globalization of finance from a theoretical point of view. In consideration of our detailed discussion of Niklas Luhmann's social theory, we must point out that Luhmann's work has to be seen as one advancement among others of Parsons's legacy.

The complexity of Parsons's theory, including its various stages of development, did not end with his death in Munich in 1979. To the contrary, it seems to us that the multilayered character of his theory is kept alive in a variety of research studies conducted by his scholars and their associates. This manifold research covers and highlights aspects of action theory, functionalism, systems theory, and many other issues. Luhmann's theory of social systems is *one* effort to advance the Parsonian theory and, as such, it surely demonstrates certain strengths and weaknesses. It should also be mentioned that the boom-and-bust cycles of theory adoption follow their own rules. And while today's academic landscape is more global than ever before, regional pathways still matter. For example, in the United States, Parsons's influence declined during the late 1970s, compared to his relative dominance in the 1950s and 1960s, but his impact on German sociology was the strongest during that same period. And while the modern theory of social systems is currently one of the dominant paradigms in Germany, the reception of Luhmann's work has not even achieved a minor role in American sociology.

Our attempt to conceive both economy and finance as operationally closed universes of communication might appear a quite unusual approach; in particular with regard to the usual division of labor between sociology and economics, whose benefits are not under discussion here. Even in German sociology, which still might be reputed as being "heavy on theory," the adoption of systems-theoretical concepts such as autopoiesis and operational closure has caused extensive criticism for being too abstract. In general, we do not agree with these diffuse criticisms, and instead plead for a pragmatic use of systems-theoretical concepts. As we have argued in the last section, the dynamics of modern finance are highly characterized by self-referential, trans-intentional, and emergent properties. The financial sphere can almost be taken as a prime example of Luhmann's notions on the autonomy of social systems.

References

Abolafia, M. Y. (1998). "Markets as Cultures: An Ethnographic Approach." In *The Laws of Market*. Ed. Michael Callon. Oxford: Blackwell.
Alexander, J. C. (1984). *Theoretical Logic in Sociology. Vol. 4: The Modern*

Reconstruction of Classical Thought: Talcott Parsons. London: Routledge & Kegan.

Baecker, D. (1988). *Information und Risiko in der Marktwirtschaft.* Frankfurt: Suhrkamp.

Baudrillard, J. (1983). *Simulations.* New York: Semiotext(e).

Black, J. (2002). *Critical Reflections on Regulation.* CARR Discussion Paper Series DP 4, January.

Brunsson, N. (1989). *The Organization of Hypocrisy: Talk, Decisions and Actions in Organizations.* Chichester, UK: John Wiley & Sons.

Burchell, S., C. Clubb, A. Hopwood, and J. Hughes. (1980). "The Roles of Accounting in Organizations and Society." *Accounting, Organizations and Society* (5)1: 5–27.

Castells, M. (1989). *The Informational City: Information Technology, Economic Restructuring, and the Urban-Regional Process.* Oxford: Blackwell Publishers.

———. (1996). *The Rise of the Network Society.* Oxford: Blackwell Publishers.

Chandler, A. D. (1977). *The Visible Hand: The Managerial Revolution in American Business.* Cambridge: Belknap Press of Harvard University Press.

Clark, G. L. (2004). *Money Flows Like Mercury: The Geography of Global Finance.* Working Paper. <http://www.geog.ox.ac.uk/research/wpapers/economic/wpg04-01.pdf>.

Fligstein, N. (1990). *The Transformation of Corporate Control.* Cambridge: Harvard University Press.

Fligstein, N., and T.-J. Shin. (2004). *Shareholder Value and the Transformation of the American Economy, 1984–2001.* CSES Working Paper Series, Paper 19. <http://web.mit.edu/ewzucker/www/econsoc/Fligstein.pdf>.

Froud, J., C. Haslim, S. Johal, and K. Williams. (2000). "Shareholder Value and Financialization: Consultancy Promises, Management Moves." *Economy and Society* 29(1): 80–110.

Giddens, A. (1990). *The Consequences of Modernity.* Cambridge, UK: Polity Press.

Goldfinger, C. (2000). "Intangible Economy and Financial Markets." *Communications & Strategies* 40(4): 59–89.

———. (2002). "Intangible Economy and Electronic Money." In *The Future of Money.* Paris: OECD Publications.

Habermas, J. (1979). "Handlung und System. Bemerkungen zu Parsons' Medientheorie." In *Verhalten, Handeln und System. Talcott Parsons' Beitrag zur Entwicklung der Sozialwissenschaften.* Ed. W. Schluchter. Frankfurt: Suhrkamp.

Hannigan, J. (2002). "Culture, Globalization, and Social Cohesion: Toward a Deterritorialized, Global Fluids Model." *Canadian Journal of Communication* 27(2/3): 277–287.

Heine, M. (2001). "Die Entkopplungsthese—eine kritische Würdigung." In *Neue Weltwährungsarchitektur.* Ed. A. Heise. Marburg: Metropolis.

Knorr Cetina, K., and U. Bruegger. (2002). "Global Microstructures: The Virtual Societies of Financial Markets." *American Journal of Sociology* 107(4): 905–950.

Künzler, J. (1989). *Medien und Gesellschaft. Die Medienkonzepte von Talcott Parsons, Jürgen Habermas und Niklas Luhmann.* Stuttgart: Enke.

Langley, P. (2002). *The Everyday Life of Global Finance.* IPEG Papers in Global Political Economy. <http://www.bisa.ac.uk/groups/ipeg/ipegpapers.htm>.

Lowenstein, L. (1988). *What's Wrong with Wall Street.* Reading, MA: Addison-Wesley.

Luhmann, N. (1976). "Generalized Media and the Problem of Contingency." In *Explorations in General Theory in Social Sciences. Volume 2.* Eds. J. J. Loubser, R. C. Baum, A. Effrat, and V. Meyer Lidz. New York: Macmillan.

——. (1977). "Differentiation of Society." *Canadian Journal of Sociology* 3(2): 29–52.

——. (1987). *Soziologische Aufklärung 4. Beiträge zur funktionalen Differenzierung der Gesellschaft.* Opladen: Westdeutscher Verlag.

——. (1988). *Die Wirtschaft der Gesellschaft.* Frankfurt: Suhrkamp.

——. (1997). *Die Gesellschaft der Gesellschaft (2 Bände).* Frankfurt: Suhrkamp.

——. (2000a). *Die Politik der Gesellschaft.* Frankfurt: Suhrkamp.

MacKenzie, D. (2004a). *Opening the Black Boxes of Global Finance.* Working Paper. <http://www.sociology.ed.ac.uk/Research/Staff/Mackpaper3.pdf>.

——. (2004b). "The Big, Bad Wolf and the Rational Market: Portfolio Insurance, the 1987 Crash and the Performativity of Economics." *Economy and Society* 33(3): 303–334.

Maturana, H. R., and F. J. Varela. (1980). *Autopoiesis and Cognition: The Realization of the Living.* Dordrecht: D. Reidel.

McGoun, E. (1997). "Hyperreal Finance." *Critical Perspectives on Accounting* 8(1/2): 97–122.

Nassehi, A. (2004). *The Two Worlds of Functional Differentiation and Social Stratification.* <http://www.lrz-muenchen.de/~ls_nassehi/nassehi/orginequal.pdf>.

Parsons, T. (1968). "Social Systems." In *International Encyclopedia of the Social Sciences. Vol. 7.* Ed. D. Sills. New York: Macmillian Company & Free Press/Collier Macmillan.

Parsons, T., and N. J. Smelser, (1956). *Economy and Society: A Study in the Integration of Economic and Social Theory.* London: Routledge & Kegan Paul.

Piel, K. (2003). *Ökonomie des Nichtwissens. Aktienhype und Vertrauenskrise im Neuen Markt.* Frankfurt: Campus Verlag.

Porter, T. M. (1995). *Trust in Numbers: The Pursuit of Objectivity in Science and Public Life.* Princeton: Princeton University Press.

Sassen, S. (1999). "Spatialities and Temporalities of the Global: Elements for a Theorization." *Public Culture: Society for Transnational Cultural Studies* 2: 215–232.

Schimank, U. (2002). "Social Differentiation." In *International Encyclopedia of the Social and Behavioral Sciences.* Eds. N. Smelser and P. Baltes. Oxford: Pergamon.

Schmidt, T. (1998). *Zur Erschließung der Theorie sozialer Systeme für Untersuchungen des Finanziellen Sektors.* Berlin: Neue Betriebswirtschaftliche Studienbücher.

Sjöberg, K. (2004). "The Wall Street Culture. Market Actors and Popular Media Discourses." *European Journal of Cultural Studies* 7(4): 481–499.

Stichweh, R. (2003). *Structure Formation in World Society: The Eigenstructures of World Society and the Regional Cultures of the World.* Working Papers of the Institute for World Society Studies. <http://www.uni-bielefeld.de/soz/iw/pdf/worldsociety.pdf>.

Stockhammer, E. (2004). "Financialization and the Shutdown of Accumulation." *Cambridge Journal of Economics* 28(5): 719–741.

Strulik, T. (2000). *Risikomanagement globaler Finanzmärkte. Herausforderungen und Initiativen im Kontext der Bankenregulierung.* Frankfurt: Campus.

Weick, K. E. (1969). *The Social Psychology of Organizing.* Reading, MA: Addison-Wesley.

White, H. C. (1981). "Where Do Markets Come From?" *American Journal of Sociology* 87(3): 517–547.

Willke, H. (1993). *Systemtheorie.* Stuttgart: Gustav Fischer.

———. (2001a). *Atopia. Studien zur atopischen Gesellschaft.* Frankfurt: Suhrkamp.

———. (2001b). *Systemisches Wissensmanagement.* Stuttgart: Lucius & Lucius.

Zorn, D., and F. Dobbin. (2003). "Too Many Chiefs?: How Financial Markets Reshaped the American Firm." Paper prepared for Konstanze Conference on Social Studies of Finance: Inside Financial Markets. University of Konstanze, Konstanz, Germany.

Index

Weber, Max, 5–8, 10, 13–19, 27, 32,
36, 43, 44, 47, 50–53, 66, 67,
76–78, 81, 84–86, 90, 91, 94,
96–98, 101–103, 105, 110, 119,
163, 175, 178, 183, 203
　Status group theory of, 98
Weimar regime, 23
Wenzel, Harald, 161, 164, 168,
179
Wessen, Albert F., 1, 18
Whitehead, A. N., 14, 15, 29, 127,
169

Williams College, 4
Williams, Robin, xxv
Williamson, Keith, 1, 37
Wolf, C. Parker, 1, 16, 54
Woods Hole, 4
World War I, 6, 22
World War II, 2, 24, 25

Z

Zafirovski, Milan, x, xxi, 75, 111,
112, 120
Zurich, 209